Other books by David Wise and Thomas B. Ross

THE U-2 AFFAIR

THE INVISIBLE GOVERNMENT

The Espionage Establishment

THE
espionage

establishment

David Wise
and *Thomas B. Ross*

RANDOM HOUSE   *New York*

For CHRISTOPHER, MARIA, and ANNE

CONTENTS

CONTENTS

The Espionage Establishment

1 the espionage establishment

Since the end of World War II, powerful espionage establishments, often consisting of several interlocking yet competitive secret agencies, have grown up in every major country of the world.

Americans are familiar with the Central Intelligence Agency, and to a lesser degree with the other intelligence organizations that comprise the espionage establishment of the United States. They are perhaps less familiar with the KGB and the GRU of the Soviet Union, Britain's M.I.5 and M.I.6, and the Social Affairs Department of Communist China.

These espionage networks, and similar but smaller ones around the globe, were created to spy out the secrets of other nations. They have also engaged in clandestine political action, stirring revolt, overthrowing governments, and in general seeking to bring about political change that is viewed, by the intelligence operators at least, as advantageous to their own country.

In the process these intelligence organizations have themselves become great wellsprings of secret power within their own societies. With vast resources of talent and public money to draw upon, and with their activities conducted for the most part out of public view, the espionage establishments are much like genii that have escaped from the bottle, for they have frequently threatened the governments that summoned them up. It is not so much that they have sought directly to challenge their national leaders or seize power. Rather, the operations of the espionage establishments have provoked events to the point where the governments which they were created to serve have either teetered on the brink of disaster or actually fallen.

In the Soviet Union, Nikita S. Khrushchev was retired with the assistance of the KGB; in England, the Profumo affair eventually felled Harold Macmillan; in France, Charles de Gaulle's grandeur was tarnished by the Ben Barka case; in Israel, during the 1965 election campaign, David Ben-Gurion and Levi Eshkol still fought over a decade-old intelligence disaster known as the Lavon affair; in Canada, the government of Prime Minister Lester Pearson was shaken in 1966 by the Munsinger affair; and in the United States, John F. Kennedy had his Bay of Pigs.

Espionage establishments tend to attract the elite, privileged and better-educated members of their societies. In the West at least, intelligence officials often come from older, upper-class families whose scions, already assured of great wealth, are now more interested in public service. In England and America there runs through the higher echelons of M.I.6 and the CIA a strong unstated undercurrent of *noblesse oblige*.

And in both countries there is a close relationship between the espionage establishment and what has come, loosely, to be termed the Establishment—that larger grouping of powerful men who, in any country, seem to control its affairs. This relationship was reflected in the fact that the OSS, the wartime forerunner of the CIA, was known as "Oh So Social"; and in the fact that the first major clandestine operation of the CIA was born in the Brook Club in New York. But it was never more forcefully and publicly demonstrated than early in

1967, during the furor over the CIA's secret subsidization of student and other private groups. For it turned out that the directors of the foundations which served obligingly as conduits for CIA money were among the most distinguished members of the Establishment.

Inevitably, the espionage and intelligence establishments have given rise to a new spy subculture. President Kennedy read Ian Fleming, and so did millions of others. As the public, through news stories and imaginative fiction, has grown more aware of intelligence activities, the spymania has spilled over into virtually every facet of modern life. In the movies and on television, the secret agent threatens the supremacy of the cowboy. Cereal box tops offer spy kits for children, and James Bond spy toys crowd Pooh Bear on the store shelves. In fashion, women are urged to buy Mata Hari pants or lounging pajamas called Spy Trappers. The United Nations receives letters from children convinced that the UN has some relationship to *The Man from U.N.C.L.E.* For relaxation, Secretary of State Dean Rusk reads spy thrillers. (President Eisenhower read Westerns, but times have changed.)

No one living in the modern world can escape the impact of espionage. But few have understood that the mounting public awareness of spying has had a substantial influence on the real world of espionage. It has affected how governments act in their dealings with one another. It has, in fact, helped to bring about a revolution in espionage.

So long as the public only dimly perceived that espionage was going on in the world around it, nations acted accordingly—and disavowed their spies. Today they are openly traded for one another, publicly acclaimed, and sometimes encouraged by their governments to write their memoirs. A street in Moscow was named for one of the Soviet Union's more famous spies, and a four-kopeck postage stamp was issued in his honor.

Much of what is written about espionage is fantasy. What the authors have attempted to do is to present not an encyclopedia of spying, but a portrait of contemporary international espionage as it really is. We have attempted to do so, first, by describing the organization, personalities and operations of the espionage establishments of the four major world powers—the United States, Britain, the Soviet Union and Communist China. Next, two detailed case studies are set forth to illustrate how Soviet spies work in the United States, a subject about which surprisingly little has been available before. Then, the espionage revolution is discussed with principal focus on the background to the major spy trades of the 1960's. And finally, some personal conclusions are offered on the follies, the dangers and the necessity of the world's second oldest profession.

One word of caution may be necessary. Espionage is a singular subject where the unusual is often the norm. The reader might bear this in mind as he learns of the James Bond test given to the Director of the CIA at the LBJ Ranch in Texas; of the KGB's efforts to go into dairy farming along the United States border; and of the identity of the head of M.I.6—and his Alice in Wonderland headquarters. But first, we shall step through the looking-glass into what may be the most powerful espionage establishment of all: the KGB.

ii the soviet union

On the morning of November 1, 1956, the Soviet ambassador in Budapest hurried to the Parliament building on the Danube in answer to the urgent summons of the new Premier of Hungary.

Ambassador Yuri Vladimirovich Andropov was a big man, more than six feet, powerfully built and prematurely gray at the age of forty-two. He towered over Imre Nagy, the short, corpulent Premier with the Hungarian peasant's mustache who now confronted him angrily.

In six days of bloody fighting while the world had held its breath, the Hungarians, using Molotov cocktails and great courage against Soviet tanks, had apparently won their freedom from Russian control. Nagy, a man respected for his relatively liberal views, had emerged as Premier. Only two days earlier the Soviet government—seemingly confused and on the defensive—had publicly ordered its troops to be withdrawn from Hungarian soil.

But now disturbing reports were reaching the new government. Nagy bluntly told the Soviet ambassador he had definite information that Russian military units had re-entered Hungary; unless they were immediately recalled, Hungary would resign from the Warsaw defense pact. The Russian was a poised, urbane diplomat and his wide face remained impassive as he promised to forward the protest to his government.

At noon Andropov telephoned Nagy and told him soothingly that Soviet troops had crossed the border only to relieve those soldiers who had been fighting and to protect Russian civilians in Hungary. In any event, the Soviet government was ready to discuss the departure of its troops; he suggested that Nagy name a delegation to negotiate the details.

The Nagy government did not accept Andropov's explanations of the Soviet troop movements. There was more telephoning back and forth on that tense afternoon, and at five o'clock the Soviet ambassador was once again called to the neo-Gothic Parliament building. This time the entire Council of Ministers had assembled. Andropov was informed that Hungary had declared its neutrality and was withdrawing from the Warsaw Pact.

By November 3 Budapest was completely encircled by Russian tanks. Nevertheless, negotiations for the withdrawal of Soviet troops began in the Parliament building. Nagy had named a four-man delegation that included his new defense minister, General Pál Maléter, hero of the previous week's battle against the much more powerful Soviet forces. For the other side, General Mikhail S. Malinin headed a delegation of three Soviet generals.

Surprisingly, the talks went well. The Russians agreed to pull their troops out, and the only major point of difference was the date. The Hungarian negotiators accepted the Soviet condition that the troops leave with full ceremony, the last units marching out to the accompaniment of martial music. The talks recessed that afternoon, but in order to iron out remaining details both sides agreed to meet again that night at Soviet headquarters in Tököl, a village on Csepel Island in the Danube, south of Budapest.

At ten o'clock General Maléter and his negotiating team met with the Russians; all went smoothly. During the evening, reports of the progress of the Tököl meeting were relayed to Nagy in Budapest, but just before midnight, telephone contact with the negotiators was cut off. The Hungarians at Tököl had sat down to a Soviet banquet in their honor, but it was interrupted by the arrival of General Ivan Alexandrovich Serov, head of the KGB.

Serov, a character as ominous as his reputation, announced that the Hungarian delegation was under arrest. General Malinin, apparently dumfounded by the turn of events, started to protest forcefully. Serov leaned over and whispered in his ear. Malinin turned red in the face, then white, then red again. He shrugged, and ordered the Soviet delegation to leave the room. The revolt in Hungary was over.*

As the terrible events of those November days faded into history, the role of Ambassador Yuri Andropov was largely forgotten. As for Serov, a decade later he was in disgrace, no longer a member of the government or even of the Communist party.

On May 19, 1967, shortly after 1 A.M., the wires of Tass, the Soviet press agency in Moscow, tapped out the first news of a surprising front-page announcement to be carried in the morning edition of *Pravda,* the party newspaper.

There had been a shakeup in Soviet intelligence. Yuri V. Andropov had just been made the new chairman of the Committee for State Security of the Council of Ministers of the Soviet Union, the Komitet

---

* At 5:56 A.M. on November 4, Nagy futilely broadcast an appeal for Maléter and the other members of the negotiating team to return to their posts. By then the Russians had already set up a new Hungarian government under János Kádár. Bitter street fighting continued for another two days, in vain. Nagy took asylum in the Yugoslav embassy. Later, despite a guarantee of safe-conduct, the bus supposedly taking Nagy to his home was seized by the Russians. In June 1958 the Hungarian Justice Ministry announced that both Nagy and Maléter had been tried and executed.

Gosudarstvennoi Bezopasnosti, better known as the KGB.*

On the back page of *Pravda,* beneath the sports news, an eight-line item cryptically disclosed that Vladimir Y. Semichastny had been relieved of his post as head of the KGB and transferred to unspecified new duties. (Several days later, it was announced that Semichastny had been named a first deputy premier of the Ukraine, a lesser post that removed him from the center of power in Moscow.)

Thus the world learned of the change in command of what is generally accepted as the most sinister intelligence, espionage and secret police organization in existence today.

Few Americans and, for that matter, not many Russians had ever heard of Yuri Andropov. At fifty-two, his hair a bit grayer than in the days of Budapest, the tall former Ambassador and veteran party official could pass, with his businesslike appearance and fluent English, for an American corporation executive. But the organization he heads, while vast, bears little resemblance to IBM, Ford or General Motors.

The KGB has been described by Allen W. Dulles, who competed against it for eight years, as "a multipurpose, clandestine arm of power . . . more than a secret police organization, more than an intelligence and counterintelligence organization. It is an instrument for subversion, manipulation and violence, for secret intervention in the affairs of other countries."

That the description might, in part, also fit the Central Intelligence Agency was doubtless unintentional but not without significance. For the KGB is one of two espionage giants operating today; the CIA, which Mr. Dulles directed, being the other. The two are deeply engaged in a silent struggle involving at least thirty thousand full-time employees, a contest that takes place largely out of view, with the sounds of battle surfacing only occasionally to remind the world that it is going on at all.

The KGB is one of the two major instruments of secret power in the Russian state, but it has a bitter rival in the intelligence arm of the

---

* Pronounced *Kah Gay Beh* in Russia, where it is generally known by its initials to Soviet citizens.

Red Army, the Chief Intelligence Directorate of the General Staff, or GRU * (for Glavnoye Razvedyvatelnoye Upravlenie).

The appointment of Andropov, a Communist party Secretary since 1962, as head of the KGB came as a complete surprise to American intelligence, and very likely to the man he replaced, Vladimir Semichastny, who had held the job for six years. There were several theories within the Western intelligence community on the reason for the shakeup, but the most convincing explanation was that the leader of the Soviet Union, Communist party chief Leonid I. Brezhnev, wanted his own man to head Soviet espionage and intelligence. Semichastny, after all, was a former protégé of Nikita S. Khrushchev's (even though he had assisted Brezhnev and Alexei N. Kosygin in ousting Khrushchev as Premier on October 15, 1964). Semichastny was also a close friend and political ally of one of Brezhnev's potential rivals, the ambitious Alexander N. Shelepin, former KGB chief promoted to the party Presidium in 1964. Indeed, Brezhnev could hardly have forgotten that in 1965 the KGB under Semichastny was spreading reports that Shelepin would replace Brezhnev. Downgrading Semichastny was one way of cutting Shelepin's power in, and ties to, the KGB.

Evidence of all this came less than two months after Semichastny's removal when it was announced that Shelepin had been assigned to head Soviet trade unions, a position of little authority. No doubt there were other factors involved as well. In June 1967, a month after Andropov became chief of the KGB, he was elevated to be a candidate member of the ruling Politburo, at the same time relinquishing his duties as a party Secretary. This gave the new head of Soviet espionage greater political stature than any of his recent

---

* Many CIA and other Western intelligence experts refer to it as an acronym, "the GRU" (as in "grew"), rather than by its initials, as in the case of the KGB. In Russian, the initials would be pronounced *Geh Eh Ru*, but unlike the initials KGB, which are widely known to Soviet citizens, those of the GRU are not, since its existence is not officially admitted.

predecessors. But by the same token, the move seemed designed to tighten party control over the operations of the KGB.

Significantly, it was Andropov who accompanied Brezhnev and Kosygin on their first trip outside the Soviet Union after Khrushchev's overthrow. Less than ten days after the upheaval, Brezhnev, Kosygin and Andropov met secretly at Bialowieska Forest in remote northeastern Poland near the Soviet frontier with Polish Communist leader Wladyslaw Gomulka. As the Soviet party Secretary in charge of relations with foreign Communist parties, Andropov had obviously been brought along to help reassure the Poles that the change in leadership in Moscow was no cause for alarm for them.

An impressive public speaker, Andropov might best be described as a dependable ideological administrator. He was born in 1914 and educated at the State University in Petrozavodsk, an industrial city and capital of the Karelo-Finnish Republic, the area of northwest Russia that borders on Finland.

As a teen-ager he worked as a telegraph operator and motion picture projectionist, but by his early twenties he was an organizer for the Komsomol, the Communist Youth League. He joined the party in 1939 and was soon the Komsomol boss in the city of Yaroslavl. During most of World War II he was the party man in charge of the Komsomol in the Karelo-Finnish Republic. In 1944 he moved up to second secretary of the Communist party organization in Petrozavodsk. After the war he climbed higher on the party ladder and by 1951 he was in Moscow as head of a political department of the Central Committee. In 1953 he was sent to the Soviet embassy in Budapest as an "adviser" and the following year he became ambassador.

In the brief thaw in Hungary that preceded the tragic revolt of 1956, Andropov seemed to come into his own. An outgoing and at least superficially pleasant envoy, he appeared much more at ease than most Russian officials and apparently enjoyed the round of diplomatic parties, at which he frequently mixed with Western diplomats.

To those who met him then, Andropov and his rather attractive wife both appeared to come from a middle-class background. If he was not as polished as his Western colleagues, Andropov was nevertheless a man with some intellectual interests and a sense of humor, Soviet style.

One who came to know him fairly well during this period was N. Spencer Barnes, the chargé d'affaires at the U.S. legation in Budapest before and during the Hungarian revolt. (The American ambassador-designate, Edward T. Wailes, was never permitted to present his credentials.) According to protocol Andropov, as an ambassador, outranked Barnes. But at diplomatic dinners he made a point of slapping the U.S. chargé on the back and saying, "Let's go in together." It was Andropov's way of trying to preserve an atmosphere of friendship with the American legation, although relations were soon to cool off during the revolt.

Andropov also demonstrated that he knew how to preserve the social amenities. Once, during the period of thaw, the Russian ambassador mentioned that his wife suffered from neuralgia. Since Barnes had a similar ailment, he sent around to Andropov a bottle of pills which had been prescribed for him by a doctor in Vienna. Whether they cured the headaches of the wife of the future head of the KGB is not known, but soon afterward Andropov reciprocated by having a copy of Tolstoy's *War and Peace* delivered to Barnes.

Andropov's importance as Moscow's overseer in Hungary was underscored by the fact that he had a direct, untappable telephone line to the leading Communist party and government officials in Hungary. After the revolt had been crushed, Andropov could not comfortably stay in Budapest. Early in 1957 he was replaced by Yevgeny I. Gromov and returned to Moscow. That November, Andropov was named head of the Central Committee department for liaison with foreign Communist parties, a job that entailed much travel—to Mongolia, Yugoslavia, Bulgaria, Poland, Communist China and Albania. In 1962 he was promoted to the party Secretariat, and as a Secretary, he was outspoken in his attacks on Mao Tse-tung and the Red Chinese. He still remained in charge of relations with other Communist parties and journeyed to Hanoi in 1962 and 1963.

Andropov obviously enjoyed the confidence of Brezhnev, as shown by their trip to Poland in 1964 and, even more dramatically, by his appointment in 1967 as head of the still-feared KGB.

This vast espionage, intelligence and police organization has its headquarters near the Kremlin at 2 Dzerzhinsky Street,* named for the first head of the Cheka, of which the KGB is the lineal descendant.

Lubianka, the KGB building, is really two buildings, with the façade remodeled to conceal where they join. One is the KGB prison, where U-2 pilot Francis Gary Powers was initially held. The other contains the KGB administrative offices. The massive stone structure, although once a hotel, resembles an office building; indeed, it housed an insurance company in czarist times.

Oddly, one of the very few Americans who got inside Soviet intelligence headquarters and emerged to tell about it was Major General William J. Donovan, head of the wartime Office of Strategic Services. Donovan did so during a special trip in December 1943. He conferred in Lubianka with Soviet intelligence officials about a plan to exchange OSS and Soviet intelligence missions in Moscow and Washington, as wildly improbable as that may sound in the light of postwar developments. The stated purpose was to trade information about sabotage operations behind German lines.

Averell Harriman, the U.S. ambassador, supported the plan as a fantastic opportunity to get an American intelligence team into Moscow. He argued that since the Russians already had hundreds of officials in the United States on various missions, many of whom were spying, the NKVD mission in Washington would probably be completely "clean" and, at any rate, easily watched. But Admiral William D. Leahy, chief of staff to President Roosevelt, and J. Edgar Hoover, Director of the Federal Bureau of Investigation, were appalled at Donovan's plan. President Roosevelt, concerned over their opposition

---

* Across the street from the KGB headquarters is Detsky Mir (Children's World), a toy and department store.

and the possible domestic political reaction, killed the scheme.* Donovan, at least, had benefited by a peek inside the lion's mouth.

Soviet intelligence has expanded considerably since the days when Donovan breached the citadel. It is true that two weeks before Shelepin stepped up and out of his post as KGB head, he insisted at the Twenty-second Party Congress that the size of Soviet intelligence had "been cut down substantially." But, perhaps with a smile, he neglected to say from what to what.

One of the problems in assessing the size of the KGB is that it combines under one roof the functions of the CIA, the FBI, the Secret Service, the U.S. Border Patrol, and several agencies that don't even exist in the American governmental structure. For example, Soviet experts in the U.S. government believe that there are three hundred thousand KGB border troops, although the estimate fluctuates and is revised from time to time. If these troops and the security guards responsible for the safety of the Soviet leadership are excluded, the KGB would probably be roughly comparable in size to the CIA, perhaps somewhat larger.†

In testimony made public in 1959, Peter Deriabin, a former KGB ‡ agent "surfaced" by the CIA, was questioned about the KGB by a House committee:

---

* The United States and the Soviet Union did continue to exchange daily intelligence information on the German order of battle during World War II. But the Russians never would divulge to the United States their own troop movements and dispositions.

† For a discussion of the CIA's size and budget, see Chapter IV. In an unusual report, the State Department on June 13, 1960, estimated that the Soviet Union, Communist China and other Communist nations combined had a total of three hundred thousand intelligence operatives in twenty-seven espionage and security services. The document also said that "some 18,300 persons" had been arrested in West Germany as Soviet spies since 1952. The report was submitted by Secretary of State Christian A. Herter to Senator J. William Fulbright, Arkansas Democrat and chairman of the Senate Foreign Relations Committee, at a time when the Eisenhower Administration was attempting to publicize Soviet espionage to counterbalance U.S. embarrassment over the U-2 incident.

‡ Actually MGB. Deriabin defected to American intelligence in Vienna in February 1954. His former service became the KGB the following month. Soviet intelligence has undergone a very complex series of splits, mergers and name changes since 1917. Where possible, the correct initials will be given for the time period referred to. But where this might only serve to confuse the reader, "the KGB" will be used in a broader, generic sense, meaning Soviet civilian intelligence.

Q. Can you tell us something about its size, responsibilities, and methods?

A. I would say the size of the foreign section of the Soviet civilian intelligence is about three thousand officers in headquarters in Moscow and about fifteen thousand officers around the world, working as representatives of the Soviet government abroad. The foreign section of the Soviet civilian intelligence is responsible for espionage and counterespionage abroad; also for surveilling Soviet and satellite citizens who travel abroad; and is responsible for carrying out occasional assassinations, kidnaping, blackmail, and similar activities.

Allowing for the fact that Deriabin's estimate is several years old, and applying Parkinson's Law (it is probable that despite Shelepin's cryptic remarks the KGB has grown, not diminished, in size in the past decade), the figure today might be twenty to twenty-five thousand KGB men and women in the espionage and intelligence section.

Nothing can be taken at face value in the espionage business. It should always be borne in mind by the reader that what *any* intelligence agency, East or West, permits to surface publicly, through a defector, or by any other means, may be doctored to confuse the opposition service, or to mislead public opinion at home. Deriabin's estimate may have been inaccurate, possibly even deliberately so, if the CIA wished to mislead the Soviets on the question of how it estimated the size of the KGB. On the other hand, intelligence organizations, and government departments in general, on both sides of the Iron Curtain, tend to overestimate, not underestimate, the size of their opponents in order to justify higher budgets and more personnel.

Defector information is a prime source of the CIA's intelligence on the size and workings of the Soviet apparatus, as Allen Dulles has indicated:

"Oh yes. I would say, looking back on my work in intelligence, that this was one of the two or three most important sources of intelligence. Because . . . when you get a man—and we have got several—who have worked inside the KGB, their Secret Service, or the GRU, their military service, it's just almost as though you had somebody inside there for a time." *

Deriabin was no ordinary defector. Although under CIA protection, he was permitted to collaborate with writer Frank Gibney on a book called *The Secret World,* published by Doubleday in 1959. In a CIA document circulated on Capitol Hill in September of 1965 the Deriabin memoir was described by the CIA as "probably the most authoritative public account of KGB organization and activity." †

How much the Soviet Union spends on intelligence each year is another figure that can only be estimated. CIA officials have indicated that the Russians spend $2,000,000,000 a year on their espionage apparatus, a figure that would not include electronic spying.

In testimony to a House subcommittee in January 1964, Hoover cited an estimate by "a former officer of the KGB" that the Soviet Union "spent about one and a half billion dollars a year" on foreign intelligence activities.‡ While the FBI chief did not directly adopt the figure as his own, the fact that he cited it might be given some weight.

Dulles has talked along the edges of the question, too, and his comments, taken together, suggest that the Soviets spend more than the CIA: "I think we have now an intelligence service that is on very sound ground and as competent as any intelligence service in the world, even including the Soviets, although we haven't as much funds as they do." §

"They have a very wide-flung apparatus. I think that in many

---

* CBS-TV interview with David Schoenbrun, August 18, 1963.

† Quote is from a footnote on page 9 of the original CIA document, *The Soviet and Communist Bloc Defamation Campaign.*

‡ Significantly, Shelepin, while head of the KGB, told the Twenty-first Party Congress on February 4, 1959, that the CIA employed twenty thousand persons and spent $1,500,000,000 a year on espionage primarily directed against the Soviet Union, a budget figure that was almost certainly too high in 1959 but which is accurate today. See Chapter IV.

§ Interview on Georgetown University Radio Forum, March 20, 1963.

ways we are better than they are. In massive coverage they are probably better than we." *

The KGB operates overseas chiefly through an extensive network of agents placed in its embassies, missions and official agencies. These "legal" † KGB operators have official cover and often diplomatic immunity.

A KGB officer in a Soviet embassy abroad may hold high rank, such as first secretary or counselor. He may even be the ambassador. But he might serve as chauffeur or doorman, or occupy some other seemingly menial post.

Vladimir M. Petrov, who dramatically defected with his wife, Evdokia, in Australia in 1954, was a Soviet intelligence officer with the rank of third secretary at the embassy in Canberra. One apparent factor in his decision was that his wife had thrown a pie at the wife of the Soviet ambassador, incurring the envoy's displeasure. The case caused a furor in Australia. A Royal Commission investigation ‡ disclosed widespread Soviet espionage activity, and Australia broke off diplomatic relations with Moscow.

When they were resumed in June 1959, the first diplomat sent to the embassy in Canberra was Ivan Fedorovich Skripov, who held the rank of first secretary but was actually a KGB officer sent to reestablish the espionage network in Australia. Skripov recruited a courier who turned out to be a lady agent of Australian counterintelligence. He first met with her at the Taronga Park Zoo in Sydney. There followed a series of meetings in public places, letters written in invisible ink, pickups of containers from "dead drops" § (hiding places), and the like. The Australians cracked down when Skripov sent the agent to Adelaide with a high-speed radio transmitter for

---

* *Issues and Answers*, ABC-TV, June 30, 1963.

† A somewhat misleading Soviet term. A "legal" agent normally has a "cover" job with a Soviet diplomatic mission, but his real duties as an espionage agent are certainly not "legal," in that they violate the laws of the country he is spying on.

‡ *Report of the Royal Commission on Espionage*, Government Printer for New South Wales, Sydney, 1955.

§ In England they are more commonly known as "dead letter boxes," or D.L.B.'s.

delivery to a Soviet agent. In 1963 the case was surfaced and Skripov was expelled from the country.

Pavel P. Lukianov, KGB station chief * in Washington from 1964 to 1966, had the title of counselor of the Soviet embassy. He and his wife lived at 2144 California Street, in a fashionable residential area of Northwest Washington. He was listed in the Washington telephone book (265–6734).

On the other hand Igor Ivanov, a high-ranking KGB officer caught in 1963, was a chauffeur for Amtorg, the Soviet trade agency headquartered in Manhattan.

Other "legal" covers used by KGB officers in the United States, besides Amtorg and the Washington embassy, are the Soviet Mission to the United Nations, the Byelorussian Mission to the UN, both in New York, and Tass, the official Soviet news agency. Only those at the embassy and the UN missions have diplomatic immunity from arrest, however.

The percentage of spies under legal cover in the United States is not a figure that the Russians might be expected to announce. But J. Edgar Hoover told a House appropriations subcommittee in March 1965 that "the great bulk of official positions abroad" are used by Soviet intelligence for cover. He estimated that "over half" of the Soviet nationals in press positions in the United States "were known to be intelligence agents," that "over half" of Amtorg's employees "were known or suspected to be actually connected with the Soviet intelligence services," and that "over twenty percent" of Soviet students enrolled for that school year were either "suspected of being agents with specific KGB assignments" or officers of Soviet intelligence. Hoover declared that as of February 1965 there were 108 Soviet employees of the UN, "of whom half were agents or officers of the Soviet intelligence services." In testimony a year later he added:

"The head of the New York residency of the KGB is a member of the Soviet Mission to the United Nations and as such he is immune

---

* "Station chief" is the term used by the CIA for the top official under diplomatic cover in a U.S. embassy abroad. The actual Soviet term is *resident,* and the network he directs is the *residentura.*

to arrest and prosecution . . . I might say over one hundred personnel engaged in espionage activities are attached to the KGB in New York City."

He gave no precise estimate, at least in his on-the-record testimony, of the number of KGB agents in the Soviet embassy and UN missions.*

Amtorg was created in 1924 in New York as the Soviet Union's export-import center in America, and from the beginning it has served as a cover for Russian intelligence as well.

Tass (Telegrafnoye Agentstvo Sovyetskoyo Soyouza) was founded the following year, and it has served both as the official Soviet world-wide news agency and as an espionage cover. In 1965, Tass had correspondents in ninety-two countries, and its largest bureaus, in New York, London, Paris and Helsinki, were linked to Moscow by twenty-four-hour-a-day teleprinters. The Australian Royal Commission that investigated the Petrov case called Tass a "recruiting agency for espionage agents." Three Tass correspondents were named as spies in the Australian case.

A Tass man, Nikolai Zheveinov (code name "Martin") was cited as a "cutout," or go-between, in the 1946 *Report of the Royal Commission* on the big Soviet spy ring in Canada. The case broke into the open in 1945 with the defection of Igor S. Gouzenko, a twenty-six-year-old code clerk at the Soviet embassy in Ottawa.

In 1951, Hilding Anderson, a Swedish Navy engineer, was convicted of espionage. He testified at his trial that he had passed information on Swedish military installations to Viktor Anisimov, the genial Tass correspondent in Stockholm. While aboard the Swedish icebreaker *Ymer,* Anderson had sketched military sites on the Karlskrona peninsula in invisible ink, and delivered the results to Anisimov. In a similar case two years later the Dutch government arrested and expelled the Tass man in The Hague, Lev Pisarev, for espionage. In April 1967 the Tass man in Brussels, Anatoli T. Ogorodnikov, thirty-

---

* As of 1966, the Russians had 321 persons in the United States with diplomatic immunity; 205 at the Soviet embassy in Washington and 116 attached to their UN missions. Since January 1, 1957, 28 Soviet officials in the United States have been arrested or expelled. (Figure includes embassy, UN missions and UN Secretariat employees.)

two, was arrested and expelled for "endangering the security of the state." He had attempted to pressure a Belgian woman into obtaining a job at the new NATO headquarters which had just moved from France to Belgium.*

No Tass correspondents have been charged with espionage in the United States, although Mikhail R. (Mike) Sagatelyan, Tass correspondent in Washington during President Kennedy's Administration, was widely regarded within the government as a KGB man.

"Legal" agents under diplomatic cover at the Soviet embassy in Washington, and at the two Russian UN missions in New York, can operate with relative ease. Because they enjoy diplomatic immunity they can at worst be caught, but not arrested or imprisoned. The information they gather can routinely be transmitted in code to the Center† in Moscow, via normal Soviet diplomatic communications channels, or by pouch. Instructions are just as easily received.

A fascinating insight into KGB courier techniques—and the workings of the KGB mind—was provided after the assassination of President Kennedy. Premier Khrushchev had apparently developed a certain fondness for the American President despite their prickly meeting in Vienna in 1961 and their clash during the Cuban missile crisis in 1962. Khrushchev reportedly was stunned and walked around his office in a daze after receiving the flash from Dallas.

He dispatched First Deputy Premier Anastas Mikoyan to Washington for the funeral. Mikoyan left Vnukovo Airport in Moscow on November 24, 1963, aboard a gleaming Ilyushin-18 propjet. Standing off to one side, away from the rest of the dignitaries at the airport, wearing a hat, and looking very much the security man, was Vladimir Semichastny, then chief of the KGB.

---

* In February 1961 a second Soviet press agency, Novosti (News), was formed, specializing in feature stories and photographs. Its correspondents have already run into trouble for political activities in Brazil, Kenya and the Congo.

† The traditional name used by agents in the field for both KGB and GRU headquarters in Moscow. That the word is still part of current KGB intelligence jargon was confirmed, possibly inadvertently, by Soviet spy Rudolf Abel in an article published in *Molodoi Kommunist* (Young Communist), February 1966. Describing for Soviet youth the details of his arrest in New York, Abel said: "The night before, *I had had a radio session with Center* [our italics] and naturally the code materials were in the hotel room."

At the funeral, on the steps of St. Matthew's Cathedral in Washington—where moments earlier John F. Kennedy, Jr., in his powder-blue coat and bright-red shoes, had saluted his father's casket—there appeared a remarkable tableau of world leaders: Charles de Gaulle, towering over the others, erect in the khaki uniform of a brigadier general; Ludwig Erhard, the baby-faced Chancellor of West Germany, looking more like a *Braumeister* than a world leader; Prince Philip, tall and elegant in a gold-braided naval uniform; and there, among them, the short Levantine figure of Mikoyan, unmistakable with his dark mustache and hawklike features. Jacqueline Kennedy later wrote a letter thanking Khrushchev for sending him.

Mikoyan flew back on the same Il-18, and when he arrived, Semichastny was once again at Vnukovo airport, waiting. As soon as Mikoyan was off the plane, two husky Russians, each carrying a large canvas bag, charged down the ramp, ran directly over to the KGB chief and climbed with him into a limousine, which roared off. The only conclusion anyone watching the scene could reach: Semichastny had used the Ilyushin bringing Mikoyan home to Moscow from President Kennedy's funeral—as a KGB courier plane. It was a rare opportunity to ship back intelligence data from Washington direct to Moscow under totally secure conditions.

KGB "legals" in the United States are inhibited only by the travel restrictions imposed on all Soviet diplomats since 1955 (in retaliation for areas closed to American diplomats in Russia since 1941) and by the knowledge that they may be under FBI surveillance. Soviet envoys who wish to travel more than twenty-five miles from the center of Washington or New York must give forty-eight hours' notice and file a complete itinerary. They cannot hire "unchauffeured automobiles" (no Hertz or Avis rental cars, for example), use helicopters or charter planes.*

---

* As of 1966, Soviet diplomats were forbidden to visit points all the way from Kodiak Island, Alaska, to Sagadahoc, Maine. Sample counties among the dozens closed off included Yuma, Arizona; Santa Barbara, California; Okeechobee and Palm Beach, Florida; Chattahoochee, Georgia; Kootenai, Idaho; Du Page, Illinois; Pottawattamie, Iowa; Nantucket, Massachusetts; Muskegon, Michigan; Ashtabula, Ohio; and Dallas, Texas. On the other hand, they were free to go to Miami Beach—but not Las Vegas.

Despite these limitations, KGB agents under "legal" cover are relatively secure in the knowledge that the FBI, however diligent, cannot watch every Soviet diplomat in the United States all the time. Twenty-four-hour surveillance by any counterespionage agency is a complex and expensive business, involving a great deal of man power, since agents must work in three shifts.

Soviet agents in the United States do not have to move about to spy. A vast amount of data shipped from the United States by the KGB comes from open sources such as newspapers, government publications and technical magazines. Nevertheless, KGB "legals" may be, and often are, in time caught by counterespionage methods. They are much more vulnerable than spies who have no official cover at all.

It is these "illegals" who are the most interesting of Russia's agents. They are the highly trained men and women who are "inserted" into another society, much like a wartime parachutist jumping behind the lines. Sometimes they are given a completely false background, or "legend," complete with documentation.

"Illegals" are akin to actors with espionage training, although they risk death or imprisonment rather than bad reviews. At best they are brilliant men, such as Rudolf Ivanovich Abel. At worst they are incompetents, such as Abel's assistant Reino Hayhanen, the drunk who ultimately turned him in.

The good ones are artists, perhaps closer in motivation to astronauts, mountain climbers or speedboat racers, taking risks for reasons that are not entirely clear to themselves or their fellow men. The "illegal" must live out his part for long years, often away from his family, facing prison, perhaps worse, if captured or if the Center becomes disenchanted with his work.

Although there are cases where Soviet intelligence provides an "illegal" with a totally invented identity, current practice of both the KGB and the GRU is to clothe an "illegal" agent in the identity of another person—often, but not always, a dead man.

Because the United States is a nation of immigrants, the "illegal's" task in this country is easier than in others. Before World War II it was not unusual for persons of eastern European extraction to return to their homeland, either on a visit, or for good, often with small children who had been born in the United States. Some of the returning émigrés were trapped by the outbreak of war. Some died; some disappeared. In more than one instance Soviet intelligence adopted their identities for "illegals." The advantage was that a U.S. birth certificate, and often a bona-fide U.S. passport, could then be obtained for the "illegal."

Alexander Orlov, a Soviet intelligence officer who defected to the West, has described it well: "Having arrived in the country where his passport awaits him, the operative undergoes a complete metamorphosis. He sheds his old identity, leaving all possible traces behind, takes his false passport, and becomes an entirely new person. From there he starts to 'swim,' as the Soviet lingo goes, and travels to the country of his assignment." *

To understand how this works in practice, it is worth exploring the "legends" used by Abel and Hayhanen.

Two years after the war, in July 1947, a fifty-one-year-old naturalized American living in Detroit, Andrew Kayotis, received a passport to visit relatives in his native Lithuania. He was not in good health when he set out on his trip that year, and subsequently friends received letters indicating that he was in a hospital. Nothing more was heard after that and his friends assumed he had died.

More than a year later, in the fall of 1948, a tall, thin, wispy-haired man boarded a ship at Le Havre, France, bound for Canada. On November 14 he disembarked at Quebec and disappeared. His passport said he was Andrew Kayotis, American citizen.

In fact, he was Rudolf Abel,† a full colonel in the KGB. (Ranks

---

* *Handbook of Intelligence and Guerrilla Warfare* (Ann Arbor, University of Michigan Press, 1963). A short but excellent account of Soviet intelligence techniques.

† A novel published in the Soviet Union in 1965, *The Shield and the Sword*, by Vadim Kozhevnikov, indicated that Abel's real name was Alexander Ivanovich Belov. It claims he was born in Polvolog, Russia, in 1903, that he was educated as an engineer, transferred to the KGB in 1927 at the recommendation of the Komsomol and during World War II penetrated the Abwehr (German military intelligence) under the name of Johann Weiss.

corresponding to those in the Army were established in Soviet intelligence in 1945.) Abel crossed the border from Canada, not a difficult feat, and around 1949 began his espionage activities in the United States. Not all of his movements are known, but by 1954 he was living as an artist-photographer named Emil R. Goldfus in a studio at 252 Fulton Street in Brooklyn. (A child named Emil Robert Goldfus was born on August 2, 1902, in New York—a date probably close to Abel's real birthdate—but died in infancy. When arrested, Abel had a copy of this birth certificate with him.)

The KGB inserted Hayhanen into New York as an "illegal" by similar means. Hayhanen, a short, husky man, was born near Leningrad on May 14, 1920, the son of peasants. For a short period he was a schoolteacher. In November 1939 he was drafted into the NKVD. Fluent in Finnish, he was put to work as an interpreter interrogating prisoners in the Soviet-Finnish war. In 1948 he was called to Moscow and given an assignment to prepare him for entry into the United States. Accordingly, in the summer of 1949 he was sent to Finland to build up his legend as an American-born laborer, Eugene Nicolai Maki.

The real Maki was born in Enaville, Idaho, on May 30, 1919, the son of an American mother and a Finnish immigrant father who had come to the United States in 1905. In the mid-1920's his parents sold their Idaho farm and sailed with him for Estonia. There the trail fades; presumably, they were swallowed up by the war.

As Eugene Maki, Hayhanen lived in Finland, in the cities of Tampere and Turku, until October 1952. In 1951 he walked into the U.S. legation in Helsinki and produced a birth certificate indicating that he was born in Enaville, Idaho. Later that year, although he already had a wife and son in the Soviet Union, he married Hanna Kurikka, a twenty-seven-year-old girl from Siilinjärvi, who was to join him in the United States. On July 28, 1952, he was given a U.S. passport, and after a clandestine trip to Moscow * for last-minute instructions, he sailed from Southampton aboard the *Queen Mary,* arriving in New York on October 21, 1952.

---

* Hayhanen told U.S. intelligence he crossed the Finnish-Russian border in an automobile trunk.

By 1954 he had been assigned to assist Abel, whom he knew only as "Mark." But Hayhanen (code name "Vic") drank heavily, abused his attractive blond wife in public, and botched his espionage assignments. Abel ordered him home. On April 24, 1957, Hayhanen sailed for Le Havre aboard the *Liberté*. In Paris, following Abel's instructions, he dialed a special number (KLEber 33-41) and asked, "Can I send through your office two parcels to the U.S.S.R. without Mori Company?" He then had two meetings in Paris with Soviet agents, who instructed him to fly to West Berlin and then to Moscow. Hayhanen thought better of it, telephoned the U.S. embassy and defected to the CIA station in Paris. He was rushed back to the United States.

Abel, hedging his bets, or possibly warned by Dzerzhinsky Street that his assistant might not arrive in Moscow, had dropped out of sight on April 26, while Hayhanen was on the high seas en route to Europe aboard the *Liberté*.

Hayhanen did not know where "Mark" lived, but once in 1955 he had been taken by him to a storage room at the Fulton Street address in Brooklyn. This proved to be a costly mistake by Abel. The FBI staked out the neighborhood, and one night in June, Abel returned to his studio. The FBI trailed Abel back to the Hotel Latham, at 4 East Twenty-eighth Street in Manhattan, where he was arrested by immigration agents on June 21, 1957. He was registered under the name of Martin Collins and had a birth certificate (forged) in that name. All told, Abel and Hayhanen had used the identities and papers of four Americans, at least three of whom were real persons, living or dead.

The KGB collects these identities much in the manner of Tammany ward heelers who gathered "tombstone" voters to keep the Democrats in power in New York. That it has literally done so was revealed in the story, little known outside of Canada, of George Victor Spencer, an obscure postal clerk who will go down in history not for his own misdeeds but as the man who indirectly touched off Canada's explosive Munsinger case.

Victor Spencer was born in England and brought to Canada by

his parents as an infant. He was a misfit, a sad, confused and lonely little man who dabbled in Communism and Pavlovian psychology, wrote poetry, and in his own eccentric way seemed to want to improve the lot of mankind. But as an elderly lady who had known him from childhood wrote to the Commission of Inquiry, he "couldn't find the answers."

He had one shining moment in the Army during World War II when, according to the commission report, "he made some very valuable mechanical suggestions in respect to tanks, on which he was working. These suggestions were tested and adopted, with the result that he received the British Empire Medal." In everything else, Spencer was a failure. He failed as a spy (for he was caught), in his marriage, and even as a Communist, for he had been expelled from the Canadian party in 1946.

Spencer, who worked in the Vancouver post office, first met a Soviet contact in 1956. A few years later he was recruited by Lev Burdiukov, the KGB station chief in Canada.* He flew to Ottawa at Soviet expense seven times between 1960 and 1963 for meetings with Burdiukov, Rem Krassilnikov, another KGB man under Soviet-embassy cover in Ottawa, and Anatoli E. Bytchkov, embassy commercial attaché, who was also a KGB agent.

The official Commission of Inquiry into the Spencer case reported in 1966 that Spencer had been asked by his Soviet controllers to visit cemeteries around Vancouver, British Columbia, "to obtain data from headstones in the graveyards and to photograph several headstones for this purpose."

---

* Before that, Burdiukov had been an employee of the UN Secretariat in New York, where he shared an apartment with Pavel Lukianov, who later became the KGB station chief in Washington. Both men obviously were being groomed in New York for positions of high responsibility in the KGB; Washington and Ottawa are intelligence plums, not lightly assigned by Moscow. Spencer did not know Burdiukov's name at the time of their meetings. But Burdiukov made the mistake of having his picture taken for an article in *Northern Neighbors* magazine entitled "U.S.S.R. Salutes Other Lands, Other Peoples." The story described him as "L. Burdiukov," a Soviet embassy secretary, speaking to the U.S.S.R.-Canadian Friendship Society about cultural exchanges. Later, when Canadian counterespionage agents showed this photograph to Spencer, he was able to identify Burdiukov.

W. H. Kelly, director of security and intelligence for the Royal
Canadian Mounted Police and, as such, Canada's top counterespionage authority, testified that the Russians wanted the tombstone names
because "they intended to send somebody to Canada under the
names" and "this would enable them to get documentation in the
name of the person named on the tombstone . . . there was less
chance of the 'illegal' running into his namesake because that person
was known to be dead."

Kelly also testified that Spencer was asked by the Soviets "to
provide addresses of about ten farms which were for sale in the
Surrey, B.C., area," just north of the U.S. border.*

Ontario Supreme Court Justice Dalton Wells, who issued the
commission report, concluded that the Soviets wanted the farms as
"suitable property for the establishment of a Russian Intelligence
Service 'illegal' network. The location of the farms, close as they were
to the U.S. border, suggested that the 'illegal' residence . . . would be
operating chiefly espionage agents on the West Coast, possibly both in
Canada and the United States."

A farm could also serve as a safe border-crossing point for
Soviet "illegals" slipping into the state of Washington. Some of these
agents could have used the identities collected by Spencer from Vancouver graveyards.

In a statement to the Mounted Police, Spencer said he had
passed along information on the farms, as well as addresses of thirty
to forty bankrupt firms. Kelly testified that Spencer was also asked by
the Russians to provide addresses of apartment houses that no longer
existed, "schools that had been torn down," and descriptions of
"clothing worn by local people and general customs" in Vancouver.
All of this information, Kelly said, was for "providing legends for
'illegal' agents. The significance of obtaining information concerning
schools that had been destroyed, businesses that had been destroyed,

---

* Surrey is an attractive area of dairy and vegetable farms and fruit
orchards of every variety. Had it become more widely known, the KGB scheme
to purchase spy farms would particularly have offended the nearest U.S.
community, the little border town and port of Blaine in Whatcom County,
Washington. A tourist and farm center and gateway to Canada, it prides itself
in the fact that on the international line at Blaine stands a Peace Arch.

was that the . . . 'illegal' would be able to receive documentation which could not be checked."

The gravely ill Spencer was not charged or brought to trial. He claimed that he had worked for the Russians because he wanted a free visit to the Soviet Union—but he received about $3,500 for his efforts. He was eased out of his postal job in 1965 when Bytchkov was expelled from Canada. By then Spencer was dying of cancer, and in his last months he pathetically turned to the Mounted Police, to whom he had confessed, as his only friends. They helped shelter him from the press, and sympathized with him. But in 1966, after he was finally dismissed and stripped of his pension, the Conservatives attacked the Liberal government of Prime Minister Lester Pearson for allegedly mishandling the case and violating Spencer's rights.

Stung by these accusations, Pearson's Minister of Justice, Lucien Cardin, charged in March that Gerda Munsinger, a voluptuous East German blond and one-time spy, had been romantically linked with Ministers in the Conservative government of former Prime Minister John Diefenbaker. (Diefenbaker came to power in 1957, but the Liberals under Pearson had turned him out in 1963.)

Cardin added that the unfortunate Gerda had returned to Germany and died. The Toronto *Star* didn't think so, and tracked Gerda down in her Munich apartment at Ainmillerstrasse 1. "Sure, I've been out with a man for dinner," she purred as millions watched her on Canadian television. "Sure I've been out with a man to play golf. Well, why shouldn't I? I'm a woman . . . like every normal woman."

The resultant sex-and-security scandal boomeranged. Conservatives charged Cardin with "McCarthyism" in making unproved allegations, and for a time the backlash threatened the Pearson government itself. To stave off disaster, the Prime Minister quickly ordered an official inquiry, which ultimately concluded, in a ninety-three-page report,* that the Munsinger affair might well be "worse than the Profumo case." The object of all this official and unofficial attention

---

* Solemnly entitled *Report of the Commission of Inquiry Into Matters Relating to One Gerda Munsinger;* The Honourable Mr. Justice Wishart Flett Spence, Commissioner, September 1966, Queen's Printer and Controller of the Stationery, Ottawa.

was born in what is now East Germany, where her father taught at a Communist party school in Königsberg. When West German police arrested her in 1949, she admitted that she had spied for the Russians. Her "espionage activities," the Canadian inquiry said, "had included contact over a considerable period with a major in the Russian intelligence service and the carrying out of several missions upon the latter's instructions."

Under her maiden name of Fräulein Heseler, Gerda applied for a visa to enter Canada in 1952. But the Mounties discovered that she was a self-admitted spy and "a common prostitute, a petty thief and a smuggler." Turned down, she married a U.S. Army sergeant named Michael Munsinger.

The United States would not let her in, either, for the same reasons as Canada, and the marriage ended in divorce in 1954. (Michael Munsinger, a one-time pitcher for the Ottawa Athletics, was a New York City patrolman when the scandal, to which he unwittingly gave his name, broke.)

In August 1955, using her married name, Gerda somehow slipped through the net and entered Canada aboard the S.S. *Arosa Sun*. Pierre Sevigny was named Associate Minister of National Defence by Diefenbaker in August 1959, and he first met her a few weeks later in Montreal, where she was working as a call girl. The government commission reported that Sevigny had "illicit sexual relations" with Gerda. It also found that George Hees, Diefenbaker's Minister of Trade, had committed a "slight but regrettable" indiscretion in his more casual relationship with the blond divorcee.

In 1960, with backing from Sevigny, Gerda applied for Canadian citizenship. Bells began to ring all over Ottawa as the Mounties discovered she was none other than Gerda Heseler. The head of the Mounted Police called on the Justice Minister, who called on Prime Minister Diefenbaker, who called in Sevigny. The Associate Defence Minister admitted that he had enjoyed Mrs. Munsinger's services, and the Prime Minister told him that however enjoyable these may have been, the Associate Defence Minister must surely understand that he had enjoyed them for the last time. He did not, however, fire Sevigny.

The Commission of Inquiry severely criticized Diefenbaker for this, calling his decision "most imprudent." The Prime Minister should have realized, it said, that Sevigny's liaison was a "security risk requiring his retirement from the Cabinet."

In April 1966, at the height of the Munsinger uproar, Victor Spencer, the little postal worker who had photographed tombstones for the KGB, died of cancer at the age of sixty-two. The desire of Moscow to collect identities for its "illegals," had, as a totally unexpected by-product, shaken the government of Canada to its very roots.

The KGB obtains identities for some of its "illegals" from the passports of American tourists traveling in the Soviet Union, in other Communist countries or even in Western Europe. Russian and many European hotels retain the passports of tourists overnight and it is simple enough for a Soviet agent working in a hotel to photograph or copy down American passport data.

Sometimes bolder methods are employed. On June 7, 1963, Paul Carl Meyer, a tall, mustached youth walked into the Chicago field office of the CIA and confessed that he had delivered fifteen U.S. passports to Soviet officials in East Berlin the previous February.

Meyer's story was a strange one. He was a high school dropout who had taught English in Quito in 1961 and prospected for minerals. His wife, Yolanda, was Ecuadorian. Meyer ran ads in U.S. newspapers advertising job opportunities in South America, and he persuaded fifteen Americans who responded to turn over their passports to him for safekeeping. Late in 1962 he showed up in Madrid and then in Berlin, where he turned over the passports to the Russians. How much he was paid remains hazy. The twenty-five-year-old ex-Army private pleaded guilty and was sentenced in February 1965 to two years in prison.

Although all major intelligence agencies are capable of manufacturing a near-perfect passport of any nation in the world,* it is far

---

* The State Department goes to extraordinary lengths to foil KGB forgers or ordinary criminals. The Payne-Jones Company of Lowville, New York, makes the azure passport cover in a simulated plastic material called Lexide for which the manufacturing process is secret. The special paper with

easier to alter a valid passport, or to fill out a blank one, if a blank can be stolen.

Why should the KGB go to such lengths to collect real names and documentation for its "illegals"? Why not, for example, simply invent a person with a totally false legend and insert him into another country? The answer is that in today's society, with computers, punch-card identification numbers, and the like, it is simpler and safer to use someone else's identity, someone, for example, who already has a social security number, who has filed income tax returns, and who has a valid history of education and employment. The Soviet agent then literally claims to be that person. In a country with a large population, such as the United States, the danger of a Soviet "illegal" ever bumping into his namesake at a cocktail party is of course minimal, but it could happen.

KGB "illegals" communicate with the Center in Moscow by a variety of means: by courier, by ordinary mail sent to cover addresses in Western Europe, by microdots, and in some instances, by channeling information to the legal *residentura.*

A microdot is a speck of film that must be optically magnified many times to be read. With the use of microdot photography, a

---

its hard-to-duplicate sunburst pattern is made by the American Writing Paper Corporation of Holyoke, Massachusetts, under tight security conditions.

Although most tourists are unaware of it, watermarks of the great seal of the United States are invisibly embedded on every page of an American passport. (They can be seen only if held to the light.) Even the eagle superimposed on the crucial first four pages is larger than that adorning subsequent pages. The prefix to the numbers perforated into the top of each passport is coded alphabetically and changed each year, with the letter A used at the start of each decade, Z for passports issued abroad, X for the black diplomatic and Y for the maroon official passports.

Soviet technicians who specialize in forging passports are known as "cobblers." Passports, quite logically, are "shoes." (As with any jargon, that of Soviet intelligence changes, but the KGB has for years been known to its rival Soviet spy agencies as "the neighbors"; a hiding place as a *dubok* (literally "little oak"); a local Communist party, "the corporation"; a radio transmitter, a "music box"; a legal front for espionage, a "roof"; a safe house, a *yavka;* prison, a "hospital"; arrest, "illness"; and *nash,* literally, "one of us" or "ours"—a Soviet agent.)

document can be reduced to the size of the period at the end of this sentence. A microdot can be glued over a period in an ordinary typewritten letter, for example, and mailed anywhere in the world. It is almost impossible to detect.

Because meetings between agents can be risky and conspicuous, and because members of a network are not usually permitted to know one another by sight, Soviet intelligence favors a system of "dead drops" to pass along espionage data within the *apparat*. A hollow tree, a loose brick on a stairway, any small cache not likely to be disturbed by children, squirrels or passers-by generally will serve.

That the KGB must worry about such chance calamities was illustrated by an episode in the Abel case. Abel and Hayhanen had been using a hole in a flight of cement steps in Brooklyn's Prospect Park. Park Department employees noticed the hole and filled it with cement while a message from Abel was still inside. When Hayhanen arrived at the spot, he couldn't get the message out.

After he defected, Hayhanen told the FBI about the incident. The FBI cracked open the cement, and sure enough, there was the message inside a hollowed-out bolt. (An FBI witness later testified it had been typed on the typewriter found in Abel's studio.) The message reflected Abel's dissatisfaction with his alcoholic assistant:

"Nobody came to meeting either 8th or 9th at 203. 2030 as I was advised he should. Why? Should he be inside or outside? Is time wrong? Place seems right. Please check."

The lengths to which Moscow goes in selecting "dead drops" was reflected as well by a message from KGB headquarters to its *resident* in Australia. The message, one of a host of documents taken by Petrov when he defected in 1954, was made public by the Australian Royal Commission. It complained in general about poor drops selected by the KGB men in Australia, and then added: "In our opinion, a crack between the boards supporting the railroad bridge embankment cannot be used as a secret hiding place for documents,*

---

* The data passed in drops is often reduced to microfilm. Sometimes it is placed in a magnetic container that can be fastened to a steel bridge girder or other metal surface. Or it is hidden inside hollowed-out cuff links, nails, pencils, bolts or coins.

because the railway bridge is probably regularly inspected by the appropriate persons, and in exceptional circumstances might be guarded."

KGB "illegals" normally receive their instructions by shortwave transmissions from Moscow at stated intervals. Owning a shortwave radio is not unusual in the United States, a nation of ham operators and hi-fi hobbyists. Abel had one and so did Robert K. Baltch, about whom we will have more to say later.* Contrary to the popular notion about Russian spies, however, an "illegal" rarely sends information to Moscow by radio. His transmission might be overheard. And a transmitter, because of the size of the aerial required to reach the Soviet Union, might arouse suspicion of the neighbors, or even of today's spy-conscious children.

Although it is sometimes thought that an "illegal" will never go near a legal Soviet agent, that is simply not the case. Like a pre-atomic submarine that had to come up for air, or a B-52 bomber that must be refueled while aloft on a long mission, an "illegal" needs periodic "servicing." He may require new passports or other documentation, money or urgent instructions. In almost every Soviet mission abroad there is an "illegal support officer" whose job, as the title implies, is to provide this kind of assistance.

Aside from the fact that "illegals," if undetected, can operate much more freely than KGB agents under "legal" cover, Soviet intelligence is interested in building up its "illegal" networks in all countries because it would have to rely entirely upon such agents in place in the event of war or a break in diplomatic relations. In that case, "illegals" could no longer rely on embassy support officers and would have to make new arrangements.

Soviet agents communicate with the Center in code and cipher. Cryptology, the science of secret communications, is a complex subject, almost impossible to explain in detail without the use of elaborate tables and charts, and for the nonexpert, even those don't help very much. Basically, codes use symbols or groups of letters to mean whole words, phrases or thoughts. Ciphers use single letters, or pairs

---

* Both were Hallicrafters.

of letters, or numbers, as substitutes for single letters.

The Russians used code to communicate with Robert Glenn Thompson, the ex-Air Force enlisted man from Bay Shore, Long Island, who got a thirty-year sentence for espionage in May 1965. He had been told to buy a shortwave radio and listen to a specific place on the band for the code words "Amour Lenin." This alerted him to the fact that other coded messages would follow. Such short phrases can readily be memorized, but for longer messages, persons communicating in code must have identical copies of a code book. And since code books can fall into hostile hands, it is often desirable to communicate in cipher.

A simple cipher, in which one letter of the alphabet is substituted for another, can easily be deciphered, because letters appear in a language according to well-established principles of frequency.* (In English, for example, the letter *E* appears far more often than any other.)

Soviet intelligence ciphers are much more sophisticated. Both the KGB and the GRU use miniature cipher pads known as "one-time pads," or "gammas." The ciphers are unbreakable †—even by the spectacular electronic code machines and computers of the National Security Agency at Fort Meade, Maryland—because each page is used only once and then destroyed.

The Soviet "illegal" and Moscow headquarters each has a copy of a pad, usually no bigger than a postage stamp, consisting of pages of nitrated cellulose, which can be burned in an instant. Some pads contain as many as 250 pages. On each page dozens of five-digit groups are printed. The numbers on half of the pages in a pad are printed in red, on the rest of the pages they are in black. The agent uses the black pages to encipher outgoing messages, and the red to decipher incoming messages. The only other copy of the one-time pad is in Moscow; using it, the Center can encipher or decipher any message. Because the number groups vary on each page and are

---

* Edgar Allan Poe explained how to solve such simple cryptograms in his classic story "The Gold Bug."

† Or holocryptic, as the professional cryptanalyst would say.

selected at random, they are meaningless to anyone attempting to crack the cipher.

These KGB/GRU cipher pads must be used in conjunction with a complex matrix of numbers and letters known as a Monome-Dinome table. The agent commits to memory a key phrase or word from which he derives the numbers that are used as the side and top co-ordinates of the table. The letters of the alphabet are then filled in. The resultant matrix can be read much like a motorist reads the co-ordinates on a road map or on a mileage table. Using the matrix, the agent enciphers the Russian "plain text" (the message to be sent) by replacing each Russian letter with the two numbers obtained from the co-ordinates of the grid.

Suppose the first five numbers that resulted from this "map-reading" process were 07048. He would then turn to his one-time pad. (He would ignore the first five-digit group on the page he has chosen because it is transmitted to Moscow as is, to tell the Center which page of the one-time pad is being used; this is known as the "indicator group." Without it, Moscow would have to try every page on the pad to find the right one.) The agent would add 07048 to the second group of five digits appearing on the page of his cellulose cipher pad. If, for example, the second group on the pad was 36056, the cipher text sent to the Soviet Union would be 33094. This is because in adding figures, the KGB uses modular arithmetic—numbers are not "carried over" into the next column, i.e.:

$$
\begin{array}{r}
07048 \\
+\ 36056 \\
\hline
33094
\end{array}
$$

To decipher the message, Moscow simply subtracts 36056 from the total and works the whole thing backwards.

Even such elaborate precautions do not guarantee against human failure. On the evening of June 22, 1953, James F. Bozart, a newsboy for the Brooklyn *Eagle,* knocked on the door of a lady customer at 3403 Foster Avenue in Brooklyn to collect a bill. As he was leaving he dropped his change on the staircase. One of the coins, a 1948 Jefferson nickel, split apart. Inside was a tiny bit of microfilm barely more than a quarter of an inch square. The newsboy turned the coin over to the police, who gave it to the FBI. The coin contained a microscopic hole in the letter *r* in the word "Trust," through which a needle could be inserted to push open the nickel. When the microfilm was enlarged it proved to be a page with twenty-one rows of five-digit numbers, 207 number groups in all.

For four years the FBI was baffled by the cipher, and the best human and mechanical brains in the intelligence community could not unscramble it. Not until Hayhanen defected in 1957 and began talking about his cipher was the FBI able to read the message in the coin. It proved to be the first message from Moscow to the bibulous KGB man, who claimed he had no idea how the coin had gotten into circulation.*

The key word that Hayhanen had memorized and used to make up his matrix was *snegopa,* the Russian word for "snowfall." Apparently he did not have a one-time pad (as Abel did), but used a considerably more complicated, though similar system. In addition to the key word, he had also memorized three other items needed to arrive at the numbers used in the cipher. They were the first twenty letters of a Russian folk song, the date September 3, 1945 (the day Russia considers it defeated Japan in World War II) and the number 13, Hayhanen's agent number.

. . .

---

* The message had been sent on December 3, 1952, six weeks after Hayhanen's arrival in the United States. It was deciphered eighteen days before Abel's capture. It read:

1. We congratulate you on a safe arrival. We confirm the receipt of your letter to the address "V repeat V" and the reading of letter number 1.
2. For organization of cover, we gave instructions to transmit to you three thousand in local (currency). Consult with us prior to investing it in any kind of business, advising the character of this business.
3. According to your request, we will transmit the formula for the preparation of soft film and news separately, together with [your] Mother's letter.
4. It is too early to send you the gammas. Encipher short letters, but the longer ones make with insertions. All the data about yourself, place of work, address, etc., must not be transmitted in one cipher message. Transmit insertions separately.
5. The package was delivered to your wife personally. Everything is all right with the family. We wish you success. Greetings from the comrades. Number 1, 3rd of December.

Besides skill in ciphers, codes and other tradecraft, an "illegal" obviously must also have a basic knowledge of the language and customs of the country to which he is assigned. In the United States, however, a foreign accent is common enough, particularly in urban centers, so that a Soviet illegal does not have to speak flawless English to be assigned to America. There is strong evidence that both KGB and GRU "illegal" agents are invariably sent first to New York, a city of many foreigners and many accents, where they become acclimated to the United States. From New York, some are sent on to other areas of the country.

Since the early 1950's, U.S. diplomats in Moscow have heard persistent reports of so-called American villages where Soviet agents are allegedly trained in surroundings similar to any small town in America. The villages are said to be replete with Fords, Chevrolets, supermarkets, hamburgers and ice cream sodas. Only English is spoken. The existence of these villages, it should be emphasized, is entirely in the realm of speculation. But responsible U.S. officials say it is certainly possible that they exist, if not in such detailed and imaginative form. For a time U.S. intelligence suspected that there might be such a village on the route from Moscow to Kiev, since U.S. diplomats were not allowed to travel directly to that city.

The Russians get indignant when reports identifying an alleged American town crop up in the Western press. A few years back, when Moscow officials were complaining about a spate of such stories, an enterprising West German correspondent challenged them to let him see the village in question to prove or disprove the rumors once and for all.

To his surprise, the Russians took the correspondent to the village. It proved to be an ordinary Russian town, but skeptics suggested that the KGB had switched the road signs identifying the town for the benefit of the visitor.

American villages or not, there are at least three schools in Moscow where Russians can study every subject in English or German or French. And Soviet students of English, when they complete their basic course, are given a choice of continuing with either "American English" or "Oxford English." KGB men get special training at the Higher School in Moscow, also known as the KGB Institute. Although it may seem incongruous, considering the prevailing image of a beetle-browed Soviet spy, students at the school's Juridical Institute can take a four-year course in internal security, intelligence and law. A graduate receives the equivalent of a law degree, but he cannot hang it on his wall or acknowledge it in any overt way unless he is separated from the KGB and needs proof of his more advanced education to get another job.*

The KGB Higher School also teaches foreign languages, surveillance, military strategy, counterintelligence, and so forth. Officers in the foreign intelligence directorate of the KGB are trained in that section's own institute, the Higher Intelligence School.

Befitting an organization with strong ties to the campus, the KGB maintains its own soccer team, the Dynamo.† The Dynamo Sports Club is the KGB club in Moscow and one of the two biggest in the Soviet Union, its major rival being Spartak, the Red Army sports organization. Top Dynamo players, much like football scholarship students at some U.S. colleges, have nominal jobs with the KGB but are virtually professional athletes. Dynamo has local branches all over the Soviet Union.

All in all, the KGB has become an increasingly professional organization, one less identified with the personality of a particular chief than in the past, and protected to some extent from the decimation of its ranks that characterized Soviet intelligence in Stalin's time, when it was alternately the instrument and victim of terror. Since Stalin's death, important fallen political leaders in the Soviet Union have been exiled or isolated but not executed, and the life expectancy of an intelligence chief has improved accordingly.

---

* Interestingly, CIA men in the Clandestine Services face even stricter regulations. Depending on the nature of their work, in many cases they are not permitted to cite CIA employment to their prospective new employer—creating an awkward career gap on their applications.
† Rhymes with "teenamo."

But as an instrument of control, and at times of terror, the Soviet state security apparatus has always been remarkably and ironically similar to the Okhrana (Okhrannoye Otdelenie, or Department of State Protection), the secret police of the czars after the assassination of the relatively liberal Czar Alexander II in 1881, and a hated symbol of the regime overthrown by the Russian Revolution. Its record of spying in the United States goes back to 1883, the year it sent agents to America to watch Vladimir Legaev, an Okhrana defector who escaped to the United States and taught at colleges in Buffalo and Chicago. The Okhrana kept laboriously detailed cards on revolutionaries and prominent citizens. It discovered, for example, that Joseph Stalin had a webbed foot. Stalin's Okhrana card, dated May 1, 1904, recorded that the second and third toes of the future dictator's left foot were grown together.

The Soviet system which supplanted the Okhrana has operated under a succession of shifting names and initials. On three occasions it has been split into two agencies, one for the police and the other for espionage, intelligence and internal security. The following table shows in somewhat oversimplified form how the system has evolved. The table lists the chief, the name of the organization at that time, his term of office and fate.

Dzerzhinsky, F. E.: Cheka, GPU, OGPU, 1917–26, died of heart attack.

Menzhinsky, V. R.: OGPU, 1926–34, died, possibly poisoned by his successor.

Yagoda, G. G.: NKVD, 1934–36, executed in 1938.

Yezhov, N. I.: NKVD, 1936–38, vanished, presumably executed.

Beria, L. P.: NKVD, MVD, 1938–53, executed in 1953.

Merkulov, V. N.: NKGB, 1941, 1943–46, executed in 1953.

Kruglov, S. N.: NKVD, MVD, 1946–56, dismissed.

Abakumov, V. S.: MGB, 1946–51, executed in 1954.

Ignatiev, S. D.: MGB, 1951–53, dismissed.

Serov, I. A.: KGB, 1954–58, transferred to GRU, ousted 1963.

Dudorov, N. P.: MVD, 1956–60, transferred to construction post.

Shelepin, A. N.: KGB, 1958–61, promoted to Secretariat.

Semichastny, V. Y.: KGB, 1961–67.

Shchelokov, N. A.: MOOP, 1966–

Andropov, Y. V.: KGB, 1967–

The father of Soviet intelligence and espionage was Felix Edmundovich Dzerzhinsky, born in 1877 to a landed Polish family near Vilna. He was a religious child and had planned to enter the priesthood. Instead, he turned to the religion of the Bolsheviks. He was poetic and emotional, a romantic fanatic to whom the end apparently justified the bloodiest of means.

On December 20, 1917, the Cheka (Chrezvychainaya Komissiya po Borbe s Kontr-revolutisiei i Sabotazhem, or Extraordinary Commission for Combating Counterrevolution and Sabotage) was founded with Dzerzhinsky as its head. In his hands it became an unparalleled instrument of torture and terror; today KGB men are still known as Chekists. From the beginning Lubianka was its headquarters.

On February 6, 1922, the Cheka was abolished and replaced by the GPU (Gosudarstvennoye Politicheskoye Upravlenie, or State Political Administration). On November 15, 1923, while still under Dzerzhinsky's control, its name was changed to OGPU, or United (Obiedinennoye) State Political Administration.

When Dzerzhinsky died a natural death three years later, OGPU was turned over to another chief of Polish origin, Vyacheslav Rudolfovich Menzhinsky. Like Dzerzhinsky, he left much of the day-to-day operation to his deputy, Genrikh Grigoryevich Yagoda, who succeeded him, and may have created the job opening by murdering him. In any event, Menzhinsky died in May of 1934, and Yagoda took over on July 10. That month OGPU faded into history, absorbed and replaced by the NKVD (Narodnyi Komissariat Vnutrennikh Del, or People's Commissariat for Internal Affairs), (OGPU's functions were taken over by a division of the NKVD called the GUGB).

On December 1 Sergei M. Kirov, a close associate of Stalin's and boss of the Leningrad party, was assassinated with one shot by a young Communist named Leonid Nikolayev under circumstances that suggested the NKVD was responsible, acting under higher orders. The assassination was the signal for the bloody purges of the late 1930's and the excuse that Stalin used to eliminate all opposition.

In his secret speech of February 25, 1956, to the Twentieth Party Congress, in which he exposed the crimes of Stalin, Khrushchev hinted that Stalin had been behind the assassination. In his address to the Twenty-second Party Congress on October 27, 1961, Khrushchev implied Stalin's guilt even more strongly. He said the NKVD had picked up Nikolayev twice before the murder and found weapons on him but released him both times "on somebody's instruction."

Under Yagoda, the NKVD prepared the first of the great show trials. Once Yagoda and the old Chekists had served Stalin's purpose, he calmly removed and exterminated them. Yagoda was dismissed in September 1936, arrested in April 1937, found guilty in The Trial of the Twenty-one—the type of proceeding he had so often helped to prepare—and executed the following year.

On September 26, 1936, Yagoda had been replaced by Nikolai Ivanovich Yezhov, who is roughly equivalent in the annals of the Soviet secret police to Heinrich Himmler. His name provided the Russian language with a new word, synonymous with terror: the Yezhovshchina, as the second half of the Great Purge came to be called. By July 1938 it was Yezhov's turn. He was eased out and succeeded by Lavrenti Pavlovich Beria, who formally took over as NKVD chief in December. In a quaint touch, Yezhov was briefly named Commissar of Inland Water Transport before he disappeared forever.

Beria, the most powerful of Stalin's security chiefs, was a cold, ominous-looking man * whom the world came to know when he ended up, briefly, as one of Stalin's heirs.

Like Stalin, a native of Georgia, he had worked in intelligence there and in Baku during the early days of the Revolution. Beria was NKVD chief until 1946, but retained control of the secret police

---

* Although not to everybody. The story is told that when General Eisenhower returned from his visit to the Soviet Union in 1945, his son, John, said, "We met one really nice guy over there—Beria."

machinery even after moving up to the Politburo * that year. A notorious figure, Beria used to hold some of his orgies in a private upstairs room of the Aragvi, a Georgian restaurant in Moscow. (The room, adjoining a balcony overlooking one of the main dining rooms, still exists, but is in rather seedy shape.)

On February 3, 1941, the machinery was split into the NKVD and the NKGB (Narodnyi Komissariat Gosudarstvennoi Bezopasnosti, or People's Commissariat for State Security). The NKGB, a new agency, was nominally placed under the direction of Beria's deputy, Vsevolod Nikolayevich Merkulov, but Beria continued to exercise the real control over the entire system. On July 20, a month after the German invasion, the NKVD temporarily reabsorbed the NKGB and the planned split did not finally go into effect until April 1943.

In January 1946 Beria gave up the title of NKVD chief to his close associate Sergei Nikiforovich Kruglov, who had handled Soviet security arrangements at Teheran, Yalta and Potsdam. In March the NKVD became a ministry, the MVD (Ministerstvo Vnutrennikh Del, or Ministry of Internal Affairs). In the same month the NKGB became the MGB (Ministerstvo Gosudarstvennoi Bezopasnosti, or Ministry of State Security), and on October 18 Viktor Semyonovich Abakumov replaced Merkulov as its chief. Throughout the period, however, Beria remained the real boss of both ministries.†

Abakumov was supplanted late in 1951 by Semyon Denisovich Ignatiev, who played a leading role in the "Doctor's Plot" of 1952–53. In his secret speech in 1956, Khrushchev declared that on orders from Stalin, Ignatiev fabricated evidence against a number of leading Moscow physicians, chiefly Jewish, who were accused of trying to do away with Kremlin leaders. According to Khrushchev, "Stalin told him curtly, 'If you do not obtain confessions from the doctors, we will shorten you by a head.' "

---

* Stalin's Politburo became the Presidium in 1952 and was renamed the Politburo in 1966. It is the ruling body of the Communist party and hence the most powerful organ in the Soviet Union.

† Beria and Merkulov were shot in 1953. Abakumov's turn came a year later, in December 1954.

Khrushchev saved Ignatiev after Stalin's death on March 5, 1953. He was transferred to the Secretariat, then fired, then exiled to a provincial post. The payoff came in 1958, when Khrushchev used Ignatiev to attack Bulganin in the Central Committee, paving the way for Khrushchev to replace Bulganin as Premier.

Upon Stalin's death, the twin ministries merged once again, this time under the name MVD. Beria briefly resumed direct control of police and intelligence, on March 7, 1953. He was arrested on June 26 and ousted both from the MVD and as a member of the post-Stalin ruling triumvirate.*

Kruglov was immediately restored as head of the MVD and remained in the job until February 1956, when Khrushchev replaced him with Nikolai Pavlovich Dudorov, an odd choice. Dudorov had been a construction man in charge of thermal insulation, cement, structural glass and similar problems. He was the last chief of the MVD. On January 13, 1962,† the organization was abolished, only to be reborn on July 26, 1966, as the MOOP (Ministerstvo Okhranenia Obshehestvennogo Poriadka, or All-Union Ministry for the Preservation of Public Order). Nikolai Anisimovich Shchelokov, a fifty-six-year-old party careerist, was named first head of the MOOP, on September 17. A one-time carpenter, he had no police background—but he had worked with Communist party chief Leonid Brezhnev in Dnepropetrovsk in the Ukraine before and after the war.

The KGB was created the year after Beria's downfall, on March 13, 1954. Its first chief was General Ivan Serov. Small and wiry, with receding red hair and beady eyes, he wore thick-soled shoes and was so sinister a character that he might have been invented by Ian

---

* The day before Christmas it was announced that he had been executed on the previous day, but there is evidence he may have been killed when he was arrested, in June.

† Dudorov went back to more familiar ground as director of the Main Moscow Administration of the Building Materials and Components Industry. What became of Kruglov is not as clear. He probably retired. His name turns up occasionally among officials attending a funeral in Moscow but it is always far down on the list.

Fleming. During the war, over a bottle of vodka, he once declared that he would like to torture the leaders of Germany so that they would wish for death ten times before he let them die. Serov also boasted that he knew how to break every bone in a man's body without killing him.

Born of a peasant family in the village of Sokol, in 1905, he joined the Red Army and went to Frunze Academy, the Soviet West Point. He transferred to the secret police in 1939 when Stalin, having depleted the ranks of the party with purges, was forced to turn to the military to recruit reliable security officials. That year and the next, he directed the harsh Sovietization of the Baltic states. Then he worked closely with Khrushchev as security chief of the Ukraine. By the time he became head of the KGB, Serov was a veteran of fifteen years in police and intelligence work.

His reputation had preceded him to England when he flew there in March 1956 to take charge of advance security arrangements for the Khrushchev and Bulganin visit. While Serov was looking for "bugs" in the Claridge, the public protest over his presence became so great that he left three weeks before the Russian leaders arrived. It was later that same year that Serov played a key role in crushing the Hungarian revolt.

In December 1958, Shelepin replaced him as head of the KGB and Serov was named director of the rival GRU. He served in that post until 1962, when he apparently ran aground over the Penkovsky affair.*

Shelepin is short and slim, with a crew-cut. He chain-smokes cigarettes but doesn't drink much, as befits the new breed of young Soviet leaders; and he avoids Westerners at diplomatic receptions. He was born on August 18, 1918, in Voronezh, on the Don, the son of a railroad worker. He was a partisan leader behind the German lines

---

* Oleg V. Penkovsky was a GRU colonel who acted as a spy for the CIA and the British M.I.6; he was arrested on October 22, 1962, and Serov stopped appearing at Moscow receptions shortly thereafter. In May 1963, two days before Penkovsky was sentenced to be shot for treason, it was revealed that Serov had been ousted. Exiled to a minor military job in the provinces, his disgrace became complete in May 1965, when it was disclosed that he had been expelled from the party.

near Moscow during World War II and is believed to hold the award of Hero of the Soviet Union, although that is not listed in his biography. Educated in Moscow, he was a history and literature major, which is unusual for Soviet leaders; he is also interested in sports.

Shelepin has frequently traveled outside of the Soviet Union. A proud man, he had a humiliating experience on a trip to Hanoi and Peking in 1965. When he landed at the Peking airport, he had to slosh across a carpet inundated with a disinfectant against hoof-and-mouth disease, which is widespread in the Soviet Union. The Chinese like symbolism, and the implication of disinfecting Shelepin did not escape the former KGB chief, judging by the expression on his face as he crossed the wet carpet.

Shelepin joined the party in 1940. In 1943 he became a high Komsomol official in Moscow, and he was active in the youth organization for almost a decade, finally becoming its head in 1952. For six years he ran the Komsomol, impressing Khrushchev with his talents in organizing such massive programs as the draft of more than a million youths to raise cattle and plow the virgin lands of Siberia and Kazakhstan.

In April 1958 Shelepin was promoted to head the party organs department of the Central Committee, and in December Khrushchev appointed him chief of the KGB.

His successor as leader of the Komsomol, and ultimately as head of the KGB, was Semichastny, a sandy-haired, slightly beefy and highly dedicated party bureaucrat. An even-tempered man, cool and businesslike, Semichastny had an assured, easy manner toward his colleagues. He is not a jovial man; his sense of humor, when he chooses to display it, is sardonic. He is tall (about five foot eleven), of medium but solid build, weighs around one-seventy and dresses well. He is handsome but unsmiling, with a tight-lipped expression and downturned mouth.

As KGB chief, he was seen only rarely in public; he seldom attended diplomatic receptions, and only a very few Westerners ever glimpsed him. He has traveled little outside of the Soviet Union. Despite this, he acquired a detailed knowledge of the United States.

Semichastny was born in 1924, the year that Lenin died. He was one of seven boys in a family of eight children. His father, a flour mill worker, had attended only two grades in the church school of their parish in prerevolutionary Russia. Semichastny has privately expressed pride in the fact that despite his father's limited schooling, all eight children completed their education; and that among them were a teacher, a pilot, an engineer—and the head of the KGB.

Semichastny was educated at Kemerovo Chemical Technological Institute, in the coal-mining heart of western Siberia. But like Khrushchev, he made his early career in the Ukraine. He joined the Komsomol, became a party member in 1944, and rose through the ranks to take control of the youth organization in the Ukraine after the war.

During this period Khrushchev was still the Communist party boss in the Ukraine. He must have worked closely with the youthful leader of the Komsomol, and it was doubtless during these years that Khrushchev came to regard Semichastny as a bright young man who might be tapped for future advancement. When Semichastny became Komsomol chief on April 19, 1958, he took over Shelepin's desk at Komsomol headquarters in Moscow.*

In October the Nobel Prize was awarded to Boris Pasternak for his novel *Doctor Zhivago,* although the author, under pressure in Moscow for his liberal views, cabled Stockholm that he could not accept. Semichastny gained considerable notoriety by attacking Pasternak at a Komsomol gathering in the Moscow sports palace. With Khrushchev sitting nearby, Semichastny told twelve thousand cheering youths that to compare Pasternak to a pig "slanders the pig." By "dirtying" his feeding place, Pasternak had done what "even pigs will not do."

From the leader of Komsomol, this was the kind of hyperbole the Soviet leadership would expect, for the chief purpose of the youth group is to instill in its twenty million members a sense of unquestioning patriotism and complete obedience to the party.

Soviet children are eligible to become Komsomol members at the

---

* He also kept a picture of Stalin on the wall of his Komsomol office, although Khrushchev's de-Stalinization campaign was by then well under way.

age of fourteen, and are carefully selected for background and relia-bility. The organization has its own newspaper, *Komsomolskaya Pravda,* with a claimed circulation of more than three million. And the Komsomol is the prime group from which party members, and future leaders, are chosen. Komsomol activists are in the vanguard of those seeking to impose party standards on Soviet society by criticizing unreliable poetry or Beatle-style haircuts or Western jazz. They are even more doctrinaire than their elders, more royal than the king. This is the rigid background from which Semichastny, Shelepin and Andropov came.

Semichastny's personal relationship with Shelepin, only six years his senior, has always been much like that of father and son. The careers of the two men were for several years almost exactly parallel. When Shelepin moved up to head of party organs in April 1958, Semichastny replaced him as head of Komsomol. After Shelepin became head of the KGB, Semichastny in March 1959 turned up running party organs. He was then sent to Baku for a two-year interlude as second secretary of the Azerbaidzhan party. But on November 13, 1961, he was named head of the KGB by Khrushchev after Shelepin moved up to the party Secretariat.

How the KGB is internally organized is a matter of some dis-pute. U.S. intelligence receives periodic information on the subject from defectors, but the data is often fragmentary, conflicting, or out of date. In 1959 Deriabin speculated that the KGB had twelve departments, or "directorates," principally the first main directorate for domestic counterintelligence and a second main directorate in charge of foreign intelligence, as well as six technical support sec-tions.* He noted, however, that this was the numbering system used "several years ago" and added that the numbers of directorates "are constantly changing."

A later Senate study, bearing earmarks of having been prepared

---

* Deriabin and Gibney, *op. cit.*

by the CIA, refers to the KGB's foreign intelligence section as the first chief directorate.*

As chief prosecution witness for the government at the trial of Abel, Hayhanen cryptically referred to the KGB's first division as "the PGU." He named its assistant chief as Colonel Alexander Mikhailovich Korotkov, one of four co-conspirators in the Abel case. U.S. intelligence has identified a KGB "Department Nine" in charge of keeping dossiers on Soviet émigrés and, where possible, recruiting them.

Whatever the names or numbers of the various directorates at any given time, it can be safely assumed from the functions the KGB performs that it must have a division dealing with foreign intelligence and clandestine political operations; a research branch to process, analyze, catalogue and evaluate the intelligence collected, in addition to preparing intelligence estimates for the Soviet leadership; a counterespionage and counterintelligence branch, roughly equivalent to the FBI; probably a separate section to keep an eye on the Soviet armed forces (including the GRU); a division in charge of the border troops; another, roughly equivalent to the U.S. Secret Service to guard the Kremlin leaders; a communications section; and finally, a scientific and technical branch to design and manufacture the KGB's highly sophisticated audio and radio equipment, its secret inks, drugs, special weapons and other paraphernalia of the modern spy.

Which brings us to SMERSH.

In *From Russia with Love,* the late Ian Fleming popularized SMERSH as "the official murder organization of the Soviet government," with forty thousand employees, including the infamous Rosa Klebb. SMERSH, a contraction of *Smert shpionam!* (Death to spies!) did exist during World War II, but with somewhat more narrowly specialized functions than those of the James Bond version. Around

---

* *Staffing Procedures and Problems in the Soviet Union,* Committee on Government Operations, May 1963. According to the foreword, this study was compiled by the staff of a subcommittee headed by Senator Henry M. Jackson (D., Wash.), "in co-operation with the executive branch." Only one agency of the "executive branch" is responsible for watching the KGB's internal operations, and that is the CIA.

1921 the Cheka established units in the Soviet Army called *osobyi otdel* (special section), to spy on the military and root out disloyal elements. These were popularly known as the Double-0 (00) sections, and they were attached to every level of the Army. During World War II the Double-0 was greatly expanded throughout the Soviet armed forces, and redesignated SMERSH.

The new organization had much more independence and broader authority. In addition to its old duties, it was assigned responsibility for intercepting enemy paratroops and for catching Soviet deserters and enemy spies. It was given power to hand out summary espionage sentences at the front and to execute those condemned to death for spying. Where the Soviet army occupied areas that had previously been foreign territory, SMERSH was assigned the job of tracking down German agents of the Abwehr and the Gestapo.* In 1946 SMERSH was dissolved and absorbed into the state security and intelligence machinery, where it remains today as a division of the KGB under the rather misleading title of "counterintelligence." But the function is basically the same: to keep watch over the armed forces.

Although the demise of SMERSH may come as a disappointment to Fleming fans, the KGB does have Bondish types licensed to kill. Soviet state security has been in the assassination business from the beginning. As early as December 1936, a euphemistically named Administration of Special Tasks was created within the NKVD to carry out assignments in terror overseas through an elite corps known as the Mobile Group.

Walter Krivitsky, one-time chief of the GRU in western Europe, became a marked man when he defected to the West in 1938. Soon afterward, in a Forty-second Street cafeteria in New York, he recognized a Soviet agent named Sergei Bassoff. Krivitsky got up and left. Bassoff followed him, but Krivitsky escaped by slipping into the *New York Times* building, a block away.

In January 1941 a Dutch national named Hans Breusse, a Soviet

---

* In 1945, Ivan Serov served as deputy chief of SMERSH in the Soviet-occupied area of Germany.

killer who had once worked for Krivitsky, was seen boarding a bus in Manhattan. Krivitsky was warned by a friend who had received a terse message: "Inform your honorable friend K that an ominous person is in New York: Hans." Alarmed, Krivitsky visited friends in Charlottesville, Virginia, and bought a gun. His hostess drove him to Washington and dropped him off at Union Station to catch a train to New York. He did not get on the train.

The next morning, February 10, 1941, a maid entered Room 532 at the Hotel Bellevue, a few blocks from the railroad station, and found a man lying on the bed. He had registered as Samuel Ginsberg.* A dumdum bullet, fired at close range from a .38 automatic, had torn his brains out. The gun, the one Krivitsky had bought two days earlier, was on the floor, drenched in blood.

Washington police ruled Krivitsky's death a suicide, but Mrs. Leon Trotsky, whose husband had been murdered with an ice ax in Mexico six months before, disagreed. So did Krivitsky's widow, Tonya,† who said that notes found in Room 532 were written "under coercion."

Violence of the sort alleged by Mrs. Trotsky and Mrs. Krivitsky is a routine instrument of Soviet intelligence according to Nikolai Y. Khokhlov, who defected in 1954.‡ He said he quit the MVD rather than carry out an assignment in murder that year, and he told this story:

Alexander S. Panyushkin,§ who had been ambassador to the United States from 1947 to 1952, during the Truman Administration, personally ordered him to kill Georgi S. Okolovich, a leader of an

---

* Krivitsky's name at birth.

† Today she and her son, Alek, then six, live quietly in the United States under assumed names.

‡ Nikolai Khokhlov, *In the Name of Conscience* (New York, David McKay, 1959).

§ Panyushkin was briefly Soviet ambassador to Communist China after leaving Washington. Five days after Stalin's death, in March 1953, he was recalled to Moscow to head the MVD's foreign intelligence department. He occupied that post in the fall of 1953 when Khokhlov claims he received the assassination order. For the past several years Panyushkin has run the party department in charge of all travel abroad by Soviet citizens. This is a sensitive and obviously intelligence-connected post.

anti-Soviet exile organization, the NTS (National Alliance of Russian Solidarists). Panyushkin supervised the preparation of a special noiseless electric gun (disguised as a cigarette pack) that fired bullets containing potassium cyanide.

After successfully testing the cigarette-pack gun on, among other things, a leg of lamb, Khokhlov flew to Frankfurt, in February 1954, to carry out Operation Rhine, the liquidation of Okolovich. Instead, Khokhlov went straight to his intended victim and asked for NTS help in getting his wife, Yana, and their eighteen-month-old son, Al-yushka, out of the Soviet Union.

At that point, ham-handed U.S. intelligence agents entered the picture. They virtually kidnaped him, refused to believe that the blond, scholarly-looking man with glasses was a Soviet intelligence captain, and changed their minds only when he turned in the ciga-rette-pack gun and two German confederates.

An elaborate plan was worked out by the Americans to "sur-face" Khokhlov at a press conference and—so he was assured—simultaneously spirit his wife and child to political asylum at the U.S. embassy in Moscow. A State Department official flew to West Ger-many to give final approval to the scheme, and the press conference was held in Bonn on April 22, 1954. Then disaster struck.

"Nobody went to your family in Moscow," the U.S. official confessed. "Nobody went. I don't know why. It looks like at the last moment they got cold feet."

In June, Khokhlov heard that his wife and child had been arrested in Moscow.

Three years later, Khokhlov said, in September 1957, Soviet intelligence slipped radioactive thallium * into his coffee during an émigré conference in Frankfurt. His skin turned into a mass of brown stripes and dark spots, and his hair fell out in bunches. His blood turned to plasma, but with the aid of transfusions, he lived.

That is Khokhlov's story as he has related it in his book, in testimony to Congress and in lectures. If it is merely a clever plot by

---

* A malleable, rare metal, bluish white in color, used chiefly in the manufacture of rat poison, photoelectric cells and green signal lights.

the CIA to embarrass the KGB, then it is very clever indeed, for Khokhlov accuses U.S. intelligence of sacrificing the safety of his family, through duplicity or inefficiency.

One of the most sensational stories of Soviet assassination is that of Bogdan Stashynsky, a self-described professional killer for the KGB. On October 19, 1962, he was sentenced to eight years' imprisonment by the Federal High Court in Karlsruhe, West Germany. What follows is his story as it emerged in the trial and in the court's decision.

In 1957 the KGB ordered Stashynsky, a Soviet agent in Germany, to liquidate Lev Rebet, a Ukrainian exile leader living in Munich. To do the job, Stashynsky was given the name and legend of Siegfried Dräger, a West German born near Potsdam. (Stashynsky was born in the western Ukraine.) On his first reconnaissance trip to Munich in April, Stashynsky watched Rebet leave his office at No. 8 Karlsplatz. According to the West German court:

"Stashynsky followed Rebet in the tram as far as the stop Münchener Freiheit. During this tram ride, Stashynsky was wearing sunglasses, as he had been instructed to do. He noticed, however, that he was the only person on the tram who was wearing sunglasses. This made him feel uneasy, so he removed them. But his uneasiness grew because he did not know which tram stop to ask for or how much the ticket would be."

In May, and again in July, he returned to Munich to stalk Rebet. Both times he took a room at the Hotel Grünwald. From his hotel room he could watch No. 9 Dachauerstrasse, the office of a Ukrainian exile newspaper where Rebet usually worked before going to his office at the Karlsplatz.

In September, in Karlshorst, a section of East Berlin that served as Soviet administrative headquarters for East Germany, a technician arrived from Moscow to demonstrate the murder weapon. The court described it as follows:

"The weapon was a metal tube, about as thick as a finger and about 7 inches long, and consisting of three sections screwed together. In the bottom section there is a firing pin which . . . ignites a powder charge. This causes a metal lever in the middle section to move; it crushes a glass ampule in the mouth of the tube. This glass ampule . . . contains a poison that in appearance resembles water and escapes out the front of the tube in the form of vapor . . . if this vapor is fired at a person's face from a distance of about 1½ feet away, the person drops dead immediately upon inhaling the vapor. The demonstrator pointed out that since this vapor leaves no traces, it is impossible to ascertain death by violence, and added that the perpetrator suffers no harmful effects from the poisonous vapor if he swallows a certain kind of tablet beforehand as an antidote, and immediately after firing the weapon, crushes an ampule sewn up in gauze and inhales its vapor." *

Before embarking on his mission, Stashynsky was taken to a wooded area by his KGB superior and the weapons technician. He was told to try out the spray gun on a dog. The dog's carcass was left lying on the ground, but the KGB supervisor "took the leash and collar with him."

On October 9, 1957, passenger "Siegfried Dräger" took an Air France flight from Berlin to Munich, and registered at the Stachus Hotel. Three days in a row he gulped his antidote pill in the morning and stationed himself at the Karlsplatz to wait.

On the third day, October 12, he saw his quarry. He caught Rebet on the stairway of the office building, pointed the spray gun at Rebet's face and fired. There was, the court said, "no screaming, no blood, merely a low smacking sound as he pressed the trigger." Rebet reeled forward and Stashynsky "hurried down the stairs. In the entrance hall, he crushed the antipoison ampule and inhaled the

---

* The poison used in the gun was prussic acid, the colorless, liquid form of cyanide, one of the deadliest poisons known to man. The ancient Egyptians made prussic acid by boiling peach leaves and seeds. The antidotes prepared by KGB chemists and given to Stashynsky were sodium thiosulfate, $Na_2S_2O_3 5H_2O$, a white powder better known to amateur photographers as hypo; and amyl nitrite, $C_5H_{11}ONO$, a yellowish liquid used medically to dilate the blood vessels, as in the treatment of angina pectoris, a form of severe heart seizure. The amyl nitrite is inhaled.

vapor." Stashynsky, who later claimed he was highly upset by what he had done, burst out of the building, and as planned, threw the weapon into a stream at the rear of the Hofgarten.

"I suddenly noticed that the sun was shining and that people looked happy," he testified. "I felt as though I had been dreaming." Not so much, however, that he failed to notice the crowd beginning to gather in the Karlsplatz, and the police car. He caught a train to Frankfurt, stayed overnight and flew back to Berlin on Pan American World Airways.

Rebet had been found on the stairway where he dropped. Munich police pronounced him dead of a heart attack. In KGB parlance, Stashynsky said, a killing is "to greet an acquaintance" and in his report to the KGB he wrote: "In a town that I know I met the object that I know and greeted it. I am sure that the greeting was a success."

Pleased with his performance, the KGB sent him back to Munich in 1959 to find Stefan Bandera, a prominent Ukrainian exile leader. Stashynsky tracked him down at No. 7 Kreittmayerstrasse, where he was living as Stefan Popel. On October 15, equipped with a slightly improved model of the vapor gun and a skeleton key, he watched as Bandera arrived home and drove into the garage to park his car. Stashynsky used his key to enter the apartment building just ahead of Bandera. On the first-floor landing a charwoman chirruped *"Auf Wiedersehen!"* to someone and came down the stairs. Stashynsky averted his face and pressed an elevator button while the woman left.

Carrying a basket of tomatoes, Bandera—who now had about a minute to live—opened the front door; with his left hand he was trying to extract his key, still in the lock. Stashynsky pointed the poison gun, wrapped in newspaper, directly at his head, and fired. He then followed a familiar procedure. He threw the gun in the same brook, caught the next train to Frankfurt and flew to Berlin, on British European Airways. But this time an autopsy was performed on the victim. It revealed cuts on Bandera's face, caused by glass splinters. The cause of death was found to be poison: prussic acid.

Stashynsky claimed that Shelepin, then head of the KGB, personally presented him with the Order of the Red Banner in Moscow that December, in recognition of his mission. But he also testified he had become embittered and disillusioned with the KGB as a result of his assignments in murder. He had met an East German girl, Inge Pohl, and the KGB warily permitted them to marry in April 1960. That fall, Inge, now pregnant, was allowed to leave Moscow to visit her parents in East Germany. She gave birth there to a son, Peter, in March 1961. The KGB, possibly suspecting that Stashynsky was getting ready to flee, refused to let him out of Moscow.

Then, on August 9, Inge telephoned her husband that the baby had died. The KGB permitted Stashynsky to fly to East Germany for the funeral—under heavy escort. He went to Dallgow, near Berlin, to make preparations for the funeral. Stashynsky and his wife decided to make a break for it, the court said, "on the day of their child's funeral, on August 12, 1961, before the funeral, since it would have been too late to do so afterward. In spite of the fact that they were being watched by three cars in streets nearby, they managed to escape unnoticed across a stretch of land planted with trees and shrubs." At Falkensee, on the outskirts of Berlin, they took a taxi to East Berlin and, from there, an electric train into West Berlin, where Stashynsky's odyssey came to an end.*

Was his story too cinematic to be true? It could have been a script from the pen of Graham Greene or Len Deighton. Of course, Stashynsky's claim that Shelepin gave him a medal obviously could not be verified and had a slightly hollow ring. But the judge who sentenced Stashynsky said that West German authorities had gone to great lengths to verify every possible detail of the story: the hotel registrations just before each murder, the PAA and BEA flights, and the rest. Everything checked. In explaining its relatively mild sentence for double murder, the court argued that Stashynsky had come over to the West, confessed, and was "not the Eichmann type." †

---

* That escape route could not have been used even one day later. The Berlin Wall went up on August 13, 1961.

† There was a strange postscript to the Stashynsky case in 1966, when Senator Thomas J. Dodd, the Connecticut Democrat, came under fire before

• • •

Perhaps the most chilling recent KGB attack took place in September 1964, in the unlikely setting of the 626-year-old Zagorsk Monastery, one of the holiest shrines of the Russian Orthodox Church. The story has fascinating ramifications. It suggests the true power of the KGB within the Soviet government, to which it is supposedly subordinate.

Thirty-six-year-old Horst Schwirkmann, an electronics expert for West German intelligence, was flown into Moscow, ostensibly as a minor diplomat on temporary duty in the German embassy at 17 Bolshaya Gruzinskaya. His real task was to remove any KGB "bugs" from the building. (Only three months earlier, the American embassy had discovered more than forty microphones nestled in its walls.) A short, chunky man with dark hair thinning in the front, Schwirkmann was the top expert on counterbugging for the Federal Republic's intelligence organization. There were reports that he had invented a device which would give a rude electric shock to anyone trying to tap a wire in the embassy.

The West Germans were old hands at the counterbugging business. When Chancellor Konrad Adenauer visited Moscow in September 1955, he politely declined a hotel suite and lived right in his train—which had been "swept" by technicians before it left Germany and equipped with elaborate anti-eavesdropping devices.

On September 3, 1964, while Schwirkmann was still in Moscow, it was announced that Khrushchev was willing to take an unprecedented step. He would meet with Chancellor Ludwig Erhard in Bonn. It would be the first visit of a Soviet Premier to the West German Republic since its creation. It was a bold move by Khrushchev—he

the Senate Ethics Committee. Dodd was accused of taking a trip to West Germany in 1964 to help a friend of his, Chicago public relations man Julius Klein, hold on to some lucrative PR accounts. Dodd said he went to investigate the Stashynsky case. To back up his story, he called on the CIA. In a letter dated July 14, 1966, Director Richard M. Helms confirmed that Dodd had been "in contact" with the CIA before and after his trip to obtain "information on Soviet murders, assassinations and kidnapings" and on the Stashynsky case in particular. Helms also wrote that while in Germany, Dodd had conferred with "our field representative" in Bonn. However, Helms carefully avoided the question of the ultimate purpose of Dodd's trip.

would be hobnobbing with the Germans, who had devastated and nearly defeated the Soviet motherland in the Great Patriotic War. It would offend the loyal Communist regime in East Germany. Undoubtedly there were those within the Presidium in Moscow who opposed the move as another example of Khrushchev's adventurism. But the Soviet leader's prestige was committed, the more so because the way had been paved for the Bonn meeting by a visit to the West German capital the previous month by his son-in-law, the exuberant Alexei I. Adzhubei, editor of *Izvestia.*

Schwirkmann completed his assignment. On Sunday, September 6, two days before he was due to fly back to Bonn via Warsaw, he accompanied four embassy friends on a visit to the Zagorsk Monastery, an hour's drive northeast of Moscow and a major tourist attraction. At the monastery a young guide led the five Germans into the cathedral, where robed priests conduct services before a gilded altar surrounded by huge icons of Russian saints. They stopped to look at a painting of the Resurrection. A middle-aged man was kneeling by it, praying quietly. When the visitors arrived, he rose politely and stood behind Schwirkmann.

The young electronics technician suddenly felt his trousers become wet over his left buttock. "I had the impression that I was being sprinkled with holy water," he said later. "Then it suddenly became cold on the wet spot—almost like ice. As I turned around, I saw the man [who had been standing behind him] take off in a hurry."

Schwirkmann thought he detected a smell something like rotten cabbage. Within seconds he was in severe pain, a dangerous chemical eating into his skin, and his companions rushed him back to Moscow. He did not enter a Soviet hospital, because he would have been at the mercy of the KGB; they could have killed him or shot him full of truth serum to learn his secrets.

Schwirkmann's condition worsened that night. Not until Monday morning was he brought to the American embassy for medical treatment, apparently on the order of the German ambassador, Horst Groeppe. He was in agonizing pain. Captain James E. Street, the assistant air attaché and U.S. embassy doctor, took one look at the tremendous blisters in the burned, four-inch-square area, and diagnosed it as a severe injury caused by nitrogen mustard gas.* He immediately gave Schwirkmann a heavy shot of morphine.

An interpreter accompanied Schwirkmann, who apparently spoke no English. The electronics expert was secretive at first about what had happened to him.

Western intelligence, analyzing the attack later, theorized that it was carried out with an aerosol can containing the liquid nitrogen mustard gas under pressure.

The German embassy tried to step up Schwirkmann's departure. It attempted to book him on a KLM flight to Amsterdam Monday night. The Russians, apparently still stalling in the hope that Schwirkmann would be forced to enter a Soviet hospital, replied that no seats were available. Schwirkmann, his condition worse, was treated by Dr. Street again on Tuesday. Finally, later that day, he flew out of Moscow on his previously scheduled flight via Warsaw.

At the Bonn University clinic, under police guard, Schwirkmann was treated by an eminent skin specialist, Professor Arthur Leinbock. He received numerous transfusions, but doctors feared he would lose his left leg. After a long period on the critical list he recovered, however, and vanished back into the intelligence world.

Despite secrecy, the story leaked out. Six days after the attack the Foreign Ministry in Bonn confirmed it officially and disclosed that a sharp protest had been lodged with the Soviet Union. At first the

---

* The world's press unanimously, but erroneously, reported that Schwirkmann had been sprayed with conventional mustard gas (dichlorodiethyl sulfide) of the type made infamous during World War I by the Germans, who first used it in 1917. That form of mustard gas is an oily, colorless liquid, odorless when pure, but with a mustard or garlic smell if not; when fired in a shell, it forms an invisible vapor that attacks the lungs, blisters the skin and sometimes causes blindness and death. Schwirkmann was a victim of the much more modern nitrogen mustard compound, developed during World War II. It has been used medically in the intravenous treatment of malignant diseases. In the United States, for example, it has been manufactured under the trade name Mustargen by Merck, Sharp and Dohme. Nitrogen mustard gas can be lethal, although it is not nearly as deadly as some of the modern odorless nerve gases, like GB (Sarin), which has been manufactured in Denver. If inhaled, the vapor from a drop of GB smaller than the head of a pin is enough to kill a man. The only antidote is atropine, a drug obtained from the belladonna plant.

Russians rejected the Bonn protest. The West Germans delayed their invitation to Khrushchev and announced that it would not be extended unless there was a satisfactory reply to the mustard-gas affair. Finally, on October 13, the Bonn Foreign Ministry announced that the Russians had expressed regret over the attack in a note that said, ambiguously: "It can only be regretted that such deeds have been done which are difficult to evaluate except as an effort to complicate the relations between our countries."

Two days later Khrushchev was deposed as Premier. Was the KGB, in attacking Schwirkmann, deliberately attempting to scuttle the Moscow-Bonn summit, and thereby undermine Khrushchev? Only the KGB knows the answer.

There is some public disagreement today among defector and CIA sources as to what the KGB murder section is called. Deriabin testified before a Senate committee in March 1965 that until Stalin's death it was known as the Spetsburo, or special bureau. It then was renamed the ninth department of the foreign intelligence directorate, he said, and now is called the thirteenth department. "The thirteenth department is responsible for assassination and terror. This department is called the department of wet affairs, or, in Russian, Mokryye Dela. It is common among Soviet security officers that when they talk about Spetsburo No. One—formerly the ninth department, now the thirteenth department, they just use the name Mokryye Dela, which means the 'department of wet affairs' . . . to translate it into English, it means 'dirty affairs'; *mokryye* means 'wet,' and in this case *mokryye* means 'blood-wet' . . . it means a wet affair."

On the other hand, Allen Dulles has said that the Soviet murder department is called the "executive action" section. According to Dulles, its chief is General Nikolai B. Rodin, who used the alias General Korovin while attached to the Soviet embassy in London from 1953 to 1961. In that capacity, Dulles wrote, Rodin had charge of two major Soviet spies in Britain, George Blake and William John Vassall. "After the apprehension of the latter, the ground got too hot for the general and he was recalled and reassigned to the 'Murder Inc.' branch of the KGB." *

No discussion of the organization of the KGB would be complete without reference to what the CIA has called the KGB's department of disinformation, or "Department D."

According to a twenty-page double-spaced document which the CIA circulated in Congress in September 1965, Department D puts out information designed to "defame and discredit" U.S. agencies, particularly the CIA. The CIA claims the disinformation department was established in 1959, is staffed by "an estimated forty to fifty geographical and functional specialists in Moscow alone," and "produces between 350 and 400 derogatory items annually." Its ultimate objective, the report says, "is to isolate and destroy what the KGB designates as *'glavni vrag'* (main enemy), the United States." The document adds that disinformation, or *dezinformatsiya* in Soviet terminology, is "false, incomplete or misleading information that is passed, fed or confirmed to a targeted individual, group or country."

According to the CIA, the head of Department D is the nefarious "General Ivan Ivanovich Agayants," † who, if the CIA is accurate, is a cross between Kilroy and Maxwell Smart, popping up like a KGB Scarlet Pimpernel, here, there and everywhere.

As far back as 1959, Deriabin identified Agayants as Moscow chief of the western European section of the KGB's foreign intelli-

---

* *The Craft of Intelligence* (New York, Harper & Row, 1963).

† Other top KGB officials identified as of 1966 were Major General N. S. Zakharov, first deputy chairman under Semichastny; S. S. Belchenko and A. I. Perepelitsyn, deputy chairmen; Colonel General P. I. Zyryanov, chief, border troops; K. F. Sekretarev, chief of staff, border troops; Major General G. I. Zabolotny, chief of political department, border troops; M. P. Svetlichny, chief Moscow city and *oblast* (region); Vasily T. Shumilov, a forty-five-year-old lawyer who organized students into a ski brigade during the siege of Leningrad and now heads the KGB in that city; M. A. Lyakishev, chief, Omsk; Y. P. Tupchenko, chief, Rostov; A. V. Ilichev, chief, Volgograd; N. Khikmatullayev, chief, Samarkand; S. S. Marfunin, secretary, KGB party committee, and A. Manannikov, secretary, Komsomol committee.

gence directorate, an Armenian with modest expertise in French art and literature, who served as *resident* in Paris just after World War II.

Deriabin also reported that Agayants masterminded the official reaction in 1952 to Western protests over the KGB's kidnaping of Dr. Walter Linse, acting chief of an organization of anti-Communist lawyers in West Berlin.

The 1965 CIA report describes Agayants as a "senior, professional intelligence officer with long experience and well developed agent and political contacts in western Europe, especially in France, where he served under the name Ivan Ivanovich Avalov. At one time in France he controlled the French spy George Paques, who was sentenced to life imprisonment on 7 July 1964." According to the report, Agayants also became head of Department D under Khrushchev.

More recently, it was suggested that he found time as well to head the Damage Assessments Committee of the KGB that studied the harm done to Soviet intelligence by the arrest in June 1963 of Colonel Stig Wennerström, the Swedish air force officer and air attaché who spied for Moscow.

According to the CIA report, Department D has even served as a ghost writer for Khrushchev. When the Soviet Premier visited America in 1959 he boasted that he had intercepted top-secret U.S. cables. "You're wasting your money," he told Allen Dulles. "You might as well send it direct to us instead of the middleman, because we get most of it anyway. Your agents give us the code books and then we send false information back to you through your code. Then we send cables asking for money and you send it to us." A footnote to the CIA document says that these Khrushchev boasts during his tour were "designed to destroy confidence in American intelligence." The CIA assured the congressmen: "His statements and remarks made during interviews, it is known, were prepared in advance in consultation with the department of disinformation."

The CIA, of course, had its own motives in disseminating the disinformation report on Capitol Hill. By spreading the story of

Department D, it was subtly suggesting that all criticism of the CIA was somehow darkly linked to the KGB.

Chalmers M. Roberts of the Washington *Post,* wondered, in a perceptive column, whether the CIA "counteroffensive" was not actually directed at CIA's critics in the American press. He noted that the CIA report said Soviet intelligence had a "deep interest" in "the development and 'milking' of Western journalists. Americans figure prominently among these." Roberts was disturbed by the CIA's suggestion that unnamed American writers were somehow deviously in the service of General Agayants.

Regardless of whether the CIA is entirely accurate in its dramatic description of Department D and its overworked chief, there is no doubt that the KGB does engage in extensive propaganda activities, including the publication of pamphlets and news stories, forgery of supposed U.S. documents, and broadcasts by radio stations in which the hand of Soviet intelligence is hidden.

The KGB's military counterpart, the GRU, is a world-wide intelligence/espionage apparatus. But because the GRU is subordinate to the Army, it is less of an independent political force within the Soviet system than the KGB. The Red Army itself, of course, is a formidable instrument of power and counterbalance to the KGB. In general, the GRU operates in a similar fashion to the KGB. It has "legals" under diplomatic cover, and "illegals," including many who have operated in the United States. Its targets are mainly, but not exclusively, military.

GRU headquarters is believed to be at the Arbatskaya Ploshchad (Arbat Square), on the opposite side of the Kremlin from Lubianka.* GRU elements probably operate as well from the huge main building of the Ministry of Defense along the Moscow River at 34 Maurice Thorez Quay.

No good figures are available on the GRU's size, although there

---

* Arbat Street and Square have had a previous connection with military matters. Napoleon entered Moscow along the Arbat in September of 1812.

are classified estimates locked in the files of Western intelligence agencies. The GRU is probably smaller than the KGB, but it is a large and active world-wide intelligence organization in its own right.

Like its rival, the GRU has had several previous names. Its founder, first chief and director for fifteen years was General Jan Karlovich Berzin. Born Peter Kyuzis in 1890, the son of Latvian peasants, he was fighting the Cossacks by age fifteen and got fifty lashes when he was caught. A year later, in 1906, he took part in robberies of state liquor and tobacco stores to raise money for the revolutionaries. Shot while trying to escape from one such holdup, he was arrested, condemned to death but let off with a two-year sentence because of his youth. His hair turned gray, possibly as a result of that experience, earning him the life-long nickname of "Starik" (old man). Arrested again, he was exiled to Siberia, but returned to participate in the Bolshevik Revolution. By 1919 he was in the Cheka in Latvia, but the same year he switched to the Red Army. He became head of the GRU (then the fourth department of the Red Army) in 1920. He directed dozens of GRU spies abroad in the twenties and early thirties, but in 1935 he was replaced by General Semyon Petrovich Uritsky. During the early part of the Spanish Civil War, Berzin was in Madrid as a top Soviet adviser to the Republican government. But in 1937 both Berzin and his successor as GRU chief were shot during Stalin's purges. (Berzin was officially rehabilitated in 1964 and Uritsky in 1965.)

One of Berzin's most famous recruits was the German Richard Sorge, who headed the Soviet GRU spy ring in Japan from September 1933 to October 1941. Officially he was a correspondent for the *Frankfurter Zeitung* and enjoyed the complete confidence of the German embassy. He was a breakfast and chess companion of the military attaché and later ambassador, Major General Eugen Ott, and through the embassy had access to the plans of the German High Command. In 1964 Sorge was posthumously awarded the U.S.S.R.'s highest decoration, Hero of the Soviet Union. A street in Moscow and a tanker have been named for him, and in 1965 the Russians issued a four-kopeck postage stamp showing his face against a blazing scarlet background.

After the war, in 1947, the Soviets tried to merge the GRU and the MGB into a single central agency, the Committee of Information, or KI. It was to have been run by Vyacheslav Molotov as a rival to the just-created CIA. It didn't work, and the KI was dissolved. Marshal Matvey V. Zakharov, Chief of Staff of the Armed Forces, reportedly headed the GRU briefly around 1950, succeeded by General Mikhail A. Shalin and then by General Sergei M. Shtemenko.

Today almost all GRU officers are graduates of the Military Academy of the Soviet Army, an elite school that teaches, besides more conventional subjects, secret writing, microdots and agent handling. The GRU has several separate schools in and around Moscow for training "illegals." One is located in an apartment building on Dorogomilovskaya Bolshaya Street in Moscow. No GRU establishments, including its headquarters, are publicly listed.

By far the most interesting episode of KGB-GRU rivalry surfaced when Igor Gouzenko wrecked the GRU network in Canada. When the Canadian government investigated, it uncovered strands leading directly to a GRU network that had operated in Switzerland during World War II under Alexander Rado (code names "Albert" and "Dora"), a short, fat Hungarian Communist who had worked as a Russian agent since World War I. He first posed in Vienna as a journalist and then in Paris as a cartographer, where his cover was Geopress, a map service financed by Soviet intelligence. In 1936 he was sent to Switzerland as the GRU *resident*. When war broke out, the Swiss listening post became an invaluable source of intelligence to Moscow. Through Rahel Dubendorfer ("Sisi"), a female agent, Rado recruited the fabulous spy Rudolf Rössler, a German expatriate who ran a book-publishing firm in Lucerne. Under the code name "Lucy," Rössler—through sources in the German High Command which he never revealed—supplied fantastic intelligence to Moscow, including the date of the Nazi attack on Russia. Hemmed in by Swiss intelligence and the Gestapo, the ring fell apart toward the end of the war. When the network ran short of funds, "Sisi," unable to communicate directly with Moscow, hit on the idea of getting word out through

Canada. From Geneva, she cabled Hermina Rabinowitch, a contact in Montreal, and asked her to get the Soviet embassy in Ottawa to arrange for a transfer of funds to the impoverished Swiss network.

In December 1943 Miss Rabinowitch, a Lithuanian-born employee of the International Labor Organization, went to the Ottawa embassy. She was not a professional agent, and the Russians were suspicious of the stout, unknown woman, lame in both legs, who hobbled into the embassy with the aid of two canes to tell her strange story. They did nothing—and the GRU section in the embassy was not even told of her visit.

Meanwhile, "Sisi" sent her friend a letter asking guardedly how things were going: "We live in the former apartment and are working as previously in the old firm. Some two weeks ago Sisi sent you a telegram. Tell us how did your journey to Gisel's parents [the GRU in Ottawa] turn out . . ."

In March 1944 Miss Rabinowitch sent this letter to the Ottawa embassy to back up her story. Apparently it finally galvanized Vitali G. Pavlov, who was NKVD *resident* for Canada under the cover title of embassy second secretary. Pavlov asked his director in Moscow for instructions and was told to do nothing, because Rabinowitch was a GRU problem.*

Four months had now gone by since Miss Rabinowitch's visit. Pavlov had not seen fit to say a word to his GRU colleagues in the embassy about what was going on.

In Switzerland, "Sisi," whose financial burdens were no doubt becoming acute, sent another letter to Hermina Rabinowitch phrased in code language: "Please inform Gisel's family that she should advise Znamensky 19 that Sisi is alive and works as of old with Lucy. Lucy wanted to change the personnel, but funds ran out. Albert is sick and is not interested in business. For the work of Sisi, Gisel's family must transfer 10,000 dollars. The transfer must be made by Hermina

---

* A much later report by the Ottawa GRU to headquarters, seeking to justify its role, explained that "Pavlov, 2nd Secr. neighbour [KGB], asked his boss, who, according to Pavlov, allegedly replied that this is *their man* and you should do nothing." All the relevant documents, including this one, were handed over to the Canadian government by Gouzenko when he defected more than a year later, in 1945. The documents appear in *The Report of the Royal Commission*.

personally through N.Y. in connection with the wishes of Mr. Helmars."

What the note, decoded, really meant was that Hermina should tell the GRU in Ottawa to advise GRU headquarters in Moscow (then at 19 Znamensky Street) that she was still operating in Switzerland with Rudolf Rössler ("Lucy"), but needed funds; that Rado ("Albert") could not continue his espionage work; and that the needed $10,000 must be transferred to Switzerland through William Helbein of the Helbein Watch Company in Manhattan ("Mr. Helmars").

Hermina duly forwarded this second letter to the embassy, where it arrived April 15, 1944. Pavlov, after waiting two more days, finally got around to advising the deputy GRU chief in Ottawa that "there is a certain Rabinovich." It was July before Hermina finally handed over the $10,000 to Helbein, and the Swiss watch company's Geneva branch paid "Sisi" the money.*

Gouzenko's defection shed light on another aspect of the troubled KGB-GRU relationship, namely that the KGB serves as a watchdog over its military rival. If Pavlov looked the other way when the GRU needed money, the minute there was trouble he stepped in to clean up the mess. Instead, he made it a good deal worse.

For weeks during the late summer of 1945, Gouzenko, the young embassy cipher clerk, had been selecting documents that he planned to take with him when he defected, by pinching their corners so that he would be able to remove them quickly from the files. When the right moment came, on September 5, he walked out of the

---

* Alexander Foote, a one-time British Communist who became a Soviet spy after service in the Spanish Civil War, wrote about his experiences as a radio operator for the Swiss GRU ring in *Handbook for Spies* (New York, Doubleday, 1949). He relates that in January 1945, he and Rado were summoned to Moscow to explain the collapse of the network. During a stopover in Cairo en route, Rado, realizing what might lay in store, fled. The Russians told the British in Egypt that he was a Soviet army deserter; he was found and shipped off to Moscow. Foote was told Rado would be shot. After the war, Rado's wife, Helene, living in Paris, was told by the Russians that her husband was in prison, but she received no letters to prove it. Foote defected to the British zone of Berlin in 1947.

embassy at 8 P.M. with the documents. He went straight to a newspaper, the Ottawa *Journal,* and announced who he was and what he had brought with him. They said they weren't interested.

The next day Gouzenko, his wife, Svetliana, and young son, Andrei, stayed away from their apartment while he desperately and unsuccessfully tried to convince various government departments that he was real. Prime Minister Mackenzie King, who heard about it, recommended that the young man return to his embassy with the papers.

Meanwhile the GRU had discovered that not only was Gouzenko gone but so were important documents. That night, when the Gouzenkos were back in their apartment, there was a knock on the door. Gouzenko recognized the voice on the other side as that of a GRU chauffeur. He did not answer, but the noise of his son running across the floor gave away their presence.

Gouzenko, who had been unable to persuade the newspapers and the Prime Minister of Canada, was finally sheltered by his next-door neighbor, a Royal Canadian Air Force sergeant, who called the police. When they arrived they found four Soviet diplomats ransacking the Gouzenko apartment. One of them was in the clothes closet. He turned out to be Vitali Pavlov.*

------

* Apparently Pavlov was not penalized for his Marx Brothers handling of the first major postwar Soviet spy case. More than a decade later he was named in the indictment as one of four co-conspirators in the Abel case, and identified at the trial as a high official of the KGB's American desk. It will be recalled that Hayhanen, before sailing for New York in 1952, was smuggled over the Finnish border in a car trunk and went to Moscow for final instructions. On the witness stand Hayhanen was asked:

Q. Now, on this trip to Moscow, did you meet Vitali G. Pavlov?
A. Yes, I did.
Q. Will you tell us about that, please?
A. Pavlov—
Q. First of all, I beg your pardon. Excuse me. Will you tell us first of all who he is?
A. Pavlov was in 1952 assistant boss to American Section of espionage work . . . Pavlov explained me that on espionage work we are all the time in war, but if real war will be . . . that I don't have to move . . . I have to do my espionage work in the country where I was assigned. And he explained that after war our country or our officials will ask everyone what he did to win this war.

When the Gouzenko case broke, Scotland Yard, the Canadian Mounties and the FBI moved in; in the uproar, the GRU Ottawa station chief, Colonel Nikolai Zabotin, slipped across the border to New York and the safety of a Soviet ship, the S.S. *Alexander Suvorov,* which sailed secretly with the night tide in violation of port regulations. A few weeks later Georgi Zarubin, Soviet ambassador to Canada, went home.

Eleven of the twenty accused members of the spy ring were sentenced to prison, but by far the biggest fish was Dr. Allan Nunn May, the British nuclear physicist who had provided the GRU in Ottawa with tiny samples of uranium 233 and 235 after the first atomic bomb was dropped on Japan in August 1945. May was sent to prison in England in 1946. It was the first of the great atomic espionage cases; the others all broke in 1950 with the arrests of Klaus Fuchs on January 27; of his American contact, chemist Harry Gold, on May 22; of Gold's Los Alamos contact, David Greenglass, on June 16; and finally of Julius Rosenberg on July 17 and his wife, Ethel, on August 11.

Gouzenko appeared at the Canadian trials under heavy police guard, and the press was forbidden to take pictures or make sketches of him, or even to publish a physical description. He subsequently wrote a book about his defection, then turned to writing novels. He is reportedly living with his family under government protection near Toronto. Although his new name, phone and car registration are closely guarded secrets, he still fears the long arm of Soviet intelligence. His wife was once quoted as saying she carried a loaded pistol in her purse at all times and could "hit a bull's-eye at a hundred yards nine times out of ten."

Obviously the Soviet intelligence services—with their worldwide communications, dossiers, thousands of agents, border troops, weapons and wiretap experts—are formidable instruments of power within the Soviet system.

How does the leader of the Soviet Union harness this vast power to serve rather than master him? The answer is he does not—at least not all the time.

Stalin obviously had tight control of the secret police and used terror as the underpinning of his dictatorship. How the police and espionage apparatus has been controlled at the top since 1953 is much less clear. The overthrow of Khrushchev was prima facie evidence that whoever rules Russia today cannot always count on the KGB as an instrument to preserve his power.

In theory, one of the functions of the KGB is to guard the Kremlin leaders, and particularly the top leader of all. Because it tightly controls all sensitive communications channels, the KGB is in a position to know what is going on. In theory, Semichastny, a protégé and creature of Khrushchev's, should have warned the Premier that trouble was brewing and used the KGB's power to frustrate the revolt in the Presidium.

In fact, he did not. At some point in the plotting, Semichastny must have made the delicate decision to go along with those in the Presidium who were about to oust Khrushchev. Indeed, there is evidence that Semichastny may have been used to bell the cat. According to information which American specialists consider reliable, when Khrushchev was summoned to Moscow from his Black Sea home at Sochi in October 1964 for the showdown, it was Semichastny who met him at the airport in Moscow. The sight of the KGB chief waiting at the plane ramp may have given Khrushchev the first indication that it was all over.*

This is not to suggest that the KGB overthrew Khrushchev, but it must have co-operated. The Schwirkmann incident, already recited, may have been one small sign of the KGB's involvement—a move to diminish Khrushchev's prestige by scuttling his plan to visit West Germany.

---

* Yet another version is that Semichastny actually flew to Sochi and brought him back. An interesting straw in the wind was that the first news of Khrushchev's fall came from Victor Louis, a Soviet journalist whom the Russians permit to write for British newspapers. Louis, who has many contacts among the Western press, telephoned the news to his London paper eight hours before it was officially announced. He is widely believed to be a KGB agent.

Of course, Khrushchev's political decline began long before 1964, perhaps even before President Kennedy forced him to pull the Soviet missiles out of Cuba in 1962. U.S. intelligence, however, had no advance warning that Khrushchev was about to be forcibly retired. Neither, it seems equally clear, did Khrushchev.

The irony was that Khrushchev had trusted the KGB and used it as his secret channel of communication with President Kennedy. Pierre Salinger, former press secretary to President Kennedy, has reported that in September 1961 he met secretly in New York in a room at the Carlyle Hotel with Georgi Bolshakov, a Soviet official who handed him a twenty-six-page letter—the beginning of an unprecedented private correspondence between the two world leaders. Bolshakov was stationed in Washington, ostensibly as editor of the English-language Soviet magazine *USSR*. He was also, "according to the CIA, a top agent for the KGB," Salinger wrote.*

Bolshakov confided to Salinger that the letter was so secret that not even the Soviet ambassador to the United States, Mikhail Menshikov, knew about it. Theodore C. Sorensen, top aide to the late President, reports a similar episode. He said that Bolshakov handed him a letter from Khrushchev to Kennedy inside a folded newspaper as the two were walking along the street in downtown Washington. Sorensen said the President's advisers speculated that Khrushchev might have used clandestine channels to keep his letters "from someone in his government, possibly someone in the Presidium or military." †

Even more dramatic is the story of how the KGB's Washington *resident,* Alexander Fomin (who had the title of embassy counselor), negotiated during the Cuban missile crisis with ABC-TV correspondent John Scali. On Friday, October 26, 1962, at the height of the crisis, Fomin telephoned Scali, who had wide contacts in the U.S. government, and urgently asked to see him. Over lunch at the Occi-

---

* Pierre Salinger, *With Kennedy* (New York, Doubleday, 1966).
† Theodore C. Sorensen, *Kennedy* (New York, Harper & Row, 1965).

dental Restaurant a block from the White House, the KGB agent proposed a formula that eventually became the settlement: Khrushchev would pull out his missiles in exchange for a pledge by Kennedy not to invade Cuba. When Scali reported this to the State Department, he was rushed to the White House to see Kennedy and get the President's reply. That night the ABC newsman met again with Fomin in the coffee shop of the Statler-Hilton, a block from the Soviet embassy, and reported that the U.S. government thought the formula would work. After Khrushchev's letter demanding removal of U.S. missiles from Turkey was broadcast in Moscow the next morning, Scali met with Fomin in a deserted banquet hall on the mezzanine at the Statler-Hilton and charged that there had been "a stinking double cross." Fomin professed to be mystified by the new Khrushchev letter. But less than twenty-four hours later the crisis had been settled on the basis of the original deal put forward by the KGB man.

Presumably there is some mechanism for co-ordinating policy inside the Soviet government when the KGB gets into the realm of nuclear diplomacy, and in fact, there does exist formal machinery for controlling the KGB and the GRU. On paper, the KGB is a committee of the Council of Ministers, whose chairman is Premier of the Soviet Union. In theory, the Council is responsible to the Presidium of the Supreme Soviet, whose chairman is head of state and "President" of the Soviet Union. Also in theory, this Presidium is elected by a joint session of the Supreme Soviet, Russia's bicameral legislature.

Actually, the true power flows from the top down and rests in the party machinery that parallels the government structure. It is here that there is provision for overseeing the KGB, somewhat as if the Democratic National Committee were in charge of the CIA.

The Communist party Presidium and the Secretariat just below it are the true wellsprings of power in the Soviet Union. Both, in theory, are chosen by the party's larger Central Committee, which is "elected" at each national party Congress to serve until the next one.

Below the Secretariat are the party departments, or *otdel,* some thirty-two as of 1966. The *otdel* specifically in charge of the KGB and the GRU is the department of administrative organs. Until four days after Khrushchev's fall on October 15, 1964, the head of this key *otdel* was Army Major General Nikolai Romanovich Mironov. He had occupied the post since 1959, after serving as a leading party official in Leningrad.

Mironov, in short, was the party official to whom Semichastny, as head of the KGB, was responsible. If the KGB was aware of the move against Khrushchev, Mironov should have known too, and in theory, he should have tipped off Khrushchev, the highest official of the party.

Whatever his role in the Byzantine maneuverings, Mironov must have known a great deal. On October 19 he joined Marshal Sergei S. Biryuzov, Chief of Staff of the Armed Forces, and as such the third ranking official of the Defense Ministry, on a trip to Belgrade to celebrate the twentieth anniversary of the liberation of the Yugoslav capital by Russian troops.

Aboard the Ilyushin-18 were five other officers and eleven crew members. Biryuzov, then sixty, had helped to liberate Belgrade as commander of the Thirty-seventh Army. He had headed Russia's strategic rocket forces until early in 1963. Then, following the Cuban missile crisis, Khrushchev named Biryuzov to replace Marshal Zakharov as Chief of Staff of the Armed Forces.

As the plane carrying the delegation approached the Belgrade airport, the pilot radioed the tower and said he was at an altitude of 5,000 feet. There was rain, a thirty-mile-an-hour wind and a heavy mist over the area.

The tower ordered the Ilyushin to descend to 3,500 feet and approach from the west. Four minutes later, at 11:34 A.M., the plane slammed into Avala Hill, which has a peak of 1,700 feet. All aboard were killed on impact as the plane tore through the wooded hillside, coming to rest a few yards from the monument to Yugoslavia's unknown soldiers of World War I atop the peak. The Soviet delegation had been scheduled to lay a wreath at the monument.

The Yugoslavs feared that Khrushchev's downfall would consign them to limbo once again, and worried that the crash would be blamed on Belgrade. On the other hand, U.S. intelligence strongly suspected that the Russians had sabotaged the plane. One Soviet air force defector told U.S. agents that the altimeter is the most unreliable piece of equipment on a Soviet aircraft and could easily be sabotaged.

Here the trail grows murky. If the sabotage theory is accepted, Mironov could have been the target, despite the fact that his career was closely linked with that of First Secretary Leonid Brezhnev, who emerged the winner after Khrushchev's fall. Or Mironov could have been sacrificed to get at Marshal Biryuzov, who may have been regarded as too close to Khrushchev.

An official Soviet-Yugoslav joint inquiry blamed the disaster on pilot error. Biryuzov got a state funeral in Moscow; ten thousand persons massed in Red Square and Brezhnev and Kosygin were in the forefront of the honor guard atop Lenin's tomb.

Most intriguing of all was the failure of the new leaders to announce replacements for some of those killed in the crash. Not until mid-February 1965 did the West learn that Zakharov was back at his old job as Chief of Staff.*

By 1967, U.S. officials had still not identified Mironov's successor as head of the KGB *otdel* (although the deputy directors were known). In December 1966 Moscow published the list of delegates to the Twenty-third Party Congress held the previous April. In the back, the head of each *otdel* was listed—except for Mironov's successor. The omission was clearly deliberate, and the reason for it was surely to be found in the fragile and complex relationship of the KGB to the Soviet leadership.

That the KGB plays a special, powerful role in the Soviet system was amply demonstrated by the Schwirkmann case; by Khrushchev's use of the KGB both as a secret channel of correspondence to Kennedy and for secret negotiations in the missile crisis; and by Semichastny's co-operation in toppling Khrushchev. The KGB con-

---

* This bit of intelligence came in the form of a listing of defense officials at a soccer game, with Zakharov appearing as No. 3, the proper rank for Chief of Staff.

tinued to play this special role in an intriguing drama that revolved around Shelepin in 1965.

One month after Khrushchev's dismissal, Shelepin had become a member of the Presidium, and during the following year he was the *only* Soviet leader to serve simultaneously on the party Presidium and the Secretariat, and as Deputy Premier. In addition, he ran the Party-State Control Committee, with some five million party members under his wing at the height of his power. Given his father-son relationship to Semichastny and his recent background as chief of the KGB, Shelepin was obviously in a very strong position, one that undoubtedly made Brezhnev and his allies nervous.

Starting in May 1965, KGB men in Moscow and eastern European capitals began to spread rumors that Shelepin would emerge as First Secretary of the party, replacing Brezhnev. The whispers increased as the summer went on and the source was always the same: the KGB.

At a background briefing a high official of the Kennedy-Johnson Administration told John Scali and a few other newsmen about the reports, but did not mention their KGB origin. (The official said that such a shake-up would be unfortunate, in view of Shelepin's KGB background and the anti-American remarks he was known to have made in private.) Scali broadcast the story from Washington over ABC prior to the September meeting of the Central Committee, at which the shake-up was supposed to occur.

Scali had struck a sensitive nerve. Alarmed over the momentum of the KGB-supported Shelepin bandwagon, news of which had now apparently even reached a Western reporter, the Soviet leadership retaliated in a manner it hoped would squelch the rumors about Shelepin. It ousted Sam Jaffe, ABC's veteran Moscow correspondent, giving Scali's broadcast in Washington as the reason. (Jaffe was due out soon, anyway, but for almost a year ABC could not get permission to send in a replacement.)

A "stop Shelepin" movement, roughly paralleling similar strategy at American political conventions, seemed to have been launched in Moscow. In December, Shelepin lost his posts as Deputy Premier and as head of the Party-State Control Committee, which was down-graded. But he retained his seats on the Presidium and the Secretariat, remaining one of only four Soviet leaders to hold such dual power. Nevertheless, Shelepin's star began to fade after 1965. First he was assigned to supervise the production of consumer goods, and then came the shake-up of 1967 and his demotion to chief of trade unions. Despite this, many Western observers felt that because of his youth, the man to watch in Soviet politics might yet prove to be the dapper, chain-smoking former head of the KGB.

All of this reflected the "Frankenstein monster" aspect of Soviet intelligence. Khrushchev had installed Shelepin as head of the KGB to bring the police and espionage organization under tighter party control. But less than a decade later Khrushchev was gone, and the KGB was whispering that Shelepin would ultimately replace him.

The nervous relationship between the party leaders and the state security machinery appears to be a built-in problem of Soviet gov-ernment, with the question of who is controlling whom ebbing and flowing like the tides. As Soviet intelligence has freed itself from the bonds of the Stalin era, it has demonstrably become more powerful within the Soviet hierarchy, an elusive and changeable force in the continuing struggle for power at the top. At the same time, as the more obvious forms of terror have been curtailed, a career in espio-nage and police work has become safer to pursue. The heads of Russian intelligence no longer are being shot. In time this is bound to improve the morale and efficiency of the KGB and the GRU, and to make Soviet espionage against the West even more effective.

"Today," Rudolf Abel has written,* "the best representatives of our youth are coming into KGB work, and absorbing the experience of the older comrades. A Soviet intelligence agent is exposed to a hazardous life but he must also be a convinced and clear-headed Marxist. The conditions of work and the situation in capitalist coun-tries requires the intelligence agent to be constantly observant and to thoroughly observe the rules of conspiracy. Devotion to his homeland, honesty and discipline, selflessness, resourcefulness, the ability to

---

* Article in *Molodoi Kommunist* (Young Communist), February 1966.

overcome difficulties and deprivation, modesty in his life—that is an incomplete listing of the demands upon the political and personal qualities of the Soviet intelligence officer. Intelligence work is not just adventure, it's not some kind of stunt, it's not gay trips abroad. Above all, it's laborious and hard work requiring great strength, resistance, restraint, will, serious knowledge and great mastery. Remember what Dzerzhinsky said: 'Clean hands, cool head and a hot heart.' "

So the Russians, clearly, will continue to spy with the ruthless fanaticism of Dzerzhinsky and the bureaucratic efficiency of Andropov. And very possibly, the crises that threaten to obliterate mankind in the nuclear age will continue to be negotiated, clandestinely, in messages conveyed in empty hotel banquet halls and inside folded newspapers by the wide-ranging agents of the Komitet Gosudarstvennoi Bezopasnosti.

III great britain

St. James's Park is really the greenest and loveliest in London. It is an island of calm in the center of the clamorous city.

The spring of 1966 was unseasonably warm, and Londoners were surprised and pleased to see the sun. They turned out to stroll in the stately park and join the tourists feeding the swans.

One block to the south, a black limousine glided discreetly along Queen Anne's Gate, a quiet backwater of a street named for England's sovereign of more than two centuries past. It is a street of once-elegant townhouses long since converted to genteel institutional use. Lord Palmerston, who became England's Prime Minister, was born at No. 20. But by 1966 the houses had been given over to such worthy organizations as the Friends of the Girls Public Day School Trust, the Keep Britain Tidy Group, and the Save the Children Fund.

The car pulled up to the curb on the south side and a white-haired, ruddy-faced man stepped out. He looked about sixty, well-tailored and self-assured, perhaps a successful banker from the City coming to a board meeting of one of the little charities in Queen Anne's Gate. Indeed, the car had stopped in front of a house where the sign read: "SOLDIERS', SAILORS' AND AIRMEN'S FAMILIES ASSOCIATION."

But the man who might have been a banker moved quickly across the sidewalk and entered the adjacent four-story house, No. 21. The black door closed behind him, its polished brass plaque gleaming for an instant in the sunlight. Oddly, the plate bore no sign to identify the house. Sir Dick Goldsmith White, the head of M.I.6, one of the most powerful but least-known men in England, was arriving for work.

The British public at large was not permitted to know his name or face. And as befits the oldest, most respected and most legendary espionage organization in the world, there was nothing about the nondescript red brick building at No. 21, with its shabby-looking white gauze curtains in the front windows, to suggest Her Majesty's Secret Service. For M.I.6 * is the most secret intelligence organization in the world. It is England's espionage arm, the stuff of fiction, of Fleming, Graham Greene and *The Ipcress File.* When he walked through the door with the plain brass plate, Sir Dick was almost literally stepping through Alice's looking-glass.

As the telephone number of 21 Queen Anne's Gate (WHItehall 2730) indicated, it was close by the major government buildings in Whitehall, including the Foreign Office, to which M.I.6 reports. Anyone strolling around the corner from No. 21 would soon have found himself on Broadway, the wide street that runs parallel to Queen Anne's Gate, one block to the south. On the north side of Broadway, at No. 54, he would have noticed an ancient and unattractive nine-story brown office structure called the Broadway Buildings.

It was listed innocuously in the London telephone directory as a

---

* Also properly known as the Secret Service, but not to be confused with the U.S. agency of that name, which performs entirely different functions. M.I.6 is roughly equivalent to the covert Plans Division of CIA, if a comparison is to be made.

subbranch of the Ministry of Land and Natural Resources (TRAfalgar 9030). The stroller would have had no way of knowing that he was in fact looking at the headquarters of M.I.6. This was not surprising, for nothing on the other side of Dick White's looking-glass was what it appeared to be: the rear of the house in Queen Anne's Gate was back to back with the rear of Broadway Buildings, and Sir Dick, the "prosperous banker" arriving for the charity board meeting, would find it easy to slip from one building to the other.

M.I.6 has many mansions. A few minutes from Queen Anne's Gate, past the houses of Parliament and across Westminster Bridge, is a twenty-story glass-and-concrete skyscraper. Hard by Waterloo Station, on the north side of Westminster Bridge Road at No. 100, it might at first glance look like a luxury apartment building; its name, Century House, adds to that impression. But its two entrances are blocked by uniformed guards, and the little signs say: "NO ENTRY. PERMIT HOLDERS ONLY." Here, too, the men and women inside worked for Sir Dick.

In yet another part of London, just off the Strand, is the 134-year-old Garrick Club. Dickens. Thackeray and Trollope were among its early members, and having been named for the actor, it is still a place where the theatrical, literary and legal professions meet. It is more convivial than the social clubs of Pall Mall (at the Garrick, members are expected to talk to one another). Along the great carved-oak staircase are colorful oil portraits by John Zoffany. Zoffany liked to paint David Garrick. (Before 7 P.M. the ladies must use the little side staircase on the right.)

At the top of the stairs, past the Rodin statue, is the morning room—so called, they like to say at the Garrick, because it is only used in the evening. It has green velvet walls, hung with paintings of actors and actresses of the London stage, and a marble fireplace. A screen discreetly shields the doorway from the landing.

This, too, was a part of Sir Dick's world.* Dining at the Garrick,

---

* In *The Anatomy of Britain Today* (New York, Harper & Row, 1965), British journalist Anthony Sampson has a wonderful chapter on London clubs, including this observation: "In all clubs, perhaps, there is an element of imposture. Everyone, as he ushers his guest through those mahogany doors,

he appeared outwardly like any other member. But to his closer friends at the club, in the more rarefied echelons of Whitehall, his real identity was known. For to them, Sir Dick was one of the legendary secret figures of modern intelligence, Britain's equivalent to Allen Dulles.

To the British government, its intelligence services, in the words of one senior diplomat, "simply do not exist." So discreet are the cover arrangements that surround the head of M.I.6, so tight the press strictures, that White's name was unknown to all but a handful of his countrymen.

There was one slip-up years ago, a tiny story that appeared in the *Daily Telegraph* on October 28, 1946. It bore the headline "TROOPSHIP HAD 'MYSTERY MAN' " and below that, "WAR OFFICE EXPLAINS." The item read:

"Messages from Liverpool last night stated that special interest had been shown by shipping officials in the departure of the 20,000 ton troopship *Duchess of Bedford* of a man described as 'an important civilian passenger.'

"He was believed to be traveling incognito, and detectives and army police were in the ship until she left last night. A double-berthed cabin had been booked in the name of D.G. White. Coded messages awaited his arrival and he was met by an army lieutenant.

"The War Office later cleared up the mystery. Colonel D. G. White, of the Intelligence Corps, had been home on leave in the normal way, it was stated. He was returning to the Middle East to rejoin his unit, and 'was entitled to travel in civilian clothes when not with his unit.' "

Twice in later years White's name appeared unobtrusively in fine print in the London *Times* among hundreds of others on the Queen's

---

becomes a slightly less real person, talks a bit louder, shakes hands a bit more heartily. The Arts Club has admen pretending to be artists. The Garrick has lawyers pretending to be actors, or vice-versa. White's has ordinary men pretending to be eccentric. The Travellers is a Foreign Office canteen pretending to be an amateurs' drawing room. Only the Athenaeum is *sui generis*—there the bishops are being bishops, the professors are professors, the eccentrics are eccentric, and the dull, distinguished men sit in their deep leather chairs in the silence room, where no one can disturb them."

Honors List: when he was knighted in 1955 the reference under KBE (Knight Commander of the Order of the British Empire) simply read: "White, Dick Goldsmith, attached War Office." In 1960, when he received a KCMG,* all that appeared was "White, Sir Dick Goldsmith, for official services."

Except for that, and for those few who knew him and his wife Kathleen socially, Sir Dick might not have existed.† He kept close to his world of Queen Anne's Gate and Broadway, the Garrick, and his country home, which he called "The White House," in the village of Pulborough, in West Sussex.

The man who rose to the top ranks of the four-hundred-year-old British intelligence establishment was born on December 20, 1906. He received a conventional British education at Bishop's Stortford College and Christ Church, Oxford, leavened by studies in the United States, at the universities of Michigan and California.

He served as a colonel in British army intelligence during World War II, and it was there that he made his unpublicized reputation as a spy master. Attached to General Dwight D. Eisenhower's Supreme Allied headquarters, White was deputy chief of the counterintelligence subdivision of Ike's G-2 (intelligence). As such he had complete charge of all the counterespionage activities at SHAEF from two months after the Normandy invasion until victory in Europe.

He brought together the counterintelligence experts of Britain, the United States and France to produce joint reports known as "Special Intelligence." As a result White and his agents were able to confuse and mislead German military intelligence as the Nazi armies were forced back through France and across the Rhine.

---

* Knight Commander of the Order of St. Michael and St. George. The CMG is irreverently referred to by British civil servants as "Call me God." The higher KCMG is known as "Keep calling me God," and the GCMG, highest of all, as "God calls me God."

† This was true until August 9, 1963, when, in the wake of the Profumo scandal, the uninhibited British satiric magazine *Private Eye* accurately suggested he was the head of "the British Secret Service." Copies were seized and carted off to the Defence Ministry for study by horrified security officers. Despite this breach of tradition, no action was taken against the magazine by the authorities. Dick White had lost his cover, but England survived.

After the war he received the U.S. Legion of Merit and the French Croix de Guerre. The war's end also meant that he had time, at the age of thirty-nine, to marry the lovely Kathleen Bellamy. Then he stepped through the looking-glass into the invisible world of M.I.6.*

As head of M.I.6, with agents reporting to him from all over the world, White in real life held the position of M, the intelligence chief known to millions of readers of the late Ian Fleming. Few of those readers realize that the heads of M.I.6 are actually known to their associates by the single initial "C." † The practice began with Sir Mansfield Cumming, the first head of M.I.6. Cumming, a commander in the Royal Navy, was put in charge about 1910. Once the tradition had been established, his successors were also called "C," even if their names did not begin with that initial.

Basically, M.I.6 is responsible for espionage overseas. Its agents operate from British embassies under Foreign Office cover, but also in a variety of other guises—as journalists and businessmen, for example.

Britain's second secret intelligence branch is M.I.5, which is responsible for internal security and counterespionage at home. It is roughly equivalent to the FBI, but has no power of arrest. When

---

* His elder brother, John Alan White, by contrast, was a well-known figure in British book-publishing circles. In 1963 he became deputy chairman of Associated Book Publishers, Ltd., a major publishing group that includes Methuen & Co. and Eyre & Spottiswoode.

† With one partial exception. During World War II the British set up Special Operations Executive to encourage resistance and sabotage in France and other Nazi-occupied countries. Its operational chief, a Scotsman named Sir Colin Gubbins, was briefly known as "M." SOE operated from 64 Baker Street and the neighboring buildings of Norgeby House, Michael House, Montagu Mansions and Berkeley Court. So secret were its headquarters that German intelligence was mistakenly convinced that all of SOE operated from a flat with a black-tiled bathroom in Orchard Court, Portman Square. Actually, it housed only one country section.

Fleming served in wartime intelligence, and some have speculated that Rear-Admiral John H. Godfrey, director of British naval intelligence from 1939 to 1943, was his model for M. Godfrey recruited Fleming into naval intelligence over lunch at the Carlton Grill in May 1939. Fleming's subsequent adventures provided many of the ideas for the James Bond books.

M.I.5 * is ready to move in on a Soviet spy ring in England, it must turn to Scotland Yard's Special Branch, with which it has close relations, to make the actual arrests.

M.I.5's formal name is the Security Service, and its chief is known as the Director-General of the Security Service, or simply as the "D.G." Probably because of the similarity between the names Secret Service (M.I.6) and Security Service (M.I.5), there is a good deal of needless confusion about the two intelligence organizations, even in England.

The secrecy cloaking everything about M.I.5 is best explained in Lord Denning's official report on the Profumo scandal, published in 1963: "The Security Service in this country is not established by Statute nor is it recognized by Common Law. Even the Official Secrets Acts do not acknowledge its existence."

Its existence and operations were so misty, in fact, that until 1963 hardly anybody in Britain, including Parliament, knew that M.I.5 was responsible not to the Prime Minister but to the Home Secretary, more or less. This too, emerged in the Denning report. For the first time the British public was told of a 1952 directive to the head of M.I.5 by the then Home Secretary, Sir David Maxwell Fyfe. It stands as a masterpiece of verbal London fog, matchless in its ambiguity:

"1. In your appointment as Director-General of the Security Service you will be responsible to the Home Secretary personally. The Security Service is not, however, part of the Home Office. On appropriate occasion you will have right of direct access to the Prime Minister."

Like the head of M.I.6, the chief of M.I.5 has always been a faceless man, his name unknown to the British public and his agency's headquarters listed nowhere. But a foreign agent with a taste for Mayfair living might well avoid the White Elephant Club, a pub at 28 Curzon Street, for it was located directly across the street from a

---

* The "M.I." designation in both 5 and 6 stands for Military Intelligence. This is an anachronism, since neither agency currently performs military intelligence functions.

massive but unmarked building called Leconfield House, which occupied the block between South Audley Street and Chesterfield Gardens. Its telephone number was unlisted, and London guidebooks simply make no mention of it, as would be expected for a building serving as headquarters of M.I.5.*

Sir Roger Henry Hollis, the chief of M.I.5 at the time of the Profumo case, retired in the aftermath of the uproar in Britain over the affair. In the mysterious English tradition, although he was the target of violent public criticism, his name never emerged to the light of day. The opposition and the press simply vented its anger on "the Director-General of the Security Service."

Many influential Britons found all this secrecy hopelessly medieval, and a screen behind which the government could evade responsibility for the actions of its intelligence services. Attacks upon the anonymity of the chief of M.I.5 came from such critics as Malcolm Muggeridge and Rebecca West.

"As the weird, ribald Profumo-Keeler story unfolds," Muggeridge fumed in the *Daily Herald* in June 1963, "he crops up at every turn, but never makes a public appearance. Yet no one is supposed to know who he is. No press photographs of him are circulated; his obituary, if written, is enigmatically expressed. In *Who's Who* he appears innocuously as 'attached to War Office' . . . only in foreign espionage circles is his name a household word."

Rebecca West has described a hushed moment in January 1963 during Lord Radcliffe's Tribunal of Inquiry into the Vassall case, when it was announced that the Director-General of the Security Service would give evidence anonymously. Any person who recognized him, the spectators were warned, must keep that knowledge to himself.

"The tall doors opened, an impressive figure walked in, and sat down in the witness chair and answered a few questions . . . Then he

---

* In one of those unaccountable lapses that occasionally lift the curtain of British secrecy, the London *Daily Mail* informed its readers on April 23, 1963, in an article entitled "Britain's Off-beat Police," that M.I.5 operates "from Leconsfield [sic] House, Curzon Street, Mayfair, London W. The name of their chief is never mentioned."

strode out, his anonymity undoubtedly making the spectacle more enjoyable, and recalling memories of Sapper and Dornford Yates.

"But it was hard to avoid the suspicion that the enemies of our country probably have a fair idea who the head of the security services is, and probably his full name, the date of his birth, his life history, the color of his eyes and his weight are among the wonderful things known by those highly educated young people whom Sir Charles Snow meets in the Soviet Union." *

Chapman Pincher of the *Daily Express* wrote: "His identity is known to every foreign agent worth his keep. His name will be bandied about today in a score of London clubs.

"*Who's Who* reveals his suburban address. His telephone number is in the London directory. Yet his identity is secret."

Sir Roger Hollis, the object of all this ire, was born on December 2, 1905, the son of the Bishop of Taunton. He was educated at Clifton College and at Worcester College, Oxford. He married Evelyn Esme, a solicitor's daughter from Somerset in 1937, and by the following year he was discreetly listing himself as "attached Ministry of Defence."

The M.I.5 chief lived quietly in Campden Hill Square, a seventeenth-century residential section of London near Kensington. He was an equally inconspicuous member of the Travellers' Club, a stodgy, dignified Pall Mall haunt founded in 1819. To qualify, a prospective member must have traveled not less than five hundred miles in a straight line from London. (At the Travellers', members who haven't been introduced are *not* expected to talk to each other.)

He had received the Order of the British Empire at the end of the war, his Companion of the Bath in 1956, and he was knighted in 1960 ("Attached War Office," said the *Times*). The only clue that he had retired came when the Queen's Honors List was published on January 1, 1966. It disclosed that Sir Roger Henry Hollis, "lately attached to Ministry of Defence," had been awarded a KBE.†

---

* Rebecca West, *The Vassall Affair* (London, Sunday Telegraph, 1963).

† Like Sir Dick White, the covert Sir Roger had an overt elder brother who made a distinguished career in publishing. Christopher Hollis, a Conservative M.P. for ten years, was a member of the editorial board of *Punch,* an

Hollis became an anonymous casualty of the Profumo affair because of the controversial role of M.I.5 in the case and because of its espionage aspects, which involved the unfortunate confluence of a Minister of the Crown, a call girl and the atom bomb.

We will not attempt to tell the story in all its detail because Lord Denning has already done so, in the spare, highly readable English that characterizes the best of the half-dozen official reports on British security cases published in the past decade.

It will be recalled that John D. Profumo, the Secretary of State for War (married to actress Valerie Hobson), met Christine Keeler, the long-legged call girl, one summer day while she "bathed naked," as Lord Denning put it, in "a fine swimming pool in the grounds of Cliveden," Lord Astor's estate. Cliveden was "one of the great houses of the country," and Lord Astor "has upheld its tradition of hospitality." Profumo liked what he saw, for Christine, in Lord Denning's words, "had undoubted physical attractions." They subsequently had a brief, torrid affair, "simply because he was attracted by her and desired sexual intercourse with her."

Also at poolside that July 8, 1961 weekend was the Soviet assistant naval attaché, a GRU agent who has by now probably been made a Hero of the Soviet Union: Captain Eugene Ivanov, also known in the London diplomatic community by his nickname "Foxface." The weekend frolic ended with Ivanov and Christine drinking two bottles of whiskey and having, as Lord Denning cautiously phrased it, "perhaps some kind of sexual relations." Christine, less cautious, later described the Russian as "a wonderful huggy bear" of a man.

RAF veteran and author of numerous books and articles, including *Foreigners Aren't Fools* and *A Study of George Orwell*. Another brother, Arthur, was the assistant bishop of Sheffield.

As the faceless head of M.I.5, Sir Roger reportedly was succeeded by Edward M. Furnival-Jones, a Cambridge graduate who had cryptically appeared on the Honors List as "E.M.F. Jones, attached to War Office" when he got his CBE in 1957, and as "Jones, Edward Martin Furnival, attached Ministry of Defence" when he was knighted in June 1967. Furnival-Jones, fifty-four, lived in the north London suburb of Golders Green near the fashionable Hampstead Garden Suburb. He belonged to the United University Club, an exclusive preserve of Oxbridge men.

Like Ivanov, Christine had come to Cliveden as a guest of Stephen Ward, the fifty-year-old artist and osteopath with a taste for two-way mirrors and very young girls. Ward had been introduced to Ivanov over lunch at the Garrick Club, and became good friends with the naval attaché. Ward also knew Profumo.

In the background were Mandy Rice-Davies, two West Indians, one of whom slashed the other and shot at Christine (this became the shot heard around the world, for it was instrumental in surfacing the whole affair), and Harold Macmillan, who survived Peter Cook's mimicry in *Beyond the Fringe* but did not really survive Christine.

In the background as well were the Labour party, which wanted power and saw the Profumo scandal as a way to get it, and a very clever man named George Wigg, a political adversary of Profumo who became party leader Harold Wilson's shadow Minister for the Profumo Affair.

Three days after the swimming party at Cliveden, M.I.5 learned the details from Ward himself; he volunteered the information that Ivanov had asked him "to find out when the Americans were going to arm Western Germany with atomic weapons." The M.I.5 man who saw Ward had even been introduced to Christine, whom he described in a report as "a young girl whose name I did not catch."

Later that month Sir Roger went to the Secretary of the Cabinet and suggested that Profumo be warned about associating with Ward because of the osteopath's friendship with a known Soviet intelligence agent. The M.I.5 chief asked whether, incidentally, Profumo might be instrumental in turning Ivanov into a double agent. M.I.5's warning was conveyed to Profumo, but he did not think much of recruiting Ivanov, so that idea was dropped.

Profumo thought that M.I.5 was really discreetly warning him to stop seeing Christine. According to Lord Denning, M.I.5 did not know at the time that Profumo and Christine were having an affair, although it was in high gear by then, mostly at Ward's apartment. Profumo was later to claim that he had phased out the affair after M.I.5's warning and last saw Christine in December 1961.

By January 1963 Christine was peddling her story to Fleet Street. Profumo saw Sir Roger in an apparent effort to enlist M.I.5's help in suppressing the story by arranging to have issued to the newspapers an official request (known in England as a D notice) that the Keeler memoirs not be published. That effort failed and, in fact, Christine did sell her story to the *Sunday Pictorial,* handing over as well a letter from Profumo that began "Darling." But the paper warily decided not to print a story that was, to put it mildly, explosive and which it may not have been wholly convinced was true. But by this time M.I.5 undisputedly did know about the 1961 romance of Profumo and Christine, and of her simultaneous friendship with Ivanov. It also knew that Prime Minister Macmillan's office had been told the story by a newspaper executive.

The head of M.I.5 decided it was now a matter for the politicians. He also decided that the Security Service should do nothing further, despite a memo from one cagey M.I.5 man which warned: "If a scandal results from Mr. Profumo's association with Christine Keeler, there is likely to be a considerable rumpus . . . if in any subsequent inquiries we were found to have been in possession of this information about Profumo and to have taken no action on it, we would, I am sure, be subject to much criticism for failing to bring it to light. I suggest that this information be passed on to the Prime Minister . . ."

A few days later M.I.5 learned from Scotland Yard that Christine had told police of her affair and had added that Ward once asked her to find out "from Mr. Profumo" when the United States was giving atomic weapons to West Germany. M.I.5 still stuck by its decision to keep out of it.

Matters now moved to a climax. By March 22, rumors had circulated to the point where Profumo was forced to go before the House of Commons with a personal statement. In it he said there was "no impropriety whatsoever" in his "acquaintanceship" with Miss Keeler.

Next, the police began investigating Ward, allegedly for living off the earnings of his stable of girls. Ward tried to blackmail the Prime Minister of England into calling off the cops. He did so by writing letters to the government and to Harold Wilson saying Profumo had lied to Parliament.

The pressure was too much. On June 4 Profumo admitted his deception and resigned. Macmillan went before the House of Commons with a defense that rested on a single major premise: he had not known the truth because "the head of the Security Service" hadn't told him. "Nobody ever tells me nuffin!" cried a backbencher at that point. The more dignified official version, contained in Lord Denning's report issued in September, was that the head of M.I.5 had not told Macmillan about Christine, Profumo and the bomb until May 29, and then only because the Prime Minister had asked M.I.5 for a bit more information.

If so, it had taken M.I.5 four months to get around to telling the Prime Minister the key facts, at least some of which it had known for almost two years, ever since the M.I.5 officer had been introduced to the young lady whose name he didn't catch. Yet, Lord Denning found M.I.5 had not been "at fault."

On the other hand, the backbencher's cynical shout reflected a feeling that Macmillan could not have been as detached from what was going on as he maintained. Nevertheless, a key question which Lord Denning did not ask was why, after Profumo lied to Commons on March 22, M.I.5 did not *then* go to Macmillan and say, "He's not telling the truth."

In fairness to Sir Roger, there are times when men of Macmillan's authority don't *want* to know what is going on, and at those times the discreet subordinate finds it wiser not to volunteer anything for which he has not been asked.

It must have been obvious to the M.I.5 chief even by February that a political explosion of unprecedented magnitude was brewing, and that from the point of view of the Security Service it had already become far too hot an issue. It had gone beyond the realm of spies & girls and into the vital arena of the survival of the Tory government.

Ultimately, Macmillan did not survive. In October 1963 he stepped down, citing health. Sir Alec Douglas-Home took over, but a year later Wilson defeated him in the general election, and Labour returned to power after thirteen years.*

---

* Stephen Ward was convicted of living off the earnings of Christine and Mandy, but he eluded the verdict by ending his life with Nembutal. Many

When Sir Roger retired, he was of course not permitted to write his memoirs (although as Director-General he had received only $16,240 a year, considerably less than England's Postmaster-General). Nevertheless, the Profumo case had given Britons their first good, if fleeting, look at M.I.5. In the process the pitfalls of supersecrecy were clearly illustrated: when something went wrong, it seemed twice as bad. All in all, it was a time of troubles for "the Firm," as M.I.5 agents obliquely refer to their organization.

The third major branch of British intelligence is, unlike its more glamorous M.I. colleagues, overt. Its $15,400-a-year chief, who has the title of Director-General of Intelligence, is a public figure and is openly listed in the main building of the Ministry of Defence in Whitehall (cable address: DEFMIN).

Until he retired in 1966, the man who held the job was Major-General Sir Kenneth Strong, Eisenhower's intelligence chief during World War II. A tall, bulky Sandhurst graduate with a striking resemblance to the British actor Robert Morley, Strong was a bachelor, an army officer who served at Eisenhower's side through the campaigns of North Africa, France, Sicily, Italy and Germany. In 1943 Eisenhower sent him on a cloak-and-dagger mission to Lisbon to negotiate the surrender of the Italian troops under the control of the Badoglio government. In 1945 Strong interpreted for Eisenhower when General Alfred Jodl signed the German surrender in the schoolhouse at Rheims.

After the war Strong became head of Britain's Joint Intelligence

---

British intellectuals felt he had been hounded to death as a scapegoat for the Etonian society to whose secret tastes he pandered. Captain Ivanov had long since left London (in January 1963, after Ward alerted him that the scandal was surfacing). Profumo dropped out of sight, and the British press, by and large, humanely left him alone. "He did," said Mandy Rice-Davies, "no more than any man would do, given half a chance."

Christine married a twenty-five-year-old civil engineer named James Levermore on October 22, 1965, but they had separated by June. Lord Astor—his full name and title was William Waldorf Astor, Viscount Astor of Cliveden—died of a heart attack in the Bahamas in 1966. Cliveden, the forty-six-bedroom estate on the Thames where it all began, was closed in May 1967 and its contents sold at public auction.

Bureau. In 1964 he was named to the new post of Director-General of Intelligence. At the same time the separate military intelligence staffs of the three armed services were combined in a Defence Intelligence Staff under him.* (The United States had taken a similar step in 1961 with the creation of the Defense Intelligence Agency.) Strong battled to overcome interservice rivalry and achieved a large measure of integration in Britain's military intelligence.

The Director-General of Intelligence has two other, nonmilitary directorates under him; one for scientific and technical intelligence, and the other for economic intelligence. These correspond to the Research Division (for scientific and technical matters) and the Intelligence Division of the CIA.

In July 1966 Strong retired, at age sixty-six. He was succeeded by Air Chief Marshal Sir Alfred Earle, a rotund career RAF officer universally known to his friends as "Tubby."

The heads of M.I.6, M.I.5 and the Director-General of Intelligence are the three coequal chiefs of British intelligence, which has no single overlord.

M.I.6 reports to the Foreign Office, and M.I.5, hazily, to the Home Secretary; all three branches are co-ordinated by a Joint Intelligence Committee at the Foreign Office whose recent chairman was Sir Bernard Burrows, a suave career diplomat. A Deputy Undersecretary of State, Burrows, six foot three and unflappable, was Eton, Oxford, KCMG and a member of the Travellers'. He was formerly political resident for the Persian Gulf and later ambassador to Turkey. But he broke the conventional career-diplomat mold with an incongruous affection for American square dancing. Once a week, while stationed in Bahrein, Burrows cast aside oil, Arabs and empire, donned a loud checked shirt and blue jeans and called square dances for the American community in an Etonian mountain twang that would have

---

* The merger of defense intelligence was further consolidated in July 1965 when the three service intelligence directorates were abolished altogether and replaced by a directorate of service intelligence (DSI) and a directorate of management and support of intelligence (DMSI), all under Strong.

stirred the envy of a Blue Ridge mountain professional.*

The chairman of the Joint Intelligence Committee does not, however, completely call the tune for British intelligence. The heads of the three branches have considerable independence. Although the chairman wields the gavel, acts as a co-ordinator and can make his influence felt, he has no overriding authority.†

The JIC comes under the Permanent Undersecretary of the Foreign Office. Since 1965 the position has been held by Paul Gore-Booth, a teetotaler who, despite that handicap, once headed British press relations in America.

At the very top of the intelligence structure, of course, is the Prime Minister. But it is widely assumed in Whitehall that the man at 10 Downing Street who acts as Prime Minister Wilson's *éminence grise* for all British intelligence is George Wigg, the M.P. who so sagely advised him on the Profumo affair.

Wigg's formal title is Paymaster-General, but his duties are much broader. He was Wilson's campaign manager, and is a tough political professional. Given his role in the Profumo affair, it would seem certain that one of Wigg's concerns is to serve as an intelligence watchdog, if only to head off any future Profumo cases that might shake the Wilson government.

Wigg has been described by the *New York Times* as "a former army colonel with jug-handle ears and a lugubrious mouth," and by Anthony Sampson as "a big man who looks like a well-fed but angry turkey cock." Both descriptions will do.

---

* Burrows was shifted to Paris in November 1966 to be the permanent representative to NATO. His successor as Deputy Undersecretary and chairman of the Joint Intelligence Committee was Denis Arthur Greenhill, a tall, gray-haired former minister at the British embassy in Washington. Greenhill, fifty-three, was a favorite of George Brown, Foreign Secretary in the Wilson government. Before Washington, he served in Bulgaria and Singapore.

† Sir Patrick Dean, named ambassador to Washington in 1965, is another former chairman of the Joint Intelligence Committee. Tall, athletic and sandy-haired, Dean was a war-crimes prosecutor at Nuremberg. His intelligence career was foreshortened by his role in the Suez invasion, Britain's Bay of Pigs. Although he plays down his intelligence background, Dean once delighted a Washington luncheon audience which included Allen Dulles by addressing it; "Mr. Chairman, gentlemen"—and with a nod at Dulles—"fellow conspirators . . ."

Quintin Hogg (the former Lord Hailsham), who has a World War II intelligence background, once called Wigg "the Oddjob of this Goldfinger outfit." But Hogg is a Conservative and might be prejudiced.*

When British intelligence was organized in 1573, it reputedly had fifty-three agents planted in the courts of foreign monarchs. M.I.6 is considerably bigger today, but far smaller than either the American or Soviet espionage establishments.

Of M.I.5, Lord Denning has said: "The Security Service in this country is comparatively small in numbers. In some other countries there is to be found a massive organization with representatives dispersed throughout the land. Whereas in this country it is and remains a relatively small professional organization charged with the task of countering espionage, subversion and sabotage."

During the mid-1950's Britain apparently spent as little as £5,000,000 a year on intelligence.† By 1963, Chapman Pincher estimated in the *Daily Express*, British intelligence was spending £12,000,000 ($33,600,000) annually. Of that total, M.I.6 was believed to be spending about £7,000,000 ($19,600,000).

An interesting official indication of Britain's intelligence expenditures unexpectedly came to light on June 17, 1963, during an emotional debate in the House of Commons between Wilson and Macmillan over the Profumo affair. Wilson needled Macmillan by suggesting that "the security services" had first heard about the affair from the executive of a Sunday newspaper. Wilson added, "If this is true—the Prime Minister must be frank about this—this would imply

---

* Particularly since Wigg had publicly called him "a lying humbug" during the Profumo debate.
† Great Britain House of Commons, *Sessional Papers, 1953–54,* Vol. 23. Under "Civil Estimates, 1954–55, Secret Service," there appears this unusual entry on page 87: "1. Estimate of the amount required in the year ending 31 March, 1955 for Her Majesty's foreign and other secret services: £5,000,000." By 1966–67 the estimate for "foreign and other secret services" had doubled to £10,000,000.

that the sixty million pounds spent on these services under the right honorable gentleman's premiership have been less productive in this vitally important case than the security services of *The News of the World.*"

If Wilson meant to include all of Britain's intelligence branches, and he seemed to, the figure would average out to £10,000,000 ($28,000,000) a year for each of the six years that Macmillan served as Prime Minister. In any event, it is small in comparison to the $4,000,000,000 the United States spends each year on intelligence.

Most upper-level M.I.6 and M.I.5 officers come from public-school England, Oxford and Cambridge. Virtually the entire top echelon of M.I.6, for example, belongs either to the Garrick or St. James's. Many future M.I.6 agents receive their academic training at St. Antony's College, Oxford, whose warden (president) is F. W. Deakin, co-author of an excellent book published in 1966 about Richard Sorge, the Soviet agent.*

Recruits of Britain's two clandestine intelligence services receive more specialized training at schools run by their respective branches. Much of this training takes place in London. On at least one occasion it led to a fantastic mix-up in which a respectable and wholly innocent London businessman was accused of kidnaping.

The story began in the fall of 1955 when two M.I.6 recruits were assigned to a training exercise in the art of interrogation. They were given the description of a man, another M.I.6 trainee learning how to resist interrogation, and ordered to capture and question him as he tailed Sir David Maxwell Fyfe, the Home Secretary, on his way from the office. There was a certain, possibly deliberate, irony in the choice of Sir David, since as Home Secretary he was the nominal boss of Britain's other secret intelligence agency, M.I.5.

At the appointed hour Sir David, who was not in on the snatch,

---

* Deakin was also a member of the 1961 Radcliffe Committee, which investigated the Portland naval secrets and the George Blake spy cases, and had full power to delve into the most secret recesses of M.I.5 and M.I.6.

left the building. The M.I.6 trainees pounced on the man walking behind him, and over his squawks of protest, bundled him in a car and drove to a flat in Old Brompton Road. It belonged to a high Foreign Office official who had made it available for the exercise.

The kidnaped man appeared genuinely terrified, protested his innocence and begged them to let him go. But that was standard procedure for a trainee being grilled. The two M.I.6 men gave him a rough time, even removing his trousers to search for hidden messages. Despite their efforts the M.I.6 trainees could not break the man, who kept insisting he was a low-level civil servant on his way home. Finally it dawned on them that they had grabbed the wrong person. They released him, but warned him to keep silent.

The civil servant, certain that he escaped from the hands of lunatics, went straight to the police. They did not believe his story, but took him back to the building in Old Brompton Road to see for themselves. Upset and confused by his experience, the civil servant mistakenly pointed out the flat occupied by a businessman, Eric Tannock, as the one where he had been manhandled. Police began questioning Tannock, who indignantly denied any connection with the kidnaping. His wife was almost in hysterics.

In the meantime the Foreign Office official who had provided his quarters for the exercise returned to his flat, one floor above. Alerted by the confusion, he took an officer aside, explained the situation, and asked the police to warn Tannock to say nothing because "a vital matter of security" was involved.

In the interim Tannock had called the *Daily Express,* whose reporters were now swarming over the building. The Foreign Office official called the Deputy Director of M.I.6 to warn him that things were getting out of hand. M.I.6 in turn called M.I.5 and asked for help. M.I.5 called Rear-Admiral George P. Thomson, England's wartime Chief Press Censor, who acted as the government's contact with Fleet Street on security matters.

Thomson finally persuaded the paper's editor, the late Arthur Christiansen, to kill the story, on the grounds that it would prejudice American opinion of British security and jeopardize negotiations between London and Washington over the exchange of atomic secrets. The admiral also explained what had happened to the M.I.6 trainee who was supposed to have been following Sir David Maxwell Fyfe out of the building: "It was really most unfortunate. He missed his train."

Such Keystone Cop comedy clashes with the generally accepted image of British intelligence as a secret service matured by four centuries of experience and wisdom.

It began in 1573 with Sir Francis Walsingham, the dark, slender Secretary of State and adviser to Queen Elizabeth ("my Moor," she called him), who established England's first national secret service. When Mary Stuart received messages smuggled to her in kegs of beer, Walsingham's agents had already intercepted them, and it was his evidence that ultimately persuaded Elizabeth to execute her rival for the throne.

Walsingham hired the brightest students from Oxford and Cambridge and sent them abroad to infiltrate the courts of England's adversaries. Very likely, one such agent was Christopher Marlowe, who may have been working for Walsingham during a six-month absence from Cambridge in 1587. The same year, Walsingham was able to turn over to his Queen detailed and priceless information on the Spanish Armada, filched from its grand admiral by one of Sir Francis' agents * in Spain.

Seventy-six years later John Thurloe ran a similar, but much better financed espionage and intelligence service as Secretary of State to Oliver Cromwell. He frustrated the Restoration plots of Charles Stuart, and his intelligence feats were chronicled by Samuel Pepys.

Modern British intelligence has its roots in this distant past, although its current form of organization dates from a more recent period. Special Branch, Scotland Yard, was established in 1886 to put down Irish Republican activity. M.I.5 and M.I.6 were created about four years before World War I.

Sir Mansfield Cumming, the first "C," received his funds from the Foreign Office. Under him, M.I.6 had responsibility for all espio-

---

* His name was Fleming.

nage outside of the British Empire, as it still does. In his youth Cumming was a line officer in the Royal Navy, taking part in campaigns in Malaya and Egypt. Like one of his successors, Sir Dick White, Sir Mansfield belonged to the Garrick. He died in 1923 at the age of sixty-four.

Sir Vernon Kell, the first head of M.I.5, was a slight, asthmatic Sandhurst officer who had fought in the Boxer Rebellion in China in 1900; among his various decorations was something called the American Order of the Chinese Dragon. M.I.5 was financed by the War Office and responsible for all counterespionage within Britain and the Empire.*

At first Kell had no assistants and called himself, for cover, Commandant of the War Department Constabulary. But soon he was catching German spies by the handful. When the war ended he commanded eight hundred men, according to his widow, Lady Kell, in a rare newspaper interview she granted in 1962. Kell listed his hobbies in *Who's Who* as "fishing and croquet." He supposedly retired in 1924, but Lady Kell said her husband didn't play croquet and did not retire as head of M.I.5 until 1940. At that time, she indicated, his staff numbered six or seven thousand.

The pert, elderly widow had sought to publish a book she had written about her husband, who died in 1942 with the rank of major-general. "The trouble is," she said, "by the time M.I.5 finished checking the book for security there was no scandal or controversy left. And that, after all, is what people want to read about nowadays, isn't it?"

The most famous chief of M.I.6 was Major-General Sir Stewart Graham Menzies,† who held the post from 1939 to about 1951. Menzies, educated at Eton, entered the army, and after a year with the Grenadier Guards, served in the Life Guards from 1910 to 1939.

---

* M.I.5 still operates on British territory overseas, but as the Empire has shrunk it has increasingly become an internal security organization in Britain alone. In addition to its responsibility for catching spies, it periodically runs security checks on civil servants who work with secret material, a process known as "positive vetting."

† Pronounced Menghis; rhymes with "Genghis."

He won the Distinguished Service Order and the Military Cross in World War I, and in World War II directed British espionage against the Nazis. His clubs were St. James's, White's and Turf. On January 30, 1967, Menzies celebrated his seventy-seventh birthday in retirement. A handsome, tweedy man, still of erect military bearing, he lived with his third wife, Audrey, in a high-ceilinged, tapestried Elizabethan house near Chippenham, an ancient Wiltshire village ninety miles west of London. He was not supposed to give interviews, and turned down the BBC when it sought to do a program about him. He was said to be writing his autobiography—for the archives of M.I.6.

Special Operations Executive, which was independent of both M.I.5 and M.I.6, was set up on July 16, 1940, with a simple directive from Churchill to Hugh Dalton, Minister of Economic Warfare: "And now set Europe ablaze."

SOE had several cover names to protect its Baker Street head-quarters, among them the Inter-Service Research Bureau and the Joint Technical Board. Dalton, and for a time Sir Robert Vansittart, supervised SOE, but as noted before, its real driving force was Sir Colin Gubbins, a career army officer. Sir Gladwyn Jebb, who much later became familiar to Americans as Britain's ambassador to the UN, was SOE's liaison man with M.I.6 and the Foreign Office.

In New York, Sir William Stephenson ran SOE's American branch from Room 3603 at 630 Fifth Avenue, in Rockefeller Center. Stephenson was a Canadian from Winnipeg who had flown a Sopwith Camel in World War I and shot down twenty German fighter planes, including one piloted by Lothar von Richthofen, lesser-known brother of the "Red Knight," Baron Manfred von Richthofen. Stephenson was himself shot down, was captured, escaped, married an American girl from Tennessee, became a millionaire businessman in England and then went into intelligence.

In January 1946, its work done, SOE was disbanded. Like the Office of Strategic Services, its American counterpart, its files remained locked up, and its exploits the subject of scattered memoirs, some real, some fanciful. After he became Prime Minister, Macmillan authorized M.R.D. Foot, an Oxford historian, to write an official history of the wartime sabotage organization's exploits in France. He produced a 578-page book * which sold for 45s. before it went out of print. Its revelations caused an immediate storm in England, and even more of a controversy in France, where some felt it overstated the degree of British control of the Resistance. It remains, however, a massive and unique document—the *only* public account of intelligence activity the British government has ever authorized.

Another known chief of M.I.5 in addition to its founder, Sir Vernon Kell, was the late Sir Percy Sillitoe. He was the head of M.I.5 when the two Foreign Office officials Donald Maclean and Guy Burgess defected to the Soviet Union in May 1951. Later Sillitoe reportedly complained that his subordinates had not told him beforehand that the two diplomats had been under investigation by M.I.5. A former police official, Sillitoe apparently felt his background was resented by the Oxbridge types in M.I.5, who could not believe that two Cambridge men had committed treason.

There is probably some truth to this. Although England's class consciousness is sometimes conveniently blamed for subtler evils, Establishment mores have contributed to Britain's unusually bad luck with spies and traitors, starting with Burgess and Maclean and reaching an uncomfortable frequency in the 1960's. (In all, the major cases involved personnel in M.I.5, M.I.6, the Foreign Office, the Admiralty and the Defence Ministry.)

On August 30, 1963, a fifty-two-year-old patient named Jim Andreevich Elliott died in his sleep of advanced arteriosclerosis at the Botkin Hospital in Moscow. His was a strange, almost comic name, a curious Anglo-Russian mixture, and although it was not his real one,

---

* *SOE in France: An Account of the Work of the British Special Operations Executive in France, 1940–44* (London, Her Majesty's Stationery Office, 1966).

it appropriately reflected his life and death. For when he died, Guy Francis de Moncy Burgess was a long way from England, from Eton, where the headmaster had thought "he should do very well," and from M.I.6, in which, for a time, he had served. Twelve years before, on May 25, 1951, he had fled from England on the night boat for St. Malo with the head of the American department of the Foreign Office, Donald Duart Maclean, with whom his name was forever after inseparably linked.

In truth, three men were involved in England's biggest security scandal, and the "third man," as he came to be known in the press and in Parliament, was Harold Adrian Russell Philby, who had defected to Moscow before the patient in Botkin Hospital died.

The case, which spanned twelve years, should have been known by the names of all three—Burgess, Maclean & Philby—but that might have sounded too much like a firm of solicitors, and in any event, headlines seldom catch up with reality.

Burgess met Maclean at Cambridge in 1931. The older of the two, Burgess came from a more moneyed, aristocratic background and was the more brilliant student. At Cambridge both men flirted with Communism, and, apparently, with each other. Burgess was, throughout his life, openly and noisily a homosexual. Maclean married Melinda Marling, an American girl whom he met at the Café de Flore in Paris in 1938, and they had three children. When he was drinking however—which he did a great deal of—his sexual preferences seemed to become less certain. On the other hand, in their espionage activities their roles were reversed: Maclean was more clearly a Soviet agent in the Foreign Office, and Burgess, less clearly so.

The contrast between them was marked. Burgess was heavy and unkempt, Maclean tall, thin and austere in appearance. Burgess suffered from lifelong insomnia, a malady which may or may not have been related to his habit of munching garlic which he always carried in his pockets.

"Kim" Philby was born in Ambala, India, on New Year's Day, 1912, the only son of Harry St. John Philby, a friend of Lawrence of

Arabia and a famed Arabist who in time became a Moslem and adopted the name Haj Abdullah.

Philby, Burgess and Maclean were all at Cambridge together, but Philby was much closer to Burgess than to Donald Maclean. When they came down from Cambridge, the careers of the three men diverged.

Maclean, the son of a Liberal Cabinet minister, entered the Foreign Office in 1935. He was posted to Paris, where he met Melinda, who had dropped out of the Spence School for young ladies in New York, worked briefly at Macy's and gone off to France. After the wedding they returned to London and spent the war years there, until 1944, when he was made first secretary at the British embassy in Washington.

Burgess, meanwhile, dabbled in journalism and broadcast for the BBC, became involved in some minor European political intrigues and may have passed along information about them to M.I.5. Then, in 1939, he joined a war propaganda section of M.I.6. Officially, he returned to the BBC in 1941, but there is better evidence that he remained in intelligence, probably with SOE in Baker Street. He joined the Foreign Office in 1944.

Philby had gone into journalism, covering the Spanish Civil War for the *Times* of London, on the Franco side. During World War II, if not before, he served in British counterintelligence, and after that he remained an M.I.6 agent under Foreign Office cover—working secretly for the Soviets. He was posted to Istanbul in 1947, and in October 1949 he was sent to Washington.

In 1948 Maclean had been transferred from Washington to Cairo, where his drinking reached such heroic proportions that in May 1950 he was recalled, put under psychiatric care and then, astoundingly, appointed head of the American department in October.

During the summer in London when Maclean was drying out, his old friend Burgess was also there, but in August he was sent to Washington, as second secretary. He immediately moved in to live with the Philby family. By the fall of 1950, then, Burgess and Philby were both in Washington, and Maclean was running the American department back in London. The threads of their lives had once more been bound up together.

In January 1949, M.I.5 had learned that there was a leak to the Russians in the Foreign Office. By early May 1951 the principal suspect had been narrowed down to Donald Maclean.

As an M.I.6 representative in Washington, Kim Philby's work involved liaison with American security agencies, and either through those channels, or more likely directly from M.I.6, he learned of the net closing in on Maclean back in London. He warned Burgess of the danger to their old school companion.

As it happened, by this time Sir Oliver Franks, the British ambassador, had had enough of Burgess, whose overt homosexuality, alcoholism and reckless driving had involved him with the Virginia gendarmerie. He was recalled to London and arrived in England on May 7, 1951, aboard the *Queen Mary*. He was asked to resign from the Foreign Office.

On May 25, M.I.5 was authorized to confront Maclean directly, for the first time. That day Burgess visited the Reform Club, Maclean went to the Travellers'. They later drove to Southampton and boarded the S.S. *Falaise* for St. Malo just three minutes before it sailed at midnight.

In June, Philby was quietly summoned home. Since Burgess had lived in his house, and since it was either known or suspected that Philby had warned him about Maclean, he was asked to resign from the "Foreign Office" (for which read: M.I.6).

Now events took a more complex turn. No one knew for sure where Burgess and Maclean had gone, although it was assumed that they were behind the Iron Curtain. The British press spent thousands of pounds trying to find out.

On September 11, 1953, Melinda Maclean and her three children, who had gone to live in Geneva, disappeared while ostensibly on a weekend visit to the Swiss village of Territet; their trail vanished at the little Austrian town of Schwarzach St. Veit, near Salzburg. In fact, Soviet intelligence had spirited them over the Swiss-Austrian border and on to Moscow.

In April 1954, when Vladimir Petrov defected in Australia, one of the things he told the security authorities was that Burgess and Maclean had been recruited in Cambridge by Soviet intelligence, that one or both had learned they were under suspicion, and that Soviet intelligence had organized their flight to Moscow.

Petrov's information was summarized in a British white paper on Burgess and Maclean issued in September 1955. On October 25 Marcus Lipton, the veteran Labour M.P. from Brixton, a man with a bushy mustache, a Cheshire-cat grin and, apparently, excellent sources within the British security services, rose in the House of Commons to ask whether Prime Minister Anthony Eden had "made up his mind to cover up at all costs the dubious 'third man' activities of Mr. Harold Philby."

On November 7 Macmillan, then Foreign Secretary, told Commons that Philby had been asked to resign from the "Foreign Service" because of "Communist associates." But, he added, "no evidence has been found" to show that he was responsible for warning Burgess or Maclean. "I have no reason to conclude that Mr. Philby has at any time betrayed the interests of this country, or to identify him with the so-called 'third man,' if, indeed, there was one."

Mr. Lipton withdrew his charge and apologized for having made it.

In February 1956 the Russians surfaced the two missing diplomats in Moscow.* Some months afterward a very odd thing happened in London, although it did not become generally known until seven years later. The Foreign Office went to the *Observer,* the quality Sunday newspaper which is run by David Astor, Lord Astor's brother. The Foreign Office asked the *Observer* to hire Kim Philby. The *Observer* did, and splitting the cost with *The Economist,* sent Philby to the Middle East, where he was correspondent for both journals. There Philby, who drank prodigiously, took his third wife, Eleanor. She had been married to Sam Pope Brewer, the *New York Times* correspondent in Lebanon, when they met.

---

* In the statement they handed to reporters, the pair claimed they had gone to Moscow to work for "better understanding" between the Soviet Union and the West. "At Cambridge we had both been Communists . . . We neither of us have ever been Communist agents."

On January 23, 1963, Philby vanished from a dinner party in Beirut. The press remembered the 'third man' fuss of 1955, and there was speculation that he, too, had skipped to Moscow. On July 1, in the wake of the Profumo scandal, Edward Heath, a member of Macmillan's Cabinet, arose in Commons with an announcement of interest about Philby.

He recalled Macmillan's denial eight years before that Philby had warned Burgess and Maclean. But the security services, Heath said, had continued to work on the case. "They are now aware, apparently as a result of an admission by Mr. Philby himself, that he worked for the Soviet authorities before 1946 and that in 1951 he, in fact, warned Maclean, through Burgess, that the security services were about to take action against him . . . Since Mr. Philby resigned from the Foreign Service in July 1951, he has not had access to any kind of official information." The government declined to say when or how Philby had made his "admission." *

Marcus Lipton could not resist asking, "Does the statement mean that Mr. Philby was, in fact, the 'third man' . . . ?"

"Yes, sir," said Heath. Thereafter, Lipton was known to his friends as "M.I.7."

In the public uproar that followed, questions were asked, the most astute by George Brown, later Foreign Secretary in the Wilson government. He rose in the House of Commons to challenge the Tories: "The Foreign Office asked the man to resign for reasons that had to do with his past political associations. Why did the Foreign Office then take the initiative to get a newspaper to employ him in the Middle East? The Foreign Office is not normally an employment

---

* In Moscow, Burgess told Reuters that Philby had not tipped him off, and insisted that Maclean had already realized he was under surveillance. "The truth . . . is that Maclean, stopping his taxi to borrow books in St. James's Square, was bumped into by a car carrying his overeager Special Branch sleuths . . . it was this and this alone which revealed to Maclean that he was being followed . . . therefore, my dear boy, there was no 'third man,' no unnamed M.I.5 man, no unnamed diplomat—no Philby who told me in Washington what was going on . . . Disraeli, said to be the hero of Macmillan, once remarked, 'There is nothing so squalid as a patrician in a panic.' The head of M.I.6 is usually a patrician and panic seems to be universal."

At the time, Burgess had less than two months to live.

agency. Why did they do that?" Why, indeed—unless, as Brown added, the Foreign Office had an "interest in him working in the Middle East." Brown had one more question, and he suggested the answer himself: "What was that Foreign Office interest? Was it so that he should be available for work he had been doing before, which was security work?"

It was almost a classic parallel to John Le Carré's spy who came in from the cold. Kim Philby, disgraced, booted out of M.I.6, a heavy drinker, sent off to Beirut as a newspaper correspondent—a morsel of cheese in the mousetrap laid for the Russians. Perhaps Philby knew, perhaps he didn't. But like Alec Leamas, he never came back to Queen Anne's Gate.

George Brown's questions—to which he got no real answers—were too close to the mark to let the debate go on. Macmillan all but confirmed the name of the game when he warned that discussion of the Philby case would "risk destroying services which are of the utmost value to us."

Between Profumo and Philby, it was a bad time for both M.I.5 and M.I.6. On July 30 *Izvestia* announced that Philby, who held "a leading position in British intelligence," had been granted asylum in Moscow.*

For a few weeks, until the death of "Jim Andreevich Elliott," the three brilliant men who had come down from Cambridge almost thirty years before with so much bright promise, were together again—under an alien sky, in the bleak sanctuary of Communism. Only their future could be worse than their past.

The second major British security scandal of the postwar era came to be called the Portland naval secrets case. It broke in 1961 and was followed in rapid succession by the Blake, Vassall and Profumo affairs. The Portland case is a fascinating and complicated one, with links to Colonel Abel, the Penkovsky case and, weirdly, a

---

* On September 26 Eleanor Philby, traveling on her American passport, followed Melinda Maclean and joined her husband in the Soviet Union.

Polish defector to the CIA who subsequently, and to its great discomfort, announced he was the czarevich, long-lost son of Nicholas II, and rightful heir to the throne of all the Russias.

Early in 1950 Morris Cohen, a teacher at P.S. 86 in Manhattan, and his wife, Lona, gave a party in their East Seventy-first Street apartment for a man whom the guests remembered as Milton, or Mills, and who was introduced as a wealthy English businessman. Much later, in 1957, when Rudolf Abel was caught, the FBI found in his hotel room two small passport-sized photographs of a man and a woman. One was labeled "Morris" and the other "Shirley." Although Abel declined to identify them, he did admit knowing both. Abel said he had met them in 1949 in Central Park, had lunched with them several times, but had not seen them since that year. The pictures were found under the flap of a package containing $4,000 in cash, and on the backs were phrases that could have been, and probably were, a *parol,** or recognition signal, used by the KGB.

It was never discovered why Abel had these photographs with him, or whether he had intended to deliver the cash to the couple in the photos, but the FBI was able to identify the man and woman as Morris and Lona Cohen. In the course of checking into their backgrounds, the FBI learned of the dinner party the Cohens had held for Milton the Englishman, who was in fact Rudolf Abel.

In July 1950, just before the arrest of Julius Rosenberg, the Cohens vanished. Cohen was then just forty. He was born in New York, the son of a Bronx grocer, played football at James Monroe High School, attended New York University and then transferred to Mississippi State. He later did graduate work at the University of

---

* The literal meaning of *parol* in Russian is "password." Example: "Didn't I meet you in a French village?" Answer: "No. In 1961 I was in Lisbon."

This was the actual question-and-answer exchange that Frank Clifton Bossard, a forty-nine-year-old Ministry of Aviation employee used in meeting a Soviet contact at a British railroad station in 1962. Bossard was arrested in 1965 in a London hotel room where he had gone on his lunch hour to photograph guided-missile documents for the Russians, for whom he had spied for four years. Bossard had previously worked in British intelligence in Germany. He received his espionage instructions over Radio Moscow in a code utilizing five musical selections: "Moscow Nights," "Swan Lake," "Kalinka," "Saber Dance" and the "Song of the Volga Boatmen."

Illinois, and then went to Spain to fight in the Abraham Lincoln Brigade in 1937 under the name of Israel Altman. He served in the U.S. Army during World War II, and got an M.A. from Columbia in 1947. In high school and college he was known as "Unc," for he had all the genial enthusiasm of a head counselor at a Catskill Mountain summer camp for boys.

He had met Leontina Petka, known as Lona, a Polish girl from Adams, Massachusetts, while she was governess in a family living on Park Avenue. They were married in Norwich, Connecticut, on July 13, 1941. Both were Communist party members. Morris began teaching in the New York City public school system on September 9, 1949. It was during this period, 1948–50, that the Cohens were involved with Abel.

In June 1950 the Cohens let it be known that they were leaving New York, for Morris claimed he had a screen-writing job in California. The Cohens closed their bank accounts, cashed $1,075 in savings bonds, attended a farewell party given by friends on July 5—and disappeared. How involved they were in the Rosenberg spy ring, if at all, is uncertain; the FBI had arrested David Greenglass (Ethel Rosenberg's brother) on June 16 and Soviet intelligence may have decided to pull back other agents from the field.

The Cohens were, in fact, highly trained Soviet agents, with a collection of seven passports, some real, some not. They are believed to have gone to Australia, New Zealand, Hong Kong, Austria and France before they entered England in 1954. By October 1955 they were living in a house at 45 Cranley Drive in Ruislip, a London suburb, as Peter John and Helen Joyce Kroger. As Peter Kroger, Cohen became well established in London's antiquarian-book trade, operating from a room at No. 190, the Strand.

On March 3, 1955, a Soviet "illegal" using the name Gordon Arnold Lonsdale and posing as a Canadian, had sailed from New York to Southampton on the *America* to join the Krogers in England.

The real Lonsdale was born in Cobalt, Ontario, on August 27, 1924. His father was Jack Emmanuel Lonsdale, the son of a Scotsman and a pure-Indian mother.* Jack Lonsdale married a Finnish girl named Olga Bousu. They separated, and in 1932 Olga left Canada and took the boy with her to Finland. That is the last heard of the real Gordon Arnold Lonsdale.

In 1954 the KGB agent using Lonsdale's name materialized in Vancouver. Possibly he slipped off one of the Soviet freighters that landed there to pick up wheat.† The Soviet agent claimed "his" birth certificate at Cobalt, and using it, obtained a valid Canadian passport on January 21, 1955. He entered the United States at Niagara Falls on George Washington's Birthday, a date that may have been chosen because there would have been many tourists in the area that day. Then he sailed for England.

There Lonsdale played the role of a Canadian businessman purveying jukeboxes and bubble-gum machines. He established contact with the Krogers and with Henry Frederick Houghton, who was working at the Portland Naval Base, near Southampton.

From the middle of 1951 until October 1952, Houghton, a much-torpedoed seaman in the British Navy during World War II, had been a clerk in the naval attaché's office at the British embassy in Warsaw. He drank, broke his wife's leg, played the black market and got involved with Polish girls. He was recalled and, surprisingly, reassigned to the Underwater Weapons Establishment at Portland, a center for NATO's research into antisubmarine warfare.

The middle-aged Houghton and his dowdy spinster girl friend, Ethel Elizabeth Gee, who was also employed at Portland, sold naval secrets to Lonsdale. On January 7, 1961, Detective-Superintendent George Gordon Smith of Scotland Yard arrested Harry Houghton,

---

* After his arrest in England and subsequent return to Russia, the Soviet agent—attempting to cling even then to his blown cover as Gordon Lonsdale—claimed that people told him he looked as if he had "Red Indian" blood. It was an interesting illustration of the lengths the Russians go to in building their legends.

† The Soviet grain freighters that visited Vancouver figured in the George Victor Spencer case, for it was aboard one of them, in 1956, that Spencer met his first Soviet contact. The chief of Canadian counterintelligence testified at the 1966 inquiry that Lonsdale's documentation came from the Haileybury area of Ontario where, as the Russians knew, records had been destroyed by a forest fire.

"Bunty" Gee and Gordon Lonsdale in London as they walked near the Old Vic with a shopping bag full of Royal Navy secrets. Among the documents was information about the *Dreadnought,* Britain's first atomic submarine.

Then Superintendent Smith went to Ruislip, where he arrested the Krogers. The suburban house proved to be a squirrel's cage of espionage gadgets, hidden away inside talcum-powder cans, a Ronson lighter, and other hollow hiding places. Among the most important equipment was a high-frequency transmitter and an automatic keying device for Morse transmissions at 240 words a minute (cutting down on the time that the Krogers would have to be on the air broadcasting to Moscow); lenses to reduce 35-mm. film to microdots; two microdot readers, resembling high-powered microscopes; and six one-time cipher pads made of cellulose nitrate. These were the tools which Lonsdale used to transmit the Portland naval secrets to Moscow.

In March all five defendants were tried at the Old Bailey before Lord Parker, the Lord Chief Justice of England, and all received heavy sentences: Lonsdale, twenty-five years; the Krogers, twenty years each; Houghton and Gee, fifteen years each. Their capture had been the culmination of an elaborate M.I.5 surveillance of their movements over several months. But how had M.I.5 picked up their traces?

Some speculated it was because Houghton was overly free in spending his money at The Elm Tree and other local pubs. In fact, it was the CIA which first learned about Houghton from Michal Goleniewski, a defector from the Polish intelligence service. The tip was passed on to M.I.5. Goleniewski was in a position to know because Houghton, while serving at the Warsaw embassy, had either compromised himself with Polish intelligence or had certainly come to its attention as a likely recruit.* When he took the stand in his own

---

* Goleniewski defected in April 1958; interestingly, the CIA brought him to the United States on January 12, 1961, just five days after the arrests of the Portland spy ring. In 1963 Goleniewski became a U.S. citizen under HR 5507, a special immigration bill sponsored by Senator Olin D. Johnston (D., S.C.), at the request of the CIA.

Goleniewski accurately disclosed to the CIA that fifteen U.S. embassy employees in Warsaw had gone abed with ladies working for Polish intelli-

defense, Houghton claimed that in 1957, five years after his return to England, Polish agents in Britain had coerced him into spying with threats against his life, some of them made at a pub in Tolworth with the cozy name of the Toby Jug. He also testified that they hired "London thugs" who beat him up to prove that they meant business. On November 24, 1961, U.S. Attorney General Robert F. Kennedy disclosed that an "intensive investigation" by the FBI had established Lonsdale's true identity as Conon Trofimovich Molody, a Moscow-born Soviet citizen who was brought to the United States in 1933, at age eleven, by an aunt who passed him off as her own son.

They lived in Berkeley, California, where the boy attended the A to Zed, a now-defunct private school, until 1938, when he returned to the Soviet Union. The FBI said he was believed to have served in the Red Army prior to the espionage assignment that brought him to Canada in 1954, posing as Gordon Arnold Lonsdale.

In November 1962 Superintendent Smith of Scotland Yard added some details in an article in *Police College Magazine*. He gave Lonsdale's birth date as January 17, 1922, and identified him as the son of a prominent Soviet science writer.

Leads to Lonsdale's true background had been revealed at the Old Bailey trial. Microdot correspondence between Lonsdale and his wife had been found in the Kroger home. One letter disclosed that their young son's name was Trofim. In another he recalled that in 1932, when he was ten, "Mother decided to dispatch me to the nether

---

gence. As a result, five State Department employees, including one fairly high official, were recalled and ousted, and ten Marines, the entire complement of the Warsaw embassy, were hauled back to the United States for the same reason. These events took place in 1958–60.

Later, after he became a U.S. citizen, Goleniewski proclaimed that he was really the czarevich, the Grand Duke Alexei, and the last of the Romanovs. He began writing open letters to CIA Director Admiral William F. Raborn, and to Richard M. Helms, his successor, which appeared in fine print as paid advertisements in the Washington *Daily News*. All of this was very awkward, since, as the CIA told Immigration when the special citizenship bill was up, Goleniewski had in fact made "truly significant" contributions "to the security of the United States . . . he has collaborated with the government in an outstanding manner and under circumstances which have involved grave personal risk." The CIA also informed Immigration that Goleniewski was "a native and citizen of Poland . . . born August 16, 1922, in Niewswiez."

regions." A postscript to the same letter said mournfully, "I will be thirty-nine shortly. Is there much left?"

This was a bad slip, for the real Gordon Lonsdale would have been thirty-six at the time this letter was written. M.I.5 assumed that the Soviet Lonsdale had learned his colloquial English in the United States or Canada, and that this was what was meant by the phrase "nether regions."

How many ten- or eleven-year-old boys had immigrated to North America from the Soviet Union around 1932? One? A dozen? In any event, the answer would have been possible to dig out, in time, from immigration records. This is what the FBI did in the investigation disclosed by Robert Kennedy. In time it was discovered that the aunt who brought Molody to California was alive and living in France as a ballet dancer. Her name was Tatiana Piankova. She disclosed that her sister, Molody's mother, was still living in Moscow under the name of Evdokia Constantinova Naumova.

On April 22, 1964, Lonsdale was exchanged for Greville Wynne, M.I.6's British businessman who had been sentenced to eight years by a Soviet court as Penkovsky's courier. In October 1965 the KGB permitted Lonsdale to publish a book about his adventures.* It is a heavy-handed but interesting propaganda exercise, in which Molody sticks to his false legend as Lonsdale, though it had been exposed in U.S. newspapers and *Police College Magazine* which the KGB must have read. He even embellishes the legend—to cover the missing middle years, from 1932 to 1954—with the highly dubious claim that after fighting the Nazis as a partisan, he served from 1950 to 1954 as a Soviet spy and radio operator in the United States—for Rudolf Abel.

In late March 1961, a week after the Portland trial ended, Macmillan had appointed a committee under Sir Charles Romer to find out what had gone wrong with British naval security.† That seemed to be the end of the security scare.

---

* Gordon Lonsdale, *Spy: Twenty years in Soviet Secret Service* (London, Neville Spearman, 1965).

† Sir Charles reported back on June 13. "The Admiralty," he wrote in the style favored by the British, "are to blame."

But less than a month later, on April 25, the London press carried a small item: "George Blake, 38, a government official, of no fixed address, was sent for trial on charges under the Official Secrets Act." (If there was anything George Blake did not like, as later events were to prove, it was a fixed address; his whole life gave testimony to that fact.)

On May 3 Lord Chief Justice Parker was back at the Old Bailey listening to the same prosecutor who had sent the Portland spies to their reward, Sir Reginald Manningham-Buller, Q.C.,* the Attorney General of England. This time the charges were even more serious, for Blake, as it gradually became clear, was an important veteran M.I.6 agent who had sold out Queen Anne's Gate and the Broadway Buildings from top to bottom. As Sir Reginald put it to the court, Blake, in his "complete and detailed confession," had said: "I must freely admit that there was not an official document of any importance to which I had access which was not passed to my Soviet contacts."

According to Sir Reginald's brief public statement at the trial, Blake had confessed that "in the autumn of 1951 . . . he resolved to join the Communist side . . . for the past nine and a half years while employed in the Government service and drawing his salary from the state, he had been working as an agent for the Russians, as a spy for them, and communicating a mass of information to them. In short . . . betraying his country."

For the next fifty-three minutes the case was heard in camera. Heavy wooden shutters swung into place over the windows of Old Bailey. When the press was readmitted, Blake pleaded guilty and Lord Parker told him, "Your full written confession reveals that for some nine years you have been working continuously as an agent and spy for a foreign power. Moreover, the information communicated, though not of a scientific nature, was clearly of the utmost importance to that power and has rendered much of this country's efforts completely useless."

---

* Who was disrespectfully known by some less hyphenated Britons as "Sir Reginald Bullying-Manner."

He gave Blake forty-two years, the longest prison sentence ever handed down in modern British legal history.

M.I.6, of course, had not been mentioned in court, and the Macmillan government attempted to hush up the full import of the case. But U.S. newspapers began to publish details, identifying Blake as an M.I.6 agent who had worked in Berlin and betrayed several British agents to the Russians. Questions were asked in Parliament, and within a few days British papers were printing the details already known overseas.

Many of the facts remain obscure, but this much is known: George Blake was born George Behar in Rotterdam, Holland, on November 11, 1922, to Catherine Beijderwellen, the daughter of a distinguished Dutch family, and Albert William Behar, an Egyptian Jew who was a descendant of the Sephardim, the Jews expelled from Spain the year Columbus discovered America. Behar had fought in the British army during World War I (he later became a British subject), and died in 1936 while George was staying with an aunt in Cairo.

George was an introspective, highly imaginative boy who liked to play at make-believe games; these often included a trial in which he always played the judge. After he returned to Rotterdam in 1939 he attended the Lutheran church and planned to become a clergyman.

Then the Germans invaded the Low Countries in 1940. George survived the terrible Nazi air raid on Rotterdam, but was interned as the son of a British national. He escaped, joined the Dutch underground, and in 1943 made his way to England via France and a trek over the Pyrenees into Spain. In England he changed his name to Blake.

He served briefly in the Royal Navy, and then joined the Dutch section of Special Operations Executive, which ran Operation North Pole. (In this ill-fated operation, fifty Dutch agents who parachuted into Holland fell into German hands. The Germans had used captured SOE radios to lure Baker Street into dispatching the stream of agents. Three survived.)

For a time after the war Blake interrogated Nazi U-boat commanders in Hamburg, then was sent to Downing College, Cambridge, to learn Russian. By 1949 he was in Seoul, South Korea, with the cover title of vice-consul in the Foreign Office. During the Communist invasion he was captured and interned in North Korea, suffering almost unbelievable hardships—including a death march—which have been memorably portrayed by Blake's friend and fellow prisoner Philip Deane,* then a correspondent for the *Observer.*

According to the charges at the Old Bailey, Blake's treason began in November 1951, while he was in the North Korean prison camp. Deane finds this "ludicrous" in view of the brutal treatment they received and the amateurish brainwashing efforts of the Soviet indoctrinator, whom the prisoners nicknamed Kuzma Kuzmitch and who, according to Deane, "has since defected to our side."

In April 1953 Blake and his fellow prisoners were freed by the North Koreans and returned to London by way of Peking and Moscow. In 1954 the bearded and dashing Blake married a pretty Foreign Office secretary named Gillian Allan, the daughter of a retired army lieutenant-colonel.† They had three children—the third born after his conviction for espionage. By April 1955 Blake and his family were in Berlin, where he worked as an M.I.6 agent for four years, operating from the Olympia Stadium Buildings.

Those were busy years in the espionage business in Berlin. Not only did the West and the Soviets compete—the Bonn government's own two intelligence agencies competed with each other. After the end of World War II the CIA had set up Reinhard Gehlen, one of Hitler's generals, as head of a shadowy West German spy organization. Gehlen had been responsible for the Abwehr's intelligence operations against the Soviet Union. He remained in business with CIA funds as chief of what became known as the West German Federal

---

* Philip Deane, *Captive in Korea* (London, Hamish Hamilton, 1953).

† In the inevitable first-person newspaper series that followed Blake's conviction, Gillian Blake, who said, "I had no idea that my husband was acting as an agent for the Russians," seemed to indicate that she, too, may have worked in M.I.6. "I had myself worked in George's department for two years," she wrote in the *Sunday Telegraph,* December 3, 1961, "so I know the type of work that goes on. Rushing off to odd places to meet odd people didn't seem strange."

Intelligence Agency (FIA), or the Bundesnachrichtendienst. M.I.6, not to be outdone, backed Dr. Otto John as head of a rival intelligence organization, the Office for the Protection of the Constitution, or the Bundesamt für Verfassungsschutz. John, who had been active in the bomb plot on Hitler's life, was in charge of all counterintelligence in West Germany. It was an extraordinary situation. To find a parallel in the United States, it would be as though one foreign power had established and subsidized the CIA and the other put its money in the FBI.

Otto John, M.I.6's man, defected to East Berlin in 1954. The British were appalled, the more so because it was suspected that the defection may have been prompted, in part, by the fact that John was engaged in a losing competition with the CIA's Gehlen organization. On December 13, 1955 (while Blake was in Berlin), John returned to the West and served a prison sentence for treason. This was the background of intrigue in which Blake was operating.

One of Gehlen's ex-agents, a man named Horst Eitner, was hired by British intelligence in Berlin during this period, and worked directly with Blake. Eitner, as it turned out, was a double agent secretly working for the Russians. It has been suggested that he found out that Blake was, too.

A double agent, Philip Deane wrote after Blake's conviction, "has to give away some genuine secrets from time to time; if he gives away more than he brings back he is a traitor—if he brings back more than he gives away, he is a hero." Deane was suggesting that M.I.6 used Blake in this tricky role of double agent, by having him pretend to be working for Russian intelligence while actually penetrating it for London. If so, his confession indicates he deceived M.I.6 and was actually loyal to Moscow.

In 1959 Blake left Berlin for London. He was assigned the next year as a student at the Middle East College for Arabic Studies in Shemlan, a picturesque mountain village near Beirut. The school, run by the British Foreign Office, was periodically assailed by pro-Nasser politicians as a "breeding ground" for British spies. Blake was of course already a spy. (So was Philby, who was in Beirut at the same time.)

Horst Eitner was arrested in October 1960 and, possibly, he fingered Blake.* In any event, at Easter 1961 Blake was summoned home from Beirut by a telegram which his superiors tried to phrase as casually as possible so as not to alarm him. Macmillan and M.I.6 must have been nervous as they waited, with visions of another Burgess-Maclean case. But early in April, Blake flew home. He must have broken quickly, for by April 18 he was being secretly arraigned at the Bow Street Magistrates' Court. Soon after came the trial at the Old Bailey.

In the storm that followed, one plaintive statement to the House of Commons by Prime Minister Macmillan somehow stood out. "Such cases as this are, I hope, extremely rare," he said. That wish was not to be. Macmillan was to become an Edwardian victim of a new age of espionage.

The Prime Minister, groping unsuccessfully for an answer, announced that he would set up a committee, in addition to the Romer Committee, to study security problems brought on by the Portland and Blake cases. "I remember," he said, almost nostalgically, "the debate on Burgess and Maclean, when we were torn between our natural tradition of liberalism and demands of security in this new kind of battle we have come into."

Thus was born the first of two security inquiries headed by Lord Radcliffe. The Radcliffe Committee took the view that no one held captive by the Communists for more than three months should be re-employed, or employed, by the government. But not even Lord Radcliffe could look inside the mind of George Blake and explain why he betrayed M.I.6. Gillian thought it might be her husband's misplaced "fanatical religious feeling," a confusion of Communism and Christ. And she offered this explanation, too: "George liked to be a power behind the scenes, but not to be obviously powerful. He wanted to know all sorts of things that were going on and liked to have a hand in them, though nobody need know it. He did not want power for himself." Philip Deane thought the explanation lay in

---

* Some evidence that he might have done so is provided by the fact that Eitner was held quietly for more than a year before he was brought to trial and sentenced. In the interim, Blake was arrested and convicted. Eitner drew three years from a West Berlin court on November 30, 1961.

Blake's penchant for make-believe: "He had Walter Mitty dreams."

It was not the end of the story. On the rainy night of October 22, 1966, just short of his forty-fourth birthday, Blake sawed through the bars of a second-story window in London's Wormwood Scrubs prison, swung to the ground and went over the wall on a fifteen-foot nylon rope ladder, its rungs reinforced with knitting needles. A pot of pink chrysanthemums was found outside the wall; it may have been a marker, or an accomplice may have carried it to look like a visitor to the Hammersmith Hospital across the road.

Special Branch put an immediate watch on Russian ships in port and on Communist embassies. But Blake had an hour-and-a-half head start before prison guards noticed, at seven o'clock, that he was missing. He could have been on a plane leaving the London airport by then. Scotland Yard issued new photographs of Blake, beardless and looking, full face, vaguely like actor Kenneth More. The Krogers were moved from their separate prisons to more secure separate prisons.

A bitter debate broke out in Commons. During the Macmillan years, Labour had been relentless in its attacks over security breaches. Now the tables were turned, and the Wilson government had to beat down a Conservative censure motion over Blake's escape. It fell back on the same time-honored device used by Macmillan: it named a committee, headed by Earl Mountbatten, to study prison security.

Wilson's difficulties were compounded by the fact that criminals had been escaping with regularity from British prisons, among them two masterminds of the Great Train Robbery of 1963.* After Blake escaped a cartoon was published with one prisoner asking another: "Are you staying in for Christmas?"

Some persons in England seriously advanced the theory that

---

* A caper which the Russians had tried to blame on the British Secret Service. On October 19, 1965, a Moscow broadcast by one Boris Belitsky suggested that M.I.6 had pulled the $8,000,000 mail train robbery because it was short of funds. The broadcast suggested that this explained who had helped two of the robbers, Charles Wilson and Ronald Biggs, break out of British jails. The Foreign Office, while not ordinarily prone to displaying humor in public, replied: "At this junction, while there are many points of interest in the main lines of this story, the train of argument would appear to carry many signal misrepresentations."

Blake had been loyal to Britain all along, that his imprisonment was a trick aimed at the KGB and that he was deliberately freed by M.I.6. It is possible, although the mind boggles at the thought of triple agentry.

Lord Parker charged that Blake had rendered much of M.I.6's operations "useless," but there were more security scandals to come. In March 1962, possibly through a Soviet defector, M.I.5 learned that there was a spy inside the Admiralty. On April 4—the very day before the Radcliffe Committee issued its report growing out of the Portland naval secrets case—the head of M.I.5, in the utmost secrecy, contacted the Admiralty, still reeling from that case, to inform it that an unidentified spy was at work inside the building.

The spy's name was revealed in September when Special Branch officers arrested a thirty-eight-year-old Admiralty clerk. William John Vassall, a homosexual, was apprehended on the eve of his annual vacation, which he had planned to spend on Capri with an American boyfriend. Vassall had been handing over top-secret Admiralty material to Soviet intelligence for seven years. At first the Russians photographed the documents and returned them to Vassall. After a while they gave him an Exakta * camera, and Vassall photographed the documents himself. He usually took them home overnight and handed the undeveloped film to his Soviet controllers.

On October 22, 1962, Lord Chief Justice Parker sentenced Vassall to eighteen years. That same day President Kennedy announced the Cuban missile crisis, the Russians arrested Oleg Penkovsky, and Harold Macmillan appointed a committee, this one headed by Sir Charles Cunningham, to study security in the Admiralty.

Vassall, like Stephen Ward, was a clergyman's son, but the family was not well off and he had no university education. During the war he was a photographer in the RAF, a skill that he later put to lucrative use as a Soviet agent.

He went to work at the Admiralty in 1947, and in 1954 was sent

---

* The Russians almost invariably use an Exakta for this type of work; the same make of camera figured in the Portland case, and many others. The Exakta, manufactured in Dresden, East Germany, is a 35-mm. single-lens reflex, excellent for close-up and microscopic photography.

to Moscow as clerk to the naval attaché, a Captain Bennett, who reported that Vassall's work was satisfactory despite "an irritating, effeminate personality." His fellow employees called him "Vera" behind his back, and the ambassador, Sir William Hayter, admitted after Vassall's arrest that he had always thought him "a bit ladylike." But apparently no one, except a Soviet agent named Sigmund Mikhailsky, a jack-of-all-trades at the British embassy,* realized that Vassall was a homosexual who might be blackmailed. In his statement to Special Branch, Vassall said Mikhailsky and three Russian friends "plied" him with brandy one night. "I remember the lighting being very strong. More of my clothes were removed . . . I remember two or three getting on the bed with me in a state of undress. Then several compromising sexual actions took place. I remember someone of the party taking photographs."

Vassall claimed that the Russians used the prints to force him to spy. It began in Moscow and continued after he returned to the Admiralty in July 1956 and went to work in the naval intelligence branch. He had two ways to get in touch with "Nikolai" or "Gregory," his Soviet contacts in London. He would draw a circle on a tree with, appropriately, pink chalk, or telephone KENsington 8955 and ask for "Miss Mary."

Vassall's arrest and trial, however, was only the beginning. He had worked from 1957 to 1959 as clerk to Thomas "Tam" Galbraith, a kindly and aristocratic M.P. from Glasgow who was Civil Lord of the Admiralty. Galbraith sent a series of chatty "My dear Vassall" letters to his clerk, who also wrote to him, and Vassall had a photograph of Galbraith on his dresser at home. On such gossamer evidence as this, the press and the Opposition built a carnival of innuendo that forced Galbraith to resign from the government.

For the second time in as many years, Lord Radcliffe was called on by Macmillan to head an official security inquiry, this time under the 1921 Tribunals of Inquiry Act, giving the investigation very broad

---

* Mikhailsky had been hired through Burobin, a branch of the KGB that provides foreign embassies in Moscow with local employees. The embassies have little choice over whom they get.

powers. The tribunal questioned 142 witnesses, and sat in camera about twice as often as it held public hearings.*

The first of four questions the Radcliffe Tribunal was directed to answer regarding Vassall was whether the government had known ever since the Portland case that another spy was at work inside the Admiralty. The charge had first been made by Percy Hoskins of the *Daily Express* in a story headlined: "DON'T FORGET THEY KNEW FOR 18 MONTHS THERE WAS A SPY AROUND . . ."

Hoskins alleged that among the microdot films found in the Krogers' home in 1961 was a copy of a secret document that had never been sent to the Portland base and therefore must have come from the Admiralty itself. The Radcliffe Tribunal found that "there was no such film of any Admiralty document" and that "no films or documents of any kind found at the Krogers' home . . . suggested or implied that there was another spy operating in the Admiralty." †

The Tribunal completely cleared Galbraith of any improper relationship with Vassall. It also sent three Fleet Street reporters to court to be cited for contempt because they refused to reveal news sources: Reginald Foster and Desmond Clough of the *Daily Sketch,* and Brendan Mulholland of the *Daily Mail.* All three received jail sentences but only Foster and Mulholland actually went to prison.

The sentencing of the three newsmen was extremely important, for the hostility between Fleet Street and Macmillan had now reached a warlike stage; the unfortunate Galbraith episode left the press very wary of damaging a Minister's moral character and public reputation—but loaded for bear in case a vulnerable, *guilty* Minister should

---

* The first Radcliffe Committee was appointed in May 1961 as a result of the Portland and Blake cases, and its report, *Security Procedures in the Public Service* (Cmnd. 1681), was published on April 5, 1962. The second Radcliffe panel, formally known as a Tribunal of Inquiry, was named on November 15, 1962, under an Act of Parliament, and its *Report of the Tribunal appointed to Inquire into the Vassall Case and Related Matters* (Cmnd. 2009), was released on April 25, 1963. Both reports were published in London by Her Majesty's Stationery Office.

† However, in an article published in the 1963 *Britannica Book of the Year,* Allen Dulles stated of the Krogers: "Microfilms found in their apartment eventually led to the apprehension of John Vassall, another Admiralty employee." It would seem that either the Radcliffe Tribunal or the former CIA Director was wrong on this point.

happen along. In the spring of 1963, one did, and his name was John Dennis Profumo.

It may be remembered that when Christine Keeler was hawking her memoirs earlier in the year, Profumo asked Sir Roger Hollis, the head of M.I.5, to meet with him. And "the head of the Security Service," as Lord Denning reported, "formed the impression that Mr. Profumo's object in asking to see him was to get a D notice or something to stop publication, which was a vain hope."

The D notice system first came to wide public attention during the Blake case. It is the machinery by which the British government is able, as a rule, to suppress information which it desires to keep out of British newspapers, books, and radio and television broadcasts. It is a system which has great attraction for Americans of an authoritarian turn of mind. They would like to substitute it for the First Amendment to the Constitution, although fortunately, they cannot. It has not, as a matter of fact, worked in an altogether satisfactory way even for Britain.

"A D notice," the first Radcliffe report explained, "is a formal letter of request which is circulated confidentially to newspaper editors . . . a notice has no legal force and can only be regarded as a letter of advice or request . . . it gives an editor warning that an item of news, which may well be protected under the Official Secrets Act, is regarded by the defense authorities as a secret of importance and . . . whether or not any legal sanction would attach to the act of publication, publication is considered to be contrary to the national interest."

In other words, although the D notice is "advisory," the editor who disregards it may just find himself breaking the law. As Oxford law professor David Williams has written in this regard: "There is no more effective censor than an uncertain law." *

Britain's Official Secrets Act prohibits all forms of espionage, bars government officials from divulging secrets and unauthorized persons from receiving them. The trick is that the Secrets Act is

---

* *Not in the Public Interest* (London, Hutchinson, 1965). A thoughtful study of the point at which Britain's legal, security and press censorship problems meet.

hitched to the D notice system. Since a D notice warns an editor that publication of a given news item may violate the Act, the effect is almost indistinguishable from compulsory censorship.

That the D notice system is a generally effective club over Fleet Street was conceded delicately by the Radcliffe Committee: "There have been cases of nonobservance but, according to our informants, such cases have been relatively few."

The D notices are issued by the Services, Press and Broadcasting Committee, a sixteen-member group that includes government and news-media representatives. But the notices are normally initiated by the government, acting through the committee. As a practical matter, the committee's central figure is its secretary. In 1945 Rear-Admiral George Thomson, the wartime Chief Press Censor, was appointed to the post and held it for almost two decades. He was succeeded as committee secretary by Colonel L. G. "Sammy" Lohan, a former SOE man with a handlebar mustache, gray hair, a gold-rimmed monocle and Savile Row tailoring.

Britain's original Official Secrets Act was passed in 1889, but the present law was enacted in 1911 and amended twice. Until the Blake case, however, most Britons were unaware of the D notice machinery. Britain not only had a system of censorship to protect secrets, but the system itself was secret.

On May 1, 1961, two days before Blake was tried, a D notice went out to Fleet Street asking that his M.I.6 affiliation and many other facts be suppressed. The London correspondent of the New York *Herald Tribune,* Richard C. Wald, who was unaware of the D notice, was able to learn details of the case. When his story appeared in London the next day in the European Edition, it caused a furor.

Another D notice went out on May 4 advising editors not to pick up stories in the foreign press, which prompted Mr. Richard Marsh, a Labour M.P., to ask Macmillan whether "members of the British public are not entitled to the same amount of information as is available to the nationals of other countries?" With the issue being discussed in Parliament, the pressure for disclosure became too great, and within a short time the British press was publishing the forbidden details.

The real question, foreshadowing the D notice aspect of the Profumo case, had also been voiced by Mr. Marsh. "What worries a number of members," he declared, "is the belief that on this occasion this procedure was used not to protect British security but to protect Ministers."

In 1963 Harold Wilson made precisely the same point, suggesting that D notices were being used "to protect the government from ridicule in the press or in the political field"—a view he has not expressed since becoming head of the government. Indeed, in February 1967 he took the unprecedented step for a Prime Minister of personally denouncing a newspaper and its reporter in the House of Commons, allegedly for violating the D notice system. The new storm broke because Chapman Pincher had disclosed in the *Daily Express* that British security men were peeking at commercial cables being sent from England by private individuals, businessmen and embassies.

The Prime Minister huffed that the cable reading had been going on since 1927 under powers derived from the Official Secrets Act, a disclosure that in itself startled a lot of Britons. The real culprit, Wilson said, was the newspaper that had violated the D notice system.

As the storm mounted, however, Wilson proved that he was not really so different from Macmillan, and that nothing really changes. He named a committee of investigation to study the Pincher article in particular and security methods in general, under a familiar chairman—Lord Radcliffe.

To Wilson's great chagrin, the committee concluded in June that the *Daily Express* had not violated any D notice. Furious, Wilson had the government write and release an extraordinary white paper that disavowed the central findings of his own investigating committee under Lord Radcliffe, whose report was published at the same time. The white paper insisted that the cable-snooping story had in fact breached the D notice procedure and two specific D notices.

In a full-scale parliamentary debate on June 22, Wilson claimed that national security had been jeopardized. He spoke mysteriously of a secret branch of the Foreign Office involved in the cable reading.

He said the story had concerned "a highly sensitive area of intelligence" and he hinted that men's lives "may have been endangered." Wilson then compounded previous errors in his handling of the whole affair by attacking Colonel Lohan, the secretary of the Services, Press and Broadcasting Committee, insinuating that he had been the source of many of Chapman Pincher's stories. Just before the debate ended at 10 P.M., the Prime Minister asserted that Lohan had been the subject of a security investigation in 1964 and had never received full clearance. He left unanswered the question of why the Wilson government had allowed Lohan to remain in his job as committee secretary, a sensitive civil service post, if the results of the check had been anything but satisfactory. Because Wilson was the last speaker, under the rules no reply could be made. Lohan, who resigned, could take no legal action to answer the innuendo against his character and reputation because statements made in the House of Commons are privileged. "I have been slandered out of business," he declared. Wilson was roundly condemned by the British press for his performance.

Books as well as newspapers have been censored in England, and once Sir Compton Mackenzie, the distinguished author, was even brought to trial at the Old Bailey. He was hauled into the dock in 1933 because the previous fall he had published *Greek Memories,* recounting some of his intelligence experiences in Athens in 1916. The book was seized and withdrawn from publication. Mackenzie was charged with using material he had acquired in government service and with mentioning the names of about a dozen people connected with the Secret Service sixteen years before.

Sir Compton gives a hilarious account of his trial in a later book.* At one point the prosecutor, Sir Thomas Inskip, condemned Mackenzie because he had "revealed the mysterious consonant by which the Chief of the Secret Service was known." Sir Compton quotes this exchange between the judge and the prosecutor:

" 'But, Mr. Attorney, if C is such a dangerous consonant, why is it still being used nearly fifteen years after the war?' "

---

* *Greece in My Life* (London, Chatto & Windus, 1960).

" 'That I couldn't say, m'lud.' "

" 'No, I shouldn't think you could. The consonant should surely have been changed by now.' "

Sir Compton was fined £100, but he got back at M.I.5 and M.I.6, and recovered his legal costs, by writing a spoof of the Secret Service called *Water on the Brain,* which could not be banned because it was supposedly fictional.*

One book that had little trouble getting published in England was *Their Trade Is Treachery,* a volume with a very limited circulation. It was compiled by M.I.5 and distributed to Foreign Office and other employees in 1964 to warn against enemy espionage. The fifty-nine-page publication has such intriguing chapter headings as "How Not to Become a Spy" and "How to Become a Spy."

"Spies are with us all the time," the Preface warns. "This booklet tells you about the great hostile spy machine that tries to suborn our citizens and turn them into traitors . . . how to recognise at once certain espionage techniques and how to avoid pitfalls, which could lead to a national catastrophe or a personal disaster—or both. Finally if you are in possession of information useful to a spy . . . this booklet tells you how to foil the spy who will certainly be seeking it. He may be closer than you think."

---

* The hero of the novel, a hen-pecked retired army major named Arthur Blenkinsop, is recruited into the Secret Service with the cover of a banana importer. At first he makes the almost unforgivable mistake of referring to N, the chief, by his name, Colonel Nutting, but he apologizes quickly and is told:

" 'I know you won't do it again. Of course, in one way, it doesn't matter in my room at the War Office. But it's against the principles of the Secret Service. You do it once in private, and then before you know where you are you'll go and do it in the middle of Piccadilly. After all, the whole point of the Secret Service is that it should be secret.' "

" 'Quite, quite, sir. I'm very sorry.' "

" 'Of course, I wouldn't go so far as to say that the secrecy was *more* important than the service, but it's every bit *as* important. Well, it stands to reason that if the Secret Service was no longer secret it would cease to be the secret service. After all, we're not cabinet ministers. We can't afford to talk.' "

Water on the Brain was first published in 1933. In the Preface to an edition two decades later, Sir Compton wrote that at the time, his novel must have seemed "a fantastic Marx Brothers affair." But during World War II, he said, "many more people discovered that those responsible for Secret Intelligence do, in very fact, as often as not behave like characters created by the Marx Brothers. *Duck Soup,* for instance, appealed to me as a film of stark realism."

It warns that Soviet intelligence has an "inborn talent" for espionage. It explains the difference between the KGB and the GRU. Although most of the cases cited use fictitious names, it also has some interesting analyses of British spies for Moscow.

"Of all spies," the book notes, "the ideological one is perhaps the hardest to uncover—especially if his conversion to the enemy cause has taken place after he has been given a position of trust . . . Such a man was George Blake of the Foreign Office.

"The mercenary spy is motivated by greed. Vassall, the Admiralty spy, claimed that at first he was blackmailed, but later he clearly became a mercenary spy. Ex-Petty Officer Houghton, in the Portland Case, was primarily a mercenary spy."

Their Trade Is Treachery was a behind-the-scenes attempt to counter the spy cases that plagued Britain in the 1960's. It was also part of a broader effort to reassure Washington. England is very conscious of the fact that its series of espionage affairs has weakened U.S. confidence in the effectiveness of British security. As a result, despite popular belief, British and U.S. intelligence do not work together as harmoniously as they should. Each complains about lack of information from the other.

Some effort is being made by the CIA and M.I.6 to divide the world into geographic areas of responsibility to avoid duplication. One problem is that in the past the CIA relied on M.I.5. to provide intelligence from Africa in areas under British control (M.I.5 rather than M.I.6 had the responsibility because these areas were considered internal). But the growth of the new nations of Africa has sharply curtailed British activity there, and the CIA has not always been able to plug the gap.

Some of the British-American difficulties go back to the rivalry between the two intelligence organizations they set up in Germany. On the other hand, before the Suez invasion the CIA knew more about the secret planning—through certain links to British intelligence—than some members of the British Cabinet who, for one reason or another, were not informed.*

---

* This was discussed in a speech delivered to a small, private audience in Washington in February 1966 by a former high official of the CIA.

Possibly more typical was a silly flare-up between the CIA and M.I.6 over a defector named Anatoli Dolnytsin. In July 1963, in the midst of the Profumo and Philby uproar, the British put out a D notice saying that a Soviet defector was in England, and please don't say that his name is Anatoli Dolnytsin.

Stories naming Dolnytsin promptly appeared in London. Enraged American intelligence officials in Washington spread the word that the Russian had defected to the United States eighteen months before and was not supposed to have been surfaced. They voiced the suspicion that the D notice had been deliberately issued not to censor but to publicize the case, and to divert attention from the security cases then embarrassing the Macmillan government. There were stories published in Britain, for example, claiming that it was Dolnytsin who had tipped off M.I.6 to the fact that Philby was the "third man."

All of this suggested that CIA-M.I.6. co-operation was, regrettably, something less than suggested by the easy relationship of James Bond and Felix Leiter in Ian Fleming's stories.* The basic reason for this is the fact that the British tend to be more tolerant of the Soviet Union and have never taken as hard a line as the United States in the Cold War. As a result, some U.S. intelligence officials are wary of taking the British into their full confidence. For their part, the British have a genuine abhorrence of McCarthyism, an attitude that is often cited as the reason why spies are not uncovered sooner. This strain runs through all of the public comments and literature on the question.

The Denning report: "The Security Service . . . are to be used for one purpose and one purpose only, *the Defence of the Realm.* They are not to be used to pry into any man's private conduct . . . Most people in this country would, I am sure, whole-heartedly support this principle, for it would be intolerable to us to have anything

---

* Fleming named the CIA agent after an American friend, the late Thomas Leiter. Much later, Fleming was surprised to learn that the land on which the CIA headquarters stand in Langley, Virginia, had been owned by Leiter's father, millionaire Joseph Leiter, who built a beautiful home there called the Glass Palace. After the senior Leiter died, in 1932, the government bought the land. The Glass Palace burned down in 1945.

in the nature of a Gestapo or Secret Police to snoop into all that we do, let alone our morals."

The Radcliffe Committee: "We have reminded ourselves that security weaknesses of this kind are part of the price we pay for having a social and political system that men want to defend."

Macmillan: "One could of course—the government of whatever complexion could—run a closely controlled, almost a police state. If you want absolute security you have to do that."

Ironically, despite the frictions between the intelligence communities in London and Washington, American intelligence was to a great extent patterned on the British. The OSS, the forerunner of the CIA, was modeled on the wartime SOE. In one important respect, however, there is a difference. The CIA combines intelligence gathering and secret operations in one organization, a practice which has often been criticized. The British separate their operators in M.I.6 from the analysts working under the overt Director-General of Intelligence in the Defence Ministry.

Historically the British have been superbly discreet in keeping their secret intelligence machinery, M.I.5 and M.I.6, out of view, partly through tradition and partly through the D notice system and the law. But Britain has turned a nineteenth-century virtue into a twentieth-century fault. Imperial England could, in a sense, afford to have hidden citadels of totally secret power within its government. Perhaps this was true even between the two World Wars. But in the modern era of high-speed communications and insistent news media—and in the light of the KGB's unpleasant activities—a clubby invisible sort of intelligence that is somehow an extension of Oxbridge becomes a political liability.

When a spy scandal does strike in England, it seems all the worse because there is no one to blame. The result is often the opposite of that desired: more, rather than less, public interest is focused on the intelligence agencies.

In the United States, when the public gets agitated over the CIA,

Time magazine can put Richard Helms on the cover, and the open discussion is some sort of safety valve. Allen Dulles understood this and never favored a faceless British-style intelligence chief for the United States. *The Economist* was perhaps thinking along these lines when it ran an editorial in October 1966 which said: "The use of the word intelligence is still pretty unfamiliar. For reasons that everyone is supposed to understand, Whitehall thinks it wise not to draw too much public attention to the word or to the activity. Because some of its methods are secret . . . it is held that everything should be secret; with the curious result that the obsolete names of our security service and secret intelligence service (M.I.5 and M.I.6) enjoy in the Western world an almost music-hall notoriety second only to that of the American CIA."

Much has been said, too, of the rampant Old Boyism that was a major contributing factor in the Burgess-Maclean and Profumo cases. In August 1963, after the Profumo dust had settled somewhat, Lord Radcliffe ruminated on the BBC that perhaps it would have been better if the Prime Minister had been told a bit sooner about Christine, Profumo and the bomb. "It is just one of those things that slipped up at the time," he said. "Of course, looking back afterwards, it seems to have been a very great pity."

A great pity indeed, but it was just this sort of languid remark that led Allen Dulles to say on a U.S. television program two weeks later that in the past, at least in the days of Burgess and Maclean, British intelligence had suffered from "too much of the old-school tie. If you went to Oxford or Cambridge you were all right. Well, it didn't turn out that way."

It was all perhaps best summed up by Harold Wilson, during an angry debate with Macmillan in the House of Commons over the Vassall case, in May 1963:

"Were our authorities too easily reassured by the school the man went to, the fact that he came of a good family . . . the fact that he was personable, had a good accent and manner, and was a member of the Conservative and Bath clubs, as Vassall was? I wonder if the positive vetting of Vassall would have been so casual if he had been a boilermaker's son and gone to an elementary school. (*Opposition cheers*)

"I think too much was taken for granted because he seemed a decent type. I cannot escape the conclusion that on this question of . . . British espionage and counterespionage, on which the security of the country depends, it is the old contest of gentlemen versus players and we are up against a ruthless, highly professionalized service.

"When you fight professionalism in the gentlemanly posture of the Establishment you are beaten before you start."

This is one of the saddest times that our government has had, in reference to public policy . . . I'm not at all happy about what the CIA has been doing and I'm sure that out of this . . . will come a reformation of that agency, with closer supervision of its activities.

—Vice-President Hubert H. Humphrey,
on CIA subsidies of students, February 20, 1967

IV the united states

On Saturday, April 10, 1965, Richard McGarrah Helms was the overnight guest of President Johnson at the LBJ Ranch in Texas. For dinner that evening there was also an unexpected guest, Senator Eugene McCarthy, the Minnesota Democrat. He had been asked to the ranch at the last moment while meeting a speaking engagement in nearby Austin.

McCarthy, an outspoken critic of the CIA but an admirer of Helms, thought it might be interesting to run a little test of the man who was to be named Deputy Director of the Central Intelligence Agency the following day. McCarthy pointed to some yellow flowers on the table and asked Helms to identify them. Helms could not. McCarthy tried a second, third and fourth variety. Helms was unable to identify any of them. McCarthy then turned to the wine and asked Helms if he could distinguish the various vintages on the table. Helms could not.

"James Bond would have known the answers," McCarthy commented dryly. Helms was not amused, perhaps because he was embarrassed at having flunked the test in such awesome company, or possibly because he shared the professional CIA man's annoyance at being associated with flamboyant, fictional spies.

But the President was not looking for a James Bond. When he later swore in Helms, on June 30, 1966, as the $30,000-a-year Director of Central Intelligence, he remarked that in all his time as President he had "yet to meet a Double-O Seven" from the CIA. He had only the highest praise for the "patriotic and dedicated" men whose "most significant triumphs come not in the secrets passed in the dark, but in patient reading, hour after hour, of highly technical periodicals. In a real sense they are America's professional students. They are unsung just as they are invaluable."

Turning to Helms, Johnson declared, "Although he has spent more than twenty years in public life attempting to avoid publicity, he has never been able to conceal the fact that he is one of the most trusted and most able and most dedicated professional career men in this capital. No man has ever come to this high critical office with better qualifications."

Helms was, in fact, the first career intelligence operator to be named head of the CIA. Allen Dulles, who had served as Director from 1953 to 1961, matched Helms in professionalism, but he had devoted more than half his working life to private law practice on Wall Street. Helms, on the other hand, entered intelligence at the age of twenty-seven and remained there. Indeed, he was the very model of the modern civil servant *—soft-spoken (but with a hearty laugh), pleasant, patient, courteous, and, most important, apolitical.

"Helms has no politics," a CIA veteran confided. "He's just a good professional intelligence man."

"Dick's so undoctrinaire," said another, "that he insists there are pros and cons to everything."

"He has no big ideological slant," an important member of the

---

* In 1965 the National Civil Service League gave him an award for "significant contributions to excellence in government."

intelligence community remarked. "He is a technician, influenced by his clandestine background."

The closest Helms's associates could come to a definition of his views was a negative one—neither "bleeding-heart liberal" nor "FBI-style anti-Communist." In any event, Johnson found Helms, as he confided privately, to be "the only one who had all the right answers."

A tall (six foot one), thin, sleekly dark-haired man, Helms is handsome and fit enough to be a Hollywood spy, though with a change in his Ivy League clothes and manner, he could easily be cast as a river-boat gambler. He was born on March 30, 1913, in St. David's, Pennsylvania, a fashionable suburb of Philadelphia, and reared in South Orange, New Jersey, a fashionable suburb of New York. While young Helms was still in school his father, Herman, a sales executive for Alcoa, retired and took his family to Europe. Helms finished his last two years in prep schools in France and Germany, becoming fluent in both languages. He came back to the United States to go to Williams College, where he was a member of Phi Beta Kappa, permanent president of his class, president of the senior honor society, and editor of both the paper and the senior year book. His classmates voted him the student who best exemplified the school's traditions, the most likely to succeed, the most respected, the man who had done most for the college, the best politician, the second most versatile and the third most popular.

After college he joined the United Press in Germany, covered the 1936 Olympics, and wangled an exclusive interview with Sonja Henie and another with Adolf Hitler. He left reporting the next year and joined the advertising department of the Indianapolis *Times*. Two years later he became its national advertising manager and married Julia Bretzman Shields,* an Indianapolis girl with two children by a

---

* Mrs. Helms, a painter and sculptress, produced Christmas creches in their house at 3901 Fessenden St. in Northwest Washington. An international network of friends supplied her with religious and folk figures for the creches. Once in Saigon she asked Madame Ngo Dinh Nhu for help in locating the Vietnamese version of her "little people"—gnomes, elves, and trolls. Madame Nhu replied coldly that she was a Roman Catholic and emancipated from such superstitions. But later she sent along a number of ancient bronzes representing "old age, wisdom and fertility."

previous marriage. The Helmses have one son of their own, Dennis, twenty-five, who was a student at the University of Virginia Law School.

During World War II, Helms served as a naval officer attached to the Office of Strategic Services. He was assigned to the European Theater because of his linguistic proficiency and worked for a while in Germany under Allen Dulles. After the war he stayed on in intelligence. When the CIA was formally established by the National Security Act of 1947, Helms was one of the small group of former OSS men clearly destined to move up in the new hierarchy. But despite his privileged position, Helms suffered a fair share of frustration in his rise to the top. He was expected to move up from No. 2 to No. 1 in the Plans Division, which runs covert (black) operations, when a vacancy developed in 1958. But Dulles passed him over for Richard M. Bissell, Jr., the tall, brilliant former Yale economics professor who ran the U-2 program and the abortive attempt to invade Cuba in 1961.

In 1962, when Bissell was eased out over the Bay of Pigs, Helms finally became deputy director for plans (DDP), only to find that Lyman Kirkpatrick,* an OSS and CIA veteran, had been inserted above him in the chain of command as executive director, a new job created by John A. McCone, Dulles' successor.

Helms also found himself confronted in the agency's hidden bureaucratic warfare by an old enemy and rival, Ray S. Cline, an OSS and Far East veteran who returned from Formosa † to become deputy director for intelligence (DDI) in 1962, a rank equal to Helms's. A scholarly Phi Beta Kappa with an A.B. and Ph.D. from Harvard, Cline had previously served as CIA's liaison with British intelligence; he started in intelligence work as a cryptanalyst in the OSS in 1942. The stocky, sandy-haired Cline gave a new thrust to the perennial

---

* Kirkpatrick, fifty, a Princeton graduate and native of Rochester, New York, had remained in the CIA despite a polio attack in July 1952 that has since restricted him to a wheelchair. He left the agency in 1965 to become a professor of political science at Brown University. His last days in the CIA were marked by open disagreement and annoyance with McCone's successors.

† Cline had run the CIA station there as "Director, United States Naval Auxiliary Communications Center, Taiwan," a cover title that was abandoned on July 1, 1965, as too transparent.

battle between the contemplative types in intelligence and the activists in plans. In the end Helms triumphed, but it took some doing. After he had served as Deputy Director, the No. 2 job in the agency, for fourteen months, he finally won the right to move into the coveted seventh-floor office, behind the door numbered 75706, the innermost sanctum of the suite marked simply "DCI" (for Director of Central Intelligence).*

Helms's promotion was, in essence, a triumph for the OSS-Ivy League establishment inside the CIA, but it was long in coming. Helms had been its candidate to succeed McCone in 1965 and he had McCone's endorsement, but President Johnson, whose formidable suspicions of cultivated Easterners had been deepened by his clash with the Kennedys, turned to an outsider and a Texan, retired Vice-Admiral William F. Raborn, Jr.

"Red" Raborn was the man primarily responsible for the development of the Polaris missile. When he left the Navy he became vice-president for project management at the Aerojet-General Corporation of California. A hearty, bluff, fifty-nine-year-old Annapolis graduate who grew roses for relaxation, he had good relations with Congress, and a reputation as a strong, efficient and inspirational executive of the Knute Rockne school. It was these qualities which were attractive to Johnson, who, like his predecessors, wanted to impress his own stamp on the CIA and at the same time keep Congress from exercising any effective control.†

---

* In addition to running the CIA, the Director of Central Intelligence also serves as chairman of the board of the entire United States intelligence community: the CIA, the Defense Intelligence Agency, the National Security Agency (which makes and breaks codes), the intelligence branches of the military services, the State Department's bureau of intelligence and research, the Atomic Energy Commission and the FBI.

The CIA is divided into four main divisions, each headed by a deputy director: Plans, Intelligence, Research (for technical and scientific matters), and Support (for equipment, logistics, security and communications).

For a more detailed description of the history, organization and operations of the CIA and the other branches of United States intelligence, see David Wise and Thomas B. Ross, *The Invisible Government* (New York, Random House, 1964).

† Johnson may also have appreciated the fact that Raborn in 1964 became a member of "Scientists and Engineers for Johnson-Humphrey," a

But Raborn failed to meet the President's expectations. From the very day he took over as Director of Central Intelligence, the admiral was a marked man. At his swearing-in ceremony in the Cabinet Room of the White House on April 28, 1965, he was literally surrounded by members of the CIA establishment. Inexplicably—almost as an ill omen—the White House issued a press release that included all of their names, identifying many of them officially for the first time.*

That afternoon President Johnson ordered the Marines into the Dominican Republic, and Raborn, unprepared, was caught in the middle of a nasty intelligence crisis. The President first justified the action as one that was necessary to save lives, American and others. Then he raised the specter of an imminent Communist uprising. The CIA supplied the supporting evidence, and critics of the intervention blamed Raborn for contriving a mishmash of hasty, self-contradictory documentation. Soon the agency's professionals were grumbling among themselves about Raborn's supposed lack of knowledge, experience and intellectual sophistication. And by the end of the year they were leaking to the press.

" 'Things have reached the point,' " an intelligence man confided to Joseph Kraft, for his column of November 1, 1965, " 'where I'm even beginning to wonder whether the Polaris can possibly be a good missile.' "

"In . . . meetings," Kraft wrote, "Admiral Raborn is supposed

---

panel organized by Dr. Donald M. MacArthur, husband of President Johnson's niece, the former Diane Taylor. Aerojet's board chairman was Dan A. Kimball, a Democratic bigwig, and Raborn became one of the few prominent retired military men not to back Senator Barry M. Goldwater, the Republican nominee. In fact, Raborn said on television two days before the election that Goldwater was "just not smart enough to be President of the United States."

* Besides Dulles, McCone, Helms, Cline and Kirkpatrick, the guest list included R. Jack Smith, a career analyst who was to succeed Cline as deputy director for intelligence; Desmond FitzGerald, Helms's successor in plans; Dr. Albert D. Wheelon, deputy director for research; Sherman Kent, head of the Board of National Estimates; John A. Bross, a deputy to the Director; Lawrence R. Houston, the general counsel; Walter Elder, a staff assistant to the Director; Cord Meyer, Jr., head of labor, student and education operations; William Egan Colby, chief of the Asian desk; J. C. King, chief of the Latin American desk (whose hobby is collecting old maps of Cuba and the Caribbean); and British-born Bronson Tweedy, who in 1966 replaced Archibald B. Roosevelt, Jr., in the prominent post of London station chief.

to mispronounce the names of foreign countries and personalities consistently. His recommendations are said to bear little relationship to the facts he presents. On occasion, apparently, he has broached, as if they were fresh matters, subjects that had been exhaustively discussed only five minutes earlier. Sometimes, it seems, his point of departure is the exact opposite of a decision just taken. Thoughtful officials complain that in the final presentation their work is badly mangled. Morale has apparently sunk in the research and analysis sections of the agency, particularly among the group preparing long-run estimates."

In a piece researched in part by a former CIA man with close connections to the agency, family and otherwise, *Newsweek* wrote on December 27 that insiders were complaining that Raborn "was a greenhorn at the spy game; he was insensitive to the professional pride of his staffers, inept at dealing in nuances, so unlettered in international politics, indeed, that he could not pronounce or even remember the names of some foreign capitals and chiefs of state . . . At one staff conference, a well-placed source said, the admiral interrupted his briefing officers to ask the meaning of the word 'oligarchy.' 'Jesus,' one sputtered afterward, 'if he doesn't know what an oligarchy is, how can he handle about two-thirds of the countries we deal with?' "

CIA professionals were annoyed, *Newsweek* reported, by Raborn's salty Navy habits and language, his tendency to ramble on interminably about his achievements in the Polaris program, and his head-coach approach to the gentlemanly art of intelligence: " 'When you walk down that hall,' he told startled staffers, 'I want to see the wind move.' . . . Gloomily recalling an old agency saying that Allen Dulles ran a happy ship and John McCone a taut ship, one CIA man added the postscript: 'Raborn's running a sinking ship.' "

The discontent was so pronounced that the old pros barely troubled to conceal it even in the presence of the Director. One reporter, invited to a briefing at CIA headquarters in Langley, Virginia, sat next to a CIA man who, throughout Raborn's presentation, kept muttering "That's wrong" and "He's hopeless."

Raborn's defense against the savage attack-by-leak was to insist that he was performing his job precisely as the President wanted him to: exercising a firm hand on the CIA's burgeoning bureaucracy, imposing managerial discipline on its increasingly technical aspects and delegating the normal intelligence functions to Helms. Applying standard Navy damage-control technique, Raborn's first response to his leaky ship was to try to find the leak. Apparently because the printed gripes had focused on intelligence analysis, he finally decided that the principal culprit must be Ray Cline. Shortly thereafter, Cline was transferred overseas.

The CIA professionals also feared that, perhaps, the choice of Raborn merely reflected the President's disinterest in the more intellectual aspects of intelligence. "Johnson's only interested in dossiers on who's doing what to whom," groused one important CIA man. Actually, the President had been disparaging Raborn privately for many months. In fact, presidential disenchantment dated back to the admiral's first week in office. At that time, talking privately around the White House, Johnson managed at once to praise and condemn Raborn: the admiral had arrived in the middle of the difficult Dominican situation and had handled himself extremely well, but he was not going to be around too long. Raborn really didn't want to come back to Washington and finally agreed to take the job only on a temporary basis; his idea of how to live was to work until 1 P.M., go home, have a bowl of soup and a nap, and play golf in Palm Springs for the rest of the afternoon. Helms would eventually take over at the CIA and that's why he had instructed Raborn to bring Helms with him whenever he came to the White House for a briefing.

These were remarkable words about a man the President had just appointed, and after such a Johnsonian assessment, Raborn's days were numbered. Fourteen months later, having served for the shortest period of any head of the CIA, the admiral returned to Aerojet-General with a medal and a mild "well done" from the President. "The lure of industry was such that I couldn't pass it up," Raborn explained.

With the admiral piped ashore, the CIA was back in the hands of the establishment, with Helms as Director. Vice-Admiral Rufus L. Taylor, a professional military man who could be expected to know his place, became the Deputy Director. R. Jack Smith, a fifty-three-year-old native of Michigan, was made deputy director for intelligence. Smith earned his B.A. at Miami University and his Ph.D. at Cornell. He joined the government in 1945, served as a "foreign affairs officer in the Department of Defense" from 1947 to 1954 and then as a "foreign service reserve" officer at the embassy in Singapore. After Cline was exiled by Raborn, Smith took over the intelligence division.

His counterpart as deputy director for plans was Desmond FitzGerald, the very personification of establishment values. A graduate of St. Mark's School, Harvard College and Harvard Law School, FitzGerald had been a prosperous Wall Street lawyer with a membership in the Racquet and Tennis Club. In 1939 he married Marietta Endicott Peabody, the beautiful granddaughter of the late Endicott Peabody, who founded the Groton School and officiated at the marriage of its most celebrated graduate, President Franklin D. Roosevelt. The FitzGeralds had one daughter, Frances; they were later divorced. Marietta then married Ronald Tree, a British multimillionaire and Conservative M.P., became active in New York liberal Democratic politics (her brother, Endicott, also a Democrat, was elected Governor of Massachusetts), and was appointed a member of the U.S. delegation to the United Nations in 1961. She was walking with Adlai Stevenson when he fell dead of a heart attack on a London street in 1965.

FitzGerald was married again in 1948 in a private ceremony on Park Avenue to another beauty, Mrs. Barbara Kent Green Lawrence of Frome, Somerset, England. As a young girl, she had caught the eye of Joseph P. Kennedy, the father of the late President, when he was U.S. ambassador to Britain. The elder Kennedy once remarked that he thought the striking English girl would be a good match for his eldest son, Joseph Jr.

During World War II, FitzGerald served on the staff of General Joseph W. "Vinegar Joe" Stilwell as liaison officer with the Chinese

Sixth Army. After the war he returned to New York and headed the Republican-dominated Committee of Five Million, which in 1949 demanded a formal investigation of the administration of Democratic Mayor William O'Dwyer. Then he slipped into the obscurity of the CIA, where he ran the Laos operation and was the agency's representative on the interagency Latin American task force, before succeeding Helms as deputy director for plans.*

Allen Dulles and many present and former members of the CIA hierarchy lived in the distinguished Georgetown section of Washington.† The wealth and social status of high CIA officials has made the agency sensitive to suggestions that it is a closed, upper-class club, a perpetuation of the caste consciousness which provoked some to describe the OSS as Oh So Social. CIA recruiters point out that the great majority of agency employees are graduates of non-Ivy League schools. But they concede that the top twenty men have always been largely drawn from Harvard, Yale, Princeton, etc. And within the twenty a substantial percentage have been members of America's first families.

The privileged background of many top CIA men has resulted in a certain Anglophilia in the agency. Their formative years were spent at the good New England prep schools which, patterned after the British public schools, have traditionally imparted a sense of class values and noblesse oblige. The CIA establishment thus tends to view itself as the caretaker of an inherited wisdom and the proper judge of sound national behavior. It is self-confident, somewhat obtuse about the yearnings of the common man and untroubled by the elitist

---

* "FitzGerald died at the age of fifty-seven on July 23, 1967. He was stricken, apparently by a heart attack, while playing tennis at his country home near The Plains, in Virginia. (He also maintained a priceless Federal house in Georgetown.) Helms issued a statement praising FitzGerald as "a professional intelligence officer of high integrity, special abilities and uncommon dedication. We in the Agency mourn the passing of a true friend and salute the memory of a gentleman unafraid."

† The Georgetown zip code, appropriately, is "twenty double-O seven" (20007).

implications of secret government. In fact, it looks with longing at Britain where the Old Boy net can run the intelligence system as it sees fit and wield the Official Secrets Act to suppress democratic scrutiny.

The attitude was concisely expressed by Robert Amory, Jr., deputy director for intelligence from 1952 to 1962, a Harvard man, the brother of society author Cleveland Amory, and a member of a family which traces its roots back to the first settlers of Massachusetts. Amory contended that press disclosures of the CIA's links with private groups early in 1967 were "a commentary on the immaturity of our society. We have a free motherland in England that has had a secret service going back to the time of Queen Elizabeth and they just don't talk about it. If something comes out like this, that is a mistake, everybody shushes up in the interests of their national security and . . . what they think is the interests of the free world civilization." *

The American espionage establishment's instinctive mode of operation reflects this frame of mind. When President Roosevelt sought advice on how to centralize U.S. intelligence in 1940, General "Wild Bill" Donovan, later the wartime head of the OSS, went to England to study the British system. In 1948, when for the first time ways were being sought to conduct covert operations in peacetime, the initial reaction of the establishment was not to turn to Congress for money and approval, but to pass the hat among wealthy friends at New York's Brook Club. Similarly, it was only natural for the CIA's Board of National Estimates to repair to the Nassau Gun Club on the Princeton campus for many of its meetings during the 1950's.

To run its fronts and offices in a score of cities,† the agency's top officials have often turned to old friends and classmates, many of whom have served a tour in the OSS or the CIA. In the fall of 1966, for example, the CIA confirmed that its man in St. Louis for the pre-

---

* *Meet the Press,* NBC-TV, February 26, 1967.

† CIA listed offices are maintained in New York, Chicago, Los Angeles, Boston, Detroit, Philadelphia, San Francisco, Miami, Pittsburgh, Houston, St. Louis, New Orleans, Seattle, Denver and Minneapolis. Their phone numbers, but not their addresses, appear in the telephone book. The CIA also has some covert offices under cover names, like Zenith Technical Enterprises, Inc., in Miami.

vious fifteen years had been Louis Werner II, an investment banker, a graduate of St. Paul's School and Princeton, and a member of a prominent and wealthy St. Louis family. Werner, an expert polo player and huntsman, died tragically on September 23, 1966, at the age of forty-two, in a private plane crash that also took the life of George Skakel, Jr., Senator Robert F. Kennedy's brother-in-law.

In Boston a trustee for the Granary Fund, a conduit for CIA money to private groups, was another agency Old Boy, George H. Kidder, who listed himself in *Who's Who* as "with Office Gen. Counsel, CIA, 1952–54." When the CIA set up its clandestine radio on Swan Island, in the western Caribbean, to attack Fidel Castro, it turned to New York attorney Richard S. Greenlee, an old OSS hand who served behind Japanese lines in Siam, to act as a civilian front man.

The list of distinguished persons who have taken part in CIA cover activities reads like the roster of the American Establishment, that informal coalition of lawyers, businessmen and financiers who, as Richard Rovere has suggested half facetiously, silently determine the course of public policy in the United States.

Morris Hadley, one-time head of the Carnegie Foundation, son of former Yale president Arthur Twining Hadley, and a senior partner in the prestigious Wall Street law firm of Milbank, Tweed, Hadley and McCloy,* permitted his family's Rubicon Foundation to be used as a CIA conduit.

Eli Whitney Debevoise, former Deputy U.S. High Commissioner in Germany and a member of the influential Wall Street law firm of Debevoise, Plimpton, Lyons and Gates, was one of the principal officers in the American Council for the International Commission of Jurists, a CIA conduit.

His partner, Francis T. P. Plimpton, former U.S. Deputy Representative to the United Nations, was a director of the Foundation for Youth and Student Affairs, a recipient of CIA funds. The foundation's president was Arthur Amory Houghton, Jr., president of Steu-

---

* John J. McCloy, an intimate adviser of Presidents and, according to Rovere, the untitled chairman emeritus of the Establishment.

ben Glass, Inc., a director of the Corning Glass Works and of the U.S. Steel Corporation, president of the Metropolitan Museum of Art, and a trustee of the Rockefeller Foundation.

John Hay Whitney, former ambassador to Great Britain and owner of the New York *Herald Tribune,* was founder of the Whitney Trust, a philanthropic organization financed in part by the Granary Fund, the CIA conduit.

The *nouveau* Texas Establishment has also been included in the CIA network. Oveta Culp Hobby, publisher of the Houston *Post* and Secretary of Health, Education and Welfare in the Eisenhower Administration, allowed the agency to use the Hobby Foundation as a conduit. John W. Mecom, the oil tycoon, was one of the original incorporators of another conduit, the San Jacinto Fund. Sarah T. Hughes, the federal judge who administered the oath of office to President Johnson, was a trustee of the Hoblitzelle Foundation, which handled CIA money,* and Leon Jaworski, a lawyer friend of the President's, was a trustee of the M. D. Anderson Foundation, another recipient.

Although it was commonly assumed when the CIA was created that it was restricted to foreign operations, the agency's home-front activity had become so extensive by 1964 that a special section, the Domestic Operations Division, was secretly created to handle it. Placed in charge of the division with an office one block from the White House was Tracy Barnes, a charming and handsome charter member of the establishment. Barnes had been a captain in the OSS during the war, parachuting behind enemy lines on several occasions and serving as one of Allen Dulles' close assistants in Operation Sunrise, which resulted in the surrender of nearly a million German and Italian troops in Italy. As Dulles tells it in *The Secret Surrender,* the "young and daring" Barnes decided on his own to assure quick

---

* The foundation was a major financial angel for the Congress for Cultural Freedom, which in turn backed *Encounter,* an intellectual political journal published in London.

delivery of the surrender terms by flying over the Swiss Alps, jumping behind the lines over Bolzano, Italy, and delivering them personally to the Germans. However, the weather turned bad, Barnes was grounded, and the terms were finally transmitted by wire.

During the Bay of Pigs planning, Barnes served as the agency's liaison with the State Department. He went to New York, and with Arthur M. Schlesinger, Jr., gave Adlai Stevenson a guarded advance briefing on the Cuban invasion plans. As director of the Domestic Operations Division (DOD), Barnes operated part of the time out of a new office building at 1750 Pennsylvania Avenue. The CIA office occupied the entire fifth floor under an elaborate, tongue-twisting cover designation: "U. S. Army Element, Joint Planning Activity, Joint Operations Group (SD 7753)." Needless to say, no such unit existed in the Army.

The very title of Barnes's division flouted the intent of Congress, which had been assured when it established the CIA—and over and over again since—that the agency would not and does not engage in domestic operations. And the huge, Madison Avenue-style secret CIA office a block from the White House was only one more tangible evidence of the agency's continual expansion.

Colonel Lawrence K. White, a high CIA official, told a House appropriations subcommittee in 1956 that if the CIA could only consolidate its several offices in Washington in one headquarters at Langley, Virginia, "we will save about 228 people who are guards, receptionists, couriers, bus drivers, and so forth." A CIA report to the lawmakers added: "Time lost shuttling between buildings will be eliminated, with a saving of over $600,000 annually, aside from the saving in bus operation and maintenance. There will be increased efficiency in the processing of intelligence information not readily measurable in monetary terms."

Alas, it did not work out that way. When the CIA moved into its $46,000,000 new home in Langley * in 1961, most people, including

---

* The eerie white concrete headquarters is partially screened from public view in a wooded, 125-acre tract in the rolling Virginia countryside. The CIA is constantly fretting about "protection" of its privacy and bought up some extra land a few years ago to assure it. To justify the land purchase, CIA agents went

members of Congress, assumed that the agency had moved out of Washington as it said it would, and that was that. But soon new CIA offices were popping up all over the downtown area. In its attempts to conceal them, the agency adopted an ostrichlike policy. On the one hand the offices were supposed to be secret, but on the other their locations were flaunted on signs in the windows of special CIA shuttle buses. The CIA listed an employment office for several years at 1016 Sixteenth Street, a nondescript eight-story buff-colored building, directly across from the Statler-Hilton and a block from the Russian embassy. Even the most myopic KGB man attached to the embassy could scarcely help but notice the signs on the shuttle buses: "LANGLEY VIA 1717 H STREET." The little buses stopped at the latter address, the Matomic Building, on the way to CIA headquarters.

For years the shuttle buses were green, but more recently a fleet of new bright-blue buses replaced them. The "Blue Birds," as they are called, still ply the route from downtown Washington to Langley. By 1966 the CIA had moved into yet another location, the Ames Building, at 1820 Fort Myer Drive in Arlington.

During the 1964 Bobby Baker hearings before the Senate Rules Committee, it was revealed that Matthew H. McCloskey, Jr., former treasurer of the Democratic National Committee, who was involved with Baker in the construction of the District of Columbia stadium, had received a multimillion-dollar contract for a mysterious CIA "Building 213" at the Naval Gun Factory in Southeast Washington. Completed about 1964, the "classified" construction project had been given to McCloskey without bids, the General Services Administration assured the committee, because "the Central Intelligence Agency stressed an urgent and compelling need for the project." At the gun

---

up on a hillside, and using telephoto lenses, took pictures of then Director John McCone's seventh-floor suite—somewhat in the manner of the shots of Vanessa Redgrave in the film *Blow-up*. The pictures were then enlarged many times their size. They were grainy, but the white-haired McCone was recognizable.

About ten thousand people work at CIA headquarters in Langley. Together with employees at the other locations in the United States and overseas, the total size of the CIA well exceeds fifteen thousand full-time employees, which does not include thousands of sub-agents and local informants around the world and persons working for CIA-financed cover organizations.

factory the guard at the gate freely pointed out the "CIA building," which contractors estimated probably cost as much as $10,000,000. "I am a little horrified," said Senator Claiborne Pell, Democrat from Rhode Island, "that the CIA has more than one building." But the disclosure of "Building 213" attracted only passing attention amidst the Baker sensations.

This multiplicity of buildings, and particularly the Domestic Operations Division at 1750 Pennsylvania Avenue, reflected the growth of the CIA's operations within the United States. Gradually a number of these domestic activities began to surface into public view, and American taxpayers began to see a bit more of the broad range of domestic projects they were unwittingly financing.

In Florida, following the Bay of Pigs, the CIA's continuing connection with the Cuban exiles was an open secret. The agency supplied money and weapons to various exile factions seeking to harass and, if possible, eliminate Fidel Castro. President Kennedy once expressed his great annoyance to the CIA at the fact that the *Rex,* one of the CIA's boats used in raids on Cuba, docked at Palm Beach while he was there on vacation. Later there were nasty diplomatic complications with Madrid when two CIA-backed Cuban exile speedboats, machine guns blazing, shot up the *Sierra Aranzuzu,* a Spanish freighter hauling almonds, toys, chicken coops and garlic to Cuba in September 1964. The captain and two members of the freighter's crew were killed and seven more fell wounded. Secretary of State Rusk blandly assured the Spanish ambassador that there was "no evidence" that the mystery raiders came from U.S. territory or waters; he promised "full co-operation" in investigating the attack.

Castro repeatedly accused the CIA of staging raids against him, plotting his overthrow and seeking to assassinate him. During Castro's visit to New York in 1960 for a meeting of the United Nations, the CIA set up a suite at the Waldorf-Astoria Hotel to entertain the New York City policemen charged with protecting him. There, as was its custom during the visit of any important foreign dignitary, the agency provided luxurious amenities, including strawberries with Devonshire sauce, for New York's Finest. Chief Inspector Michael J. Murphy (later commissioner) wandered into the suite and was approached by a CIA man with a chilling story. The agency had a plan, the CIA man recounted casually, to plant a special box of cigars at a place where Castro would smoke one. When he did so, the agent said, the cigar would explode and blow his head off. Murphy, who could scarcely believe his ears, was appalled, since his responsibility was to protect Castro, not to inter him. If the CIA man was pulling Murphy's leg it was a shockingly foolish subject to joke about. But, worse yet, the agent seemed completely in earnest. Much to Murphy's relief, however, the CIA man explained that the plan would not be carried out.

In addition to its connection with the Cubans, it also became increasingly clear that the CIA was deeply involved with other émigré groups in the United States.* In November 1964 Eerik Heine, a forty-six-year-old Estonian living in Rexdale, a suburb of Toronto, Canada, brought suit in federal court in Baltimore against Juri Raus, a thirty-nine-year-old Estonian of Hyattsville, Maryland, a suburb of Washington. Heine accused Raus of slander and demanded $110,000 in damages. Specifically, Heine charged that Raus had defamed him by publicly alleging that he was an agent of the KGB. Heine, a celebrated figure among the twenty to thirty thousand Estonians in North America, insisted he was an authentic freedom fighter who had spent seven years in Russian prisons, sometimes under torture, before escaping to the West.

Raus, national commander of the Legion of Estonian Liberation, admitted on January 3, 1965, that two years earlier he had publicly declared that "he was in possession of responsible information received from an official agency of the United States government to the

---

* Previously, even members of the CIA watchdog subcommittees in Congress apparently had not been informed of the relationship. During a hearing of the Senate Armed Services Committee on January 18, 1962, Senator Leverett Saltonstall of Massachusetts, the ranking Republican on the Senate watchdog subcommittee, remarked, "Is it not true, Mr. McCone, in your understanding of the CIA, that any work on the ethnic groups in this country would not be within the province of the CIA, in any event; am I correct in that?" McCone replied, "I cannot answer that, Senator."

effect that the plaintiff was a Soviet agent or collaborator." Raus said that he was a $10,605-a-year employee of the Bureau of Public Roads * and that he received an additional $1,000 a year as an Army Reserve captain.

But on January 11, 1966, Raus's lawyers † submitted an affidavit from Deputy Director Helms stating that Raus was a CIA employee acting on orders when he charged that Heine was a KGB agent. The lawyers asserted that because Raus was a government employee acting under orders, he had "absolute privilege." Under Supreme Court rulings, they contended, he could not be held liable even if it were proved that he spoke out of "actual malice."

Heine's lawyers objected and the judge, Roszel C. Thomsen, seemed at first to be deeply troubled. "Assume the plaintiff is a Communist," he said, "assume he is everything you say, everybody has some rights in this country . . . in the United States, just as Mr. Justice Frankfurter said, 'There are some things you cannot do to a dog' . . . you are not going to persuade this court that there is anybody in this country who does not have some rights."

On April 4 Raus's lawyers responded by producing another affidavit from Helms, stating without elaboration that Raus had accused Heine in order to "protect the integrity of the agency's foreign intelligence sources." Declaring that any further disclosure "would be contrary to the security interests of the United States," he ordered Raus not to testify.

A third affidavit from Helms was submitted on April 25. It said Raus "was instructed to warn members of the Estonian émigré groups

---

* The Bureau of Public Roads maintains two buildings adjacent to CIA headquarters in Langley, Virginia. For years the George Washington Memorial Parkway turnoff to the CIA was marked only by a sign which read "BPR." After this aroused some public mirth, the letters were painted over. By 1967 the sole indication of the CIA turnoff was a sign reading "Fairbank Highway Research Station." The Bureau of Public Roads facility was so named on June 24, 1964, in honor of its deputy commissioner for research, the late Herbert S. Fairbank.

† E. Barrett Prettyman, Jr., former Assistant U.S. Attorney General who aided James B. Donovan in negotiations for release of the Bay of Pigs prisoners in 1962; and Paul R. Connolly, who in 1966 became a partner of famed trial lawyer Edward Bennett Williams.

that Eerik Heine was a dispatched Soviet intelligence operative, a KGB agent. The purpose for this instruction was to protect the integrity of the agency's foreign intelligence sources, existing within or developed through such groups, in accordance with the agency's statutory responsibility to collect foreign intelligence and the statutory responsibility of the Director of Central Intelligence to protect foreign intelligence sources and methods."

On April 28 Admiral Raborn submitted an affidavit supporting Helms and directing Raus to "respectfully decline to answer questions." To protect the CIA's interests he also sent the agency's general counsel, Lawrence R. Houston, into court for the first time since 1952.

Raus also submitted an affidavit warning that a ruling against him "would expose every agent . . . throughout the world to the peril of an adverse judgment against him no matter how ill-founded the charge."

On arrival in Washington the day before, Heine had challenged the FBI to arrest him under the espionage laws, maintaining that "the trial would show I am innocent." His lawyers appealed for White House intervention under a little-used executive order requiring the President to "take action upon" complaints about CIA secrecy regulations. In addition they raised questions as to why Thomas W. LaVenia, a former investigator for the late Senator Joseph R. McCarthy, had been hired to look into Heine's background if the CIA already had conclusive evidence that he was a KGB agent. Heine's lawyers also alleged that the CIA had attempted to "pay off" Heine to drop the case but that he would "not auction his honor." Raus's lawyers dismissed the incident as a routine effort to settle the suit out of court.

In the end Judge Thomsen sided with the CIA, restricted the testimony of Raus and on December 8, 1966, dismissed Heine's suit. The judge cited the Supreme Court decision that it is "better to leave unredressed the wrongs done by dishonest officers than to subject those who try to do their duty to the constant dread of retaliation." *

---

* Justice John M. Harlan so ruled in the Barr v. Matteo case over which the Court split 5 to 4 in 1959.

Judge Thomsen overruled the contention of Heine's lawyers that the CIA had violated the provision of the National Security Act of 1947 which prohibited it from exercising any "internal security functions."

"It is reasonable," Thomsen declared, "that émigré groups from nations behind the Iron Curtain would be a valuable source of intelligence information as to what goes on in their own homeland. The fact that the immediate intelligence source is located in the United States does not make it an 'internal security function' over which the CIA has no authority. The court concludes that activities by the CIA to protect its foreign intelligence sources located in the United States are within the power granted by Congress to the CIA."

Judge Thomsen then revealed a remarkable series of events that had taken place in his court. During the proceedings, he said, he had asked the CIA "to submit a statement as to the legal authority of the CIA to engage in activities in the United States with respect to foreign intelligence sources." In response the CIA submitted an affidavit that included "particular paragraphs of a document which is classified 'secret' and which cannot be declassified for the purposes of this case."

The CIA had asked the Justice Department to submit the document to the court "under seal for in camera inspection." The agency said that if Heine's lawyers wanted to see the sealed document it would not object, but that they would have to go out to CIA headquarters to do so. What is more, they would not be permitted to disclose to their client "the excerpts thus made available to them."

Heine's attorneys "refused to examine the excerpts under those conditions, stating that they would not look at anything they could not communicate to their client."

The CIA was created by a public law which most Americans assumed confined it to overseas operations. Now, however, it was saying that there were additional, secret provisos, giving it the right to engage in certain domestic activities, but that these could not be disclosed to the American people.

Judge Thomsen conceded that the CIA's claim to "absolute privilege" put Heine "in a very difficult position." But he did not comment on the difficulties posed for American democracy when an act of Congress is amended by a secret executive order that can be perused only in the Langley, Virginia, headquarters of the CIA.

Heine immediately appealed, vowing to go all the way to the Supreme Court. Senator Richard B. Russell, the powerful Georgia Democrat who heads both the Armed Services Committee and the CIA subcommittee, looked into the episode and commented, "Such a far-flung organization as this is going to have a goof now and then." Russell did not elaborate, but since it seemed unlikely that the CIA had testified that Heine was falsely accused, Russell must have been implying that the agency erred in directing Raus to attack him, thereby exposing itself to an embarrassing court case. If Heine *was* a Soviet agent, it was clear that the KGB had cleverly succeeded in hauling the CIA into court, blowing the cover on its links with émigré groups and revealing to the American people its unlimited potential to make or break private citizens. On the other hand, if Heine was a true anti-Communist freedom fighter, he had been outrageously slandered and stood as testimony to the agency's "absolute privilege" to defame the innocent. Either way, it was an unpleasant episode.

While the Heine case was being argued in court, the CIA's extensive involvement in the academic community began to seep out in considerable detail. *Ramparts,* an iconoclastic California magazine founded by liberal Roman Catholic laymen, disclosed in April 1966 that Michigan State University had provided academic cover for the CIA police operation in South Vietnam. The magazine reported that the university ran a police training program for the CIA from 1955 to 1959 under a $25,000,000 contract and concealed five CIA agents in the project. John A. Hannah, president of the university and the chairman of the U.S. Civil Rights Commission, vehemently denied any knowledge of the CIA involvement. But Lyman Kirkpatrick, who had held his high position in the agency during the period, said the university had signed a contract with the CIA and had full knowledge of its role in the project.

The agency's connection with Michigan State was by no means unique. The CIA had worked out secret arrangements with individuals and institutes at dozens of colleges, universities, and research centers.* The prototype for this kind of relationship was the Center for International Studies at the Massachusetts Institute of Technology. The Center was founded in 1951 with CIA money, and the following year Max F. Millikan, assistant director of the CIA, became its head. From the start, another key figure at the Center was former OSS man Walt Whitman Rostow, an economics professor who became President Johnson's personal adviser on national security and foreign affairs, as well as his principal link with the intelligence community. MIT declared in 1966 that the Center had severed all connection with the agency, not on moral grounds but as a matter of "public relations" and "because of misunderstandings and unfounded suspicion of the character of our contracts with the CIA." In 1964, when the CIA connection was first revealed, MIT had airily implied it was a thing of the past. But when it publicly severed the CIA link it conceded that the Center was receiving fifteen to twenty percent of its budget from Langley.

Scholars from MIT and elsewhere had complained that they were being taken for CIA agents even when involved in the most innocent research projects overseas. In an effort to remove the suspicions, Stephen T. Boggs, executive secretary of the American Anthropological Society, demanded the setting up of "an absolutely impassible

---

* Including Operations and Policy Research, Inc., of Washington, which was headed by Evron M. Kirkpatrick, director of the American Political Science Association. An ex-OSS man, Kirkpatrick listed himself as an intelligence official of the State Department from 1946 to 1954.

Also the Fund for International Social and Economic Education of Philadelphia, headed by Richard M. Hunt, assistant dean of the Harvard Graduate School of Arts and Sciences and the son of the president of the Aluminum Company of America. George Lodge, son of Henry Cabot Lodge, former U.S. ambassador to Vietnam, was a member of the board of directors.

The Pentagon was also deeply involved in such classified scholarship. In June 1965 Ralph Dungan, U.S. ambassador to Chile, cabled a bitter protest to the State Department about the activities of American University of Washington, D.C. The university's Special Operations Research Office (SORO) had entered a contract with the Army to conduct "Project Camelot," an inquiry into the possibility that there would be an antidemocratic coup in Chile. The project was canceled in response to protests by the Chilean government.

barrier" between the CIA and scholars involved in foreign re-search. But the agency clearly was determined at that time to main-tain its influence, direct and indirect, in the academic world. The April 1966 issue of *Foreign Affairs,* the prestigious scholarly quar-terly, contained an article entitled "The Faceless Viet Cong." It was a defense of the government's position that the guerrilla movement in South Vietnam was controlled by the Communist party of North Vietnam. It was written by George Carver, Jr., who was identified only as a "student of political theory and Asian affairs, with degrees from Yale and Oxford; former officer in the U.S. AID mission in Saigon; author of *Aesthetics and the Problem of Meaning.*" In fact, Carver was an employee of the CIA.* His contribution to *Foreign Affairs* represented only one of the hundreds of articles and books which the CIA had got into print at home and abroad without identification of their source.

The CIA also manipulated students and scholars in a similar manner, as became abundantly clear early in February 1967, when *Ramparts* disclosed the agency's long-secret links with the National Student Association, the nation's largest student group with chapters on three hundred campuses. Confronted by the magazine's detailed accusations, NSA leaders admitted that the CIA had subsidized the association for fifteen years (covering as much as eighty percent of its budget each year), had provided it with rent-free headquarters in Washington, had obtained draft deferments for NSA officers and staff members, and in return, had acquired NSA dossiers on foreign stu-dent leaders. All told, it was estimated that the CIA had poured $3,000,000 into NSA.

Shortly after the *Ramparts* disclosure Sam Brown, a twenty-three-year-old Harvard divinity student and chairman of NSA's Na-tional Supervisory Policy Board, also accused the CIA of "trapping"

---

* Sometimes a piece of agency research is leaked out to embarrass the Administration. In August 1964 the right-wing Chicago *Tribune* was given a copy of a scholarly paper by Willard Matthias of the agency's Board of National Estimates. At a time when President Johnson was under attack by Barry Goldwater for failing to win the war in Vietnam, Matthias wrote that there was "serious doubt" that the Vietcong could be suppressed and that a "prolonged stalemate" might be the best the United States could hope for.

association leaders into co-operation with it. Each year, he explained, the CIA picked out one or two NSA leaders to be informed of the secret relationship and to serve as liaison; they would be approached, advised that there were some secrets that they should know about, and asked to sign a security statement.

"Then," Brown said, "they were told, 'You are employed by the CIA.' At that point they were trapped, having signed a statement not to divulge anything . . . This is the part of the thing that I found to be most disgusting and horrible. People were duped into this relationship with the CIA, a relationship from which there was no way out. There has been no physical intimidation, but it seems apparent that under the National Security Act—under the statements these people signed—there would be the probability of prosecution by the government . . . a twenty-year jail sentence to maintain your integrity is a very high price to pay." *

The NSA disclosures led to a rash of revelations about the CIA's involvement with virtually every important segment of American life—business, labor, government, the churches, the universities, the news media, charitable organizations, book publishers, lawyers, teachers, artists, women's organizations and cultural groups.† Quite

---

* But Lawrence Houston, general counsel for the agency, quickly made it clear in a rare public statement that the CIA had no intention of taking action against any NSA leaders.

† Organizations which received money directly or indirectly included the African American Institute, American Council for International Commission of Jurists, American Federation of State, County and Municipal Employees, American Friends of the Middle East, American Newspaper Guild, American Society of African Culture, Asia Foundation, Association of Hungarian Students in North America, Committee for Self-Determination, Committee of Correspondence, Committee on International Relations, Fund for International Social and Economic Education, Independent Research Service, Institute of International Labor Research, International Development Foundation, International Marketing Institute, National Council of Churches, National Education Association, Paderewski Foundation, Pan American Foundation (University of Miami), Frederick A. Praeger, Publishers, Radio Free Europe, Synod of Bishops of the Russian Church Outside Russia, United States Youth Council.

Foreign beneficiaries included *African Forum, Africa Report, Berliner Verein,* Center of Studies and Documentation (Mexico), Congress for Cultural Freedom, in Paris (which supported the publications *Hiwar,* Lebanon; *Forum,* Austria; *Preuves,* France; as well as *Encounter,* Britain), Frente Departamental de Campesinos de Puno, Foreign News Service, Inc., Institute of Political

aside from the moral issues involved, the CIA had neglected one of the fundamental rules of the spy business: it had failed to keep its operations distinct and separate and had used the same fronts to finance a number of projects. When the agency's connection with one of the projects was disclosed, the cover was blown on all of them.

The CIA's involvement with all these groups was defended by government officials as a necessary expedient of the Cold War dating back to a time—the early 1950's—when the Communists were bidding to capture various international groups. The financing had to be secret, it was argued, because it was necessary to deceive foreigners who might have viewed government-supported groups as puppets, and to deceive the American people, who in the McCarthy era might have rejected open government subsidies, especially for left-of-center groups.

"We obtained what we wanted," said Allen Dulles. "If we turned back the Communists and made them milder and easier to live with, it was because we stopped them in certain areas, and the student area was one of them." Robert Amory, Dulles' former deputy director for intelligence, agreed: "If we hadn't done this, we could have just been run over by the Commie front organizations."

Vice-President Hubert H. Humphrey, who had been approached by NSA leaders for help shortly before the *Ramparts* disclosure, said at Stanford University on February 20: "This is one of the saddest times that our government has had, in reference to public policy. My

---

Education (Costa Rica), Interamerica Federation of Newspapermen's Organizations, International Federation of Free Journalists, International Journalists, International Student Conference, Public Services International, World Assembly of Youth, World Confederation of Organizations of the Teaching Profession.

Conduits for CIA money included the Andrew Hamilton Fund, Beacon Fund, Benjamin Rosenthal Foundation, Borden Trust, Broad-High Foundation, Catherwood Foundation, Chesapeake Foundation, David, Joseph and Winfield Baird Foundation, Dodge Foundation, Edsel Fund, Florence Foundation, Gotham Fund, Heights Fund, Independence Foundation, J. Frederick Brown Foundation, J. M. Kaplan Foundation, Jones-O'Donnell, Kentfield Fund, Littauer Foundation, Marshall Foundation, McGregor Fund, Michigan Fund, Monroe Fund, Norman Fund, Pappas Charitable Trust, Price Fund, Robert E. Smith Fund, San Miguel Fund, Sidney and Esther Rabb Charitable Foundation, Tower Fund, Vernon Fund, Warden Trust, Williford-Telford Fund.

own view is that these organizations ought to be free and independent. I regret that they were unable to be that way. I'm not at all happy about what the CIA has been doing and I'm sure that out of this very singularly disagreeable situation will come a reformation of that agency, with closer supervision of its activities and with recommendations coming to the government of the United States that will confine the CIA to its intelligence-gathering purposes, and to keep it from being associated directly or indirectly with organizations and bodies of men and women and young people that are not needed for those purposes."

Republican Governor George Romney of Michigan thought the episode "smacks of secret government within our society."

Barry Goldwater expressed annoyance at the fact that the agency had financed "left wing" groups.* "Why didn't they spread this money around? In other words, what they have been doing with it, as far as I can see, is to finance socialism in America."

John W. Gardner, Secretary of Health, Education and Welfare, said "it was a mistake for the CIA ever to entangle itself in covert activities close to the field of education or scholarship or the universities." However, he had "little respect for critics who give themselves airs of moral superiority in attacking an activity they know to be necessary."

Senator Robert F. Kennedy thought it unfair to let the CIA "take the rap." He said the programs had been approved at the highest levels of the government in the Eisenhower, Kennedy and Johnson Administrations. "If the policy was wrong, it was not the product of the CIA but of each Administration . . . We must not forget that we are not dealing with a dream world, but with a very tough adversary."

At that, President Johnson directed his news secretary, George Christian, to tell the press that he was "totally unaware" of the CIA's links with the National Student Association. To reduce the political

---

* Although some left-of-center groups benefited from the CIA's domestic spending, reliable estimates from inside the intelligence community indicate only twenty percent of the agency's money goes to liberal causes abroad.

pressures, the President ordered an investigation by a three-man group, headed by Undersecretary of State Nicholas deB. Katzenbach and including Gardner and Helms. Katzenbach said, "The President believes strongly that the integrity and independence of the educational community must be preserved. He has directed a careful review of any government activities that may endanger this integrity and independence."

The following week, however, on February 23, the President endorsed a preliminary finding by the Katzenbach group that absolved both the CIA and the Administration. The CIA "did not act on its own initiative," the panel declared, "but in accordance with policies established by the National Security Council in 1952 through 1954. Throughout it acted with the approval of senior interdepartmental review committees, including the Secretaries of State and Defense or their representatives . . . the support provided by the Central Intelligence Agency enabled many far-sighted and courageous Americans to serve their country in times of challenge and danger to the United States and the free world. Furthermore, the Central Intelligence Agency has been, and continues to be, indispensable to the security of this nation. It is vitally important that the current controversy over its support of certain private organizations not be permitted to obscure the value or impede the effectiveness of competent and dedicated career officials serving this country."

The Johnson Administration, which had responded uncertainly at first to the storm over the CIA student subsidies, was now moving quickly to close ranks. Humphrey had made his statement, extremely critical of the CIA, to a student audience three days *before* the President endorsed the preliminary finding of the Katzenbach panel. Now, with little choice but to conform to the Administration's public pronouncement, Humphrey told a news conference in Miami Beach on February 27, one week after his Stanford speech, that the CIA "has done nothing but follow the policies of higher authority." He added: "CIA has been criticized far too much, most of it unjust. The CIA has, in the main, served our interests very well. Our government must have the ways and means to forward our interests. You need a CIA."

In the unclassified portion of its final report on March 29, the Katzenbach panel recommended that the CIA and all other government agencies be prohibited in the future from providing covert financial support to any "of the nation's educational or private voluntary organizations." It also recommended establishment of a "public-private mechanism" to provide money openly to "deserving" private groups.

The panel said there should be no exception to the ban on channeling covert government money to "any educational, philanthropic, or cultural organization." However, secret grants could still be made to private groups in other, unspecified fields when "overriding national security interests" were involved.* The arbiter of the exceptions should be the same "interdepartmental review committee" that had invoked "national security" to approve the covert financing of private groups over the previous fifteen years. The Secretaries of State and Defense would also have to give their approval.

The President adopted the panel's main recommendation and ordered all government agencies to sever their secret financial arrangements with private groups. He also set up another committee, under Secretary of State Dean Rusk, to study the panel's proposal for open funding. With that, Johnson obviously hoped that the troublesome episode would be laid to rest.

The furor over the CIA's relationship with NSA and other domestic groups was doubly embarrassing to the agency because only seven months before, Helms had told the Senate Foreign Relations Committee that the CIA did not operate in the United States and did not use the U.S. student exchange program as cover for espionage.

---

* It was generally assumed that this loophole was included principally to permit continuing CIA subsidies to the international labor movement. In May 1967 Thomas W. Braden, head of the CIA's Division of International Organization from 1951 to 1954, asserted in the *Saturday Evening Post* that he organized the agency's secret links to private groups at home and abroad. In an article entitled "I'm Glad the CIA is 'Immoral,'" Braden wrote that he had personally given $50,000 to Walter and Victor Reuther of the United Automobile Workers. He also described several additional subsidies for the foreign operations of Jay Lovestone and Irving Brown, who manage international affairs for the AFL-CIO.

Helms had been called before the committee to explain a letter he had written to the St. Louis *Globe-Democrat* praising an editorial attacking Senator J. William Fulbright, chairman of the committee. The editorial, which appeared on July 18, 1966, derided Fulbright as a "crafty Arkansan" seeking to destroy "one of our most valuable agencies in foreign affairs." The newspaper commended the Senate for having refused four days earlier to give Fulbright's committee a share in the Senate's surveillance of the CIA.

On July 27 the *Globe-Democrat* published a letter from Helms: "I want to let you know of my pleasure in reading the editorial 'Brickbats for Fulbright' . . . It reflects so well your paper's policy of 'printing the news impartially, supporting what it believes to be right and opposing what it believes to be wrong without regard to party politics.' "

The next day Senator Eugene McCarthy rose in the Senate to denounce Helms's action. "In the course of the recent debate on this agency," he said, "we were told that the CIA does not involve itself in domestic politics. I suggest that this is a new departure. If we permit the Director of that agency to take this action unchallenged by the Senate, it may well be that in every campaign hereafter, people will turn up with letters from the Central Intelligence Agency saying, 'We think Senator So-and-so is crafty,' or 'He proposes to try to destroy the CIA, to destroy this great agency.' " *

McCarthy's remarks were quickly endorsed by his colleagues, including a number of senators normally disposed to defend the agency. Fulbright thanked them for their support and suggested it might be time to question Helms about "whether or not his agency takes part in domestic affairs, for example, in the elections in our labor unions and whether or not the CIA was using the exchange program."

Senator Leverett Saltonstall, the Republican Brahmin from Massachusetts, scurried to a cloakroom phone to talk to Helms. Salton-

---

* On at least one occasion a high-ranking CIA official, during one of his frequent bouts with the bottle, had braced a congressman who was critical of the agency and threatened to move against him with CIA money in his home district unless he mended his ways.

stall, a long-time member of the CIA watchdog subcommittee and the brother of a high-ranking CIA official, returned with assurances from Helms that it was "the only letter he has written, that it was a mistake, and he feels sorry about it."

The next day Helms appeared for two hours at a closed session of Fulbright's committee. He apologized for the letter, explained that an assistant had prepared and presented it to him in a stack of other letters, and that he signed it without his full attention focusing on it. Fulbright later said he had accepted the explanation as a "very forthright, honest statement." Moreover, the senator added, Helms had assured him that the CIA "very positively" did not use the student exchange program, originated by Fulbright, as a cover for espionage and that, to the best of his knowledge, the CIA did not "intervene directly or indirectly" in domestic matters. "He said," Fulbright reported, "that under their charter they are authorized to operate only beyond the continental United States." Clearly, Fulbright had not been told of the CIA's Domestic Operations Division.

Although Fulbright appeared placated, Senator Wayne Morse, Oregon Democrat, demanded that Helms resign. Until he did so, Morse argued, "the American people cannot rest secure in the belief that the agency is living up to its legal mandate not to operate within the United States or influence or participate in affairs within the United States."

It was evident from Fulbright's reference to a "charter" and Morse's allusion to a "legal mandate" that the members of Congress had been led to believe that the CIA was prohibited by law from operating within the United States. And, indeed, a scrutiny of the committee hearings and debate on the National Security Act of 1947 indicates that most congressmen thought at the time that the agency was being limited to intelligence work and, then, only outside the United States.

In proposing the creation of the CIA, the Truman Administration had laid great emphasis on Pearl Harbor and the need for a centralized intelligence apparatus that would provide prompt and adequate warning of an impending enemy attack. Even before the National Security Act was passed, President Truman had established, by executive order on January 22, 1946, a National Intelligence Authority and under it a Central Intelligence Group. The authority's members were Secretary of State James F. Byrnes, Secretary of War Robert P. Patterson, Secretary of the Navy James V. Forrestal, and Admiral William D. Leahy, who had made a study of the intelligence system for the President at the end of the war. The Central Intelligence Group was the authority's operating arm, the successor to the OSS and the forerunner of the CIA. First head of the group was the deputy chief of naval intelligence, Rear Admiral Sidney W. Souers, who served for five months. He was succeeded by Air Force General Hoyt S. Vandenberg, who was holding the job when the CIA legislation was submitted to Congress.

Administration witnesses took great pains to emphasize that the CIA was to limit itself to overseas operations. On April 25, 1947, during a hearing of the House Committee on Expenditures in the Executive Departments, the following indicative exchange took place between Republican Congressman Clarence J. Brown of Ohio and Forrestal:

> BROWN: How far does this Central Intelligence Agency go in its authority and scope? . . . Nobody can tell from . . . this bill, if enacted into law, what power or authority this fellow had . . . Do you not think this should be set out in the statute? Intentions are fine, but intentions make good paving blocks, too . . . This chief of the Central Intelligence Agency, the director, should he decide he wants to go into my income tax reports, I presume he could do so, could he not?
>
> FORRESTAL: I do not assume he could, I think he would have a very short life—I am not referring to you, Mr. Brown, but I think he would have a very short life.
>
> BROWN: Well, he probably would, if he went into mine, but I

was wondering how far this goes. This is a very great departure from what we have done in the past in America. Perhaps we have not been as good as we should have been and I agree with that, either in our military or foreign intelligence, and I am very much interested in seeing the United States have as fine a foreign military and naval intelligence as they can possibly have, but I am not interested in setting up here in the United States any particular agency under any President, and I do not care what his name is, and just allow him to have a Gestapo of his own if he wants to have it. Every now and then you get a man that comes up in power that has an imperialistic idea.

FORRESTAL: The purposes of the Central Intelligence Authority are limited definitely to purposes outside of this country, except the collation of information gathered by government agencies. Regarding domestic operations, the Federal Bureau of Investigation is working at all times in collaboration with General Vandenberg. He relies upon them for domestic activities.

BROWN: Is that stated in the law?

FORRESTAL: It is not; no, sir.

BROWN: That could be changed in two minutes, and have the action within the United States instead of without; is that correct?

FORRESTAL: He could only do so with the President's direct and specific approval.

BROWN: I know, but even then it could be done without violation of law by the President or somebody who might write the order for him and get his approval, and without the knowledge and consent or direction of the Congress. Do you think it would be wise for the Congress of the United States to at least fix some limitation on what the power of this individual might be, or what could be done, or what should be done, and all these safeguards and rights of the citizen may be protected?

FORRESTAL: I think it is profitable to explore what you need for protection and I am in complete sympathy about the dangers of sliding into abrogation of powers by the Congress.

During a hearing of the same committee on June 24, 1947, there was this exchange between Democratic Congressman Henderson Lanham of Georgia and an Administration witness, Dr. Vannevar Bush, chairman of the Joint Research and Development Board of the War and Navy departments.

LANHAM: Do you feel there is any danger of the Central Intelligence Division becoming a Gestapo or anything of that sort?

BUSH: I think there is no danger of that. The bill provides clearly that it is concerned with intelligence outside of this country, that it is not concerned with intelligence on internal affairs, and I think this is a safeguard against its becoming an empire. We already have, of course, the FBI in this country, concerned with internal affairs, and the collection of intelligence in connection with law enforcement internally. We have had that for a good many years. I think there are very few citizens who believe this arrangement will get beyond control so that it will become an improper affair.

To conciliate Brown, Lanham, and others, the bill was amended to provide that "the agency shall have no police, subpena, law-enforcement powers, or internal security functions." * Otherwise,

---

* Despite this provision, the CIA raided the Georgetown home of Hans Tofte, fifty-nine, one of its top clandestine operators, in a bizarre episode that began with a classified ad in the Washington *Post* on July 23, 1966, advertising a $150-a-month apartment for rent. Kenneth R. Slocum, a twenty-four-year-old electronics specialist from Hollywood, California, responded. He had just come to work for the CIA. He and his wife were taken by a real estate agent to Tofte's home, and shown the advertised basement apartment. Tofte and his wife, Marlys, were in the process of moving to a larger house, and only Mrs. Tofte's mother, Charlotte Leister, eighty-six, was at home. Somehow, Slocum peeked into a third-floor room, saw some CIA papers stamped "Secret" and reported his find to the agency. (Tofte had taken the papers home to work on them, a practice which he claimed was common in the higher echelons of the

however, the legislation did not incorporate any "charter" or "mandate" prohibiting the CIA from operating within the United States. Even in the prohibited "internal security" area, an exception was made to permit the agency to take action to protect "intelligence sources and methods from unauthorized disclosure."

The act as passed by Congress and signed by President Truman became effective on September 18, 1947. It authorized the CIA:

"(1) to advise the National Security Council in matters concerning such intelligence activities of the government departments and agencies as relate to national security;

"(2) to make recommendations to the National Security Council for the co-ordination of such intelligence activities . . . ;

"(3) to correlate and evaluate intelligence relating to the national security, and provide for the appropriate dissemination of such intelligence within the government . . . ;

"(4) to perform, for the benefit of the existing intelligence agencies, such additional services of common concern as the National Security Council determines can be more efficiently accomplished centrally;

"(5) to perform such other functions and duties related to intelligence affecting the national security as the National Security Council may from time to time direct."

The fifth paragraph provided the loophole under which the CIA's role was broadened beyond the apparent intent of Congress to include special operations at home and abroad in addition to intelligence gathering. In 1948 the Administration became alarmed by the

---

agency.) The next day the Slocums returned with Charles D. Speake, a CIA security man. They tricked the elderly Mrs. Leister into letting them in by saying that Speake was interested in buying the house. Without a search warrant, they then carted out the papers. Tofte, a Danish underground hero and OSS veteran, was hauled out to CIA that night. He fought back, charged that $30,000 in jewels was missing from the house after the CIA visitation. Suspended from his $25,000-a-year job, Tofte began talking to newsmen, appearing on television and raising a huge ruckus. Before a special CIA review board, he demanded that Director Helms disclose whether the CIA had stopped entering private homes "illegally, minus a warrant and without due process of law." Tofte was fired on September 15 but he never did get an answer to his question.

Communist takeover in Czechoslovakia and the possibility of a Communist election victory in Italy, but it was uncertain whether the "other functions and duties" clause could legally be used to authorize operations. Forrestal felt that secret counteraction was vital, but his initial assessment was that the Italian operation would have to be private. The wealthy industrialists in Milan were hesitant to provide the money, fearing reprisals if the Communists won, and so the hat was passed at the Brook Club in New York.

But Allen Dulles felt the problem could not be handled effectively in private hands. He urged strongly that the government establish a covert organization. Because of the desire to finance the organization with unvouchered funds,* the decision was made to create it under the National Security Council through the "other functions and duties" clause. Accordingly, in the summer of 1948 the National Security Council issued a secret paper, NSC 10/2 (pronounced alternately as "ten-slash-two" or "ten-slant-two"). It authorized special operations, provided that they were secret and small enough to be plausibly deniable by the government, and created an operating agency under the innocuous title Office of Policy Coordination.

Frank G. Wisner,† an ex-OSS man, was brought in from the State Department to direct the operations under a cover name of his own invention—assistant director of the Office of Policy Coordination. (A separate Office of Special Operations handled covert intelligence gathering.) This machinery was in the CIA but the agency

---

* Congress formally ratified the use of unvouchered funds in the Central Intelligence Act of 1949. It empowered the Director of Central Intelligence to spend money "without regard to the provisions of the law and regulations relating to the expenditure of government funds." His signature on any check, no matter how large, was "deemed a sufficient voucher."

† Wisner contracted hepatitis at the time of the 1956 Suez and Hungary crises but insisted upon staying on the job. Later he suffered a nervous breakdown. He resigned from the agency in 1962 and killed himself with a shotgun in 1965. A group of friends issued an anonymous eulogy, declaring that "in the most literal sense [he] gave his life to public service . . . he had to meet the long prepared challenge of the vast Stalinist intelligence and subversion net . . . for about a decade, he devoted himself totally to one of the most onerous and difficult tasks any American public servant has ever had to undertake."

shared it with the State Department and the Pentagon. When General Walter Bedell Smith replaced the first Director of the CIA, Rear Admiral Roscoe H. Hillenkoetter, in 1950, he succeeded in eliminating outside control and placing Wisner's operation exclusively under the jurisdiction of the CIA. On January 4, 1951, the Office of Policy Coordination and the Office of Special Operations were merged into a new Plans Division, which has had sole control over secret operations of all types since that date.

For example, the division was responsible for the successful overthrow of the leftwing governments of Iran in 1953 and Guatemala in 1954. It obtained and published the historic speech in which Nikita S. Khrushchev secretly denounced Joseph Stalin at the Twentieth Communist Party Congress in Moscow in 1956. It ran the U-2 program. And it directed the abortive Bay of Pigs operation.

Although the CIA did not abandon its covert operation against Castro after the unsuccessful invasion, it found that the operation had left it with a surplus of men and equipment. Some of it was put to use in suppressing the Congo revolt in 1964. There, a number of the Cuban exile pilots who had flown at the Bay of Pigs again manned the B-26 bombers * in combat for the CIA under cover of a company called Caramar (Caribbean Marine Aero Corporation). This time the operation succeeded, although some of the Cuban pilots were troubled at being ordered to make indiscriminate strafing attacks on civilians in rebel territory.

Many of the weapons for such counterinsurgency operations are provided by Interarmco Limited, the International Armaments Corporation, which maintains its central warehouse in Alexandria, Virginia, just across the river from Washington and a short ride from the

---

* The B-26 had also been used by the CIA in support of the unsuccessful effort to overthrow Sukarno in 1958. In 1966 the CIA was accused of exporting the B-26 for use against the rebels in Portuguese Angola. The CIA and the State Department denied the allegation. One of the pilots arrested in the plane-smuggling episode said he had been led to believe he was working for the CIA. He and another pilot were acquitted in a federal court in Buffalo on October 13, 1966. Jury members explained that they had not been convinced that the pilots deliberately violated the law. They said their decision did not mean they accepted the allegations against the CIA.

CIA building. Interarmco, a combine of seventeen companies, also has offices in London, Geneva, Monte Carlo, Helsinki, Buenos Aires, and Pretoria, South Africa. It is run by Samuel Cummings, a forty-year-old weapons expert who worked directly for the CIA during the Korean War and then set up Interarmco in 1953. Interarmco has amassed holdings of more than $10,000,000 and Cummings lives in luxurious privacy in tax-free Monte Carlo, shunning liquor, cigarettes and the public fleshpots.

The Alexandria warehouse, which has a nearby deepwater pier, can hold more than a hundred thousand weapons in its 89,000 square feet of storage space. The weapons flow to the four corners of the world, to friendly governments seeking to suppress leftwing insurrections.

The Plans Division has also been conducting a multitude of domestic operations under several classified NSC directives authorizing CIA activity within the United States under certain conditions. For example, NSCID 7 (National Security Council Intelligence Directive No. 7) empowered the agency to question persons within the United States, provided it first checked with the FBI (a proviso that is reportedly often honored in the breach). It enabled the CIA to brief and debrief scholars, students, businessmen and tourists traveling to and from Communist countries. It allowed the CIA to sign contracts with universities and colleges to tap their fund of foreign expertise. And it established the rationale for the CIA's domestic fronts, foundations and regional offices. In short, the ambiguous "other functions and duties" clause was pushed to the limit at home as well as abroad.

Former President Harry S. Truman, who sponsored the National Security Act, declared in 1963, "I never had any thought . . . when I set up the CIA that it would be injected into peacetime cloak-and-dagger operations. Some of the complications and embarrassment that I think we have experienced are in part attributable to the fact that this quiet intelligence arm of the President has been so removed from its intended role . . . I . . . would like to see the CIA be restored to its original assignment as the intelligence arm of the President, and whatever else it can properly perform in that special field—and that its operational duties be terminated or properly used elsewhere. We have grown up as a nation respected for our free institutions and for our ability to maintain a free and open society. There is something about the way the CIA has been functioning that is casting a shadow over our historic position and I feel that we need to correct it."

The Eisenhower Administration had sought to solve the problem by exercising a greater measure of control over the agency. In December 1954 the National Security Council created a high-level coordinating body called the Special Group (or the "54/12 Group"). It consists of the Director of Central Intelligence, the President's adviser for national security affairs, the Deputy Secretary of Defense, and the Undersecretary of State for Political Affairs or his deputy.

The Special Group is supposed to authorize all black (covert) operations and any expenditure of more than $10,000 that might have embarrassing political ramifications. It is also supposed to make sure the President is personally informed of all important undertakings of the CIA. It is the Special Group to which CIA men allude when they declare, as did Allen Dulles in *The Craft of Intelligence:* "The facts are that the CIA has never carried out any action of a political nature, given any support of any nature to any persons, potentates or movements, political or otherwise, without appropriate approval at a high political level in our government *outside the CIA."*

Similarly, Richard Bissell complained in an interview on NBC in May 1965: "Those who believe that the U.S. government on occasion resorts to force when it shouldn't, should in all fairness and justice direct their views to the question of national policy and not hide behind the criticism that whereas the President and Cabinet generally are enlightened people, there is an evil, an ill-controlled agency, which imports this sinister element into U.S. policy."

The trouble with the Dulles-Bissell view is that it does not account for the instances in which important CIA operations have been conducted without the knowledge of the President. It is true that presidential approval can be cited for a number of major operations. Eisenhower publicly admitted personal authorization for the Guatemala operation and Kennedy publicly took the blame for the Bay of Pigs. It is also true, as CIA men protest, that the President, perhaps the busiest man in the world, cannot be expected to give detailed scrutiny to every CIA operation; some things must be delegated and the Special Group was set up for that purpose.

On the other hand, the control machinery is demonstrably defective if presidential approval and oversight are not solicited and obtained for operations that run the risk of grave national danger or humiliation. At the outset of the embarrassing NSA controversy in 1967, as we have seen, President Johnson spread the word that he was "totally unaware" of the CIA's involvement.

By the same token, President Kennedy objected strongly to the fact that he had not been informed in advance of a CIA plot to contaminate a shipment of Cuban sugar in Puerto Rico in August of 1962. The sugar, which was bound for the Soviet Union, had been off-loaded by a British freighter while it was undergoing repairs. Kennedy ordered the shipment impounded lest there be a setback in U.S.-Russian relations when the sugar finally arrived in the Soviet Union. The CIA complained that it was only operating under instructions from the Special Group to sabotage the Cuban economy where feasible. The President's view was that the specific action far exceeded the general mandate and that, in any event, he should have been informed.

The difficulty, as one former member of the Special Group has confessed privately, is that those who serve on it are too busy with their primary jobs to provide detailed scrutiny of operations before they are approved and to police them as they are carried out.

The difficulty is compounded for the President's Foreign Intelligence Advisory Board, a panel of distinguished private citizens headed by Clark Clifford, the prosperous Washington lawyer who served as special counsel to President Truman. The board is supposed to have complete access to the secrets of the agency, but it manages to convene only several times a year.

In Congress the agency is supposed to be watched by three informal subcommittees: one of the House Armed Services Committee; another of the House Appropriations Committee; and a third a combined panel of members from both the Senate Armed Services and Appropriations committees. Although these committees have no responsibility for foreign affairs—the CIA's principal involvement—they have asserted jurisdiction on the grounds that they handled the legislation under which the CIA was created. Several attempts have been made to supplant the informal subcommittees with a Joint Committee on Intelligence, patterned after the Joint Committee on Atomic Energy, and equipped with a professional staff. But after the proposal was defeated, 59 to 27, in the Senate in 1956, the inner "club" has prevented it from coming to another vote.

By 1966, however, considerable momentum for change had built up under the pressure of mounting disclosures of agency operations that had gone awry. In the view of the critics, the congressional subcommittees clearly exercised little meaningful control, had limited knowledge of foreign affairs, tended to protect the agency rather than police it, and allowed themselves to be informed after rather than before the event.

For example, Senator Russell, the most powerful man in the congressional control mechanism, admitted after the Bay of Pigs that while he knew Cuban exiles were being trained in Central America, he "did not know the timing" of the invasion. "I only wish I had been consulted," Russell declared, "because I would have strongly advised against this kind of operation if I had been. That may have been one reason why I was not consulted."

During the first two decades of the CIA, Senators Russell and Saltonstall constituted what agency men called a "genteel duumvirate" which let the CIA go its own way. In the House, the Armed Services subcommittee was under the direction of L. Mendel Rivers, the chaotic superhawk from South Carolina. The Appropriations subcommittee was headed by George H. Mahon, the capable—and sober—Texas Democrat. But his responsibility was money, not policy, and he was so burdened by Pentagon matters that he once told the Budget Bureau, "I count on you to really get the fat out of this [CIA] budget."

The agency's spending is monitored by the international division of the Budget Bureau, which controls the CIA's total appropriation but is not in a position to exercise fiscal control over individual operations. As of 1967, the CIA was spending $1,500,000,000 a year. Total U.S. intelligence expenditures, including aerial reconnaissance (planes and satellites) amounted to $4,000,000,000 annually.

Discontent with the congressional machinery for overseeing these huge sums had grown sufficiently strong by 1966 for Senator Fulbright to try again to reform the system. On July 14, with the backing of his committee (14 to 5), he submitted a resolution which would have created a nine-man Senate Committee on Intelligence Operations, including three members each from the Appropriations, Armed Services and Foreign Relations committees.

"Our sponsorship of this resolution," Fulbright declared, "proceeds from the belief that the CIA plays a major role in the foreign policy decision-making process and that by its activities is capable of exerting—and has exerted—a very substantial influence on our relations with other nations . . . When the CIA was created, the extent and nature of its present role could not be foreseen. From a modest beginning in an entirely different context of world politics, the operations of the CIA have grown today to exceed the Department of State in both number of personnel and budget . . .

"As is natural with any organization—particularly one staffed by intelligent and dedicated individuals—the CIA becomes a factor in the decision-making process as an advocate of its own recommendations . . .

"I believe that the failure of the Senate to take this small step in formal recognition of its duty to exercise a more comprehensive oversight of U.S. intelligence activities will evidence an abdication of our clear duty in an area where the activities of the executive branch can spell the difference between national honor and national discredit or, conceivably, between war and peace."

Senator Russell responded that Fulbright's resolution violated

Senate procedure in that it had not been first submitted to the committee with jurisdiction over the matter. With considerable heat, he accused Fulbright of "muscling in on my committee." Any expansion in the oversight machinery, Russell argued, would run the risk of causing harmful leaks of highly sensitive information. "Our intelligence sources throughout the world would dry up. It would frighten them all to death . . . The first time such methods were tried we will have destroyed the usefulness of the CIA and we might as well abolish it."

The Senate then shut its doors to the press and public to debate the issue in an extraordinary secret session, the second such meeting since World War II. Later a censored transcript was issued, revealing that most of the session had been taken up with parliamentary rather than substantive discussion. Two members of the CIA watchdog subcommittee betrayed ignorance of fundamental facts about the intelligence community. Saltonstall incorrectly stated the members of the National Security Council. Stuart Symington, the Missouri Democrat, confessed that he had not known "until recently" that the State Department maintained an intelligence branch of its own, the Bureau of Intelligence and Research (INR).

Symington also disclosed that for fear of leakage, the CIA subcommittee in the Senate had not asked a single question about the agency's "methods and sources" for five years.

"We can get information as to sources and methods," Russell declared, "but I want to be very frank . . . I do not want the information except in the very rarest of cases. And the other members of the committee do not want that information except in unusual circumstances." *

---

* Two months earlier Russell had remarked that even public debate on the CIA tended to "chill these sources of information . . . [to] cause them to clam up" for fear of their lives. At the same time, Saltonstall noted that security within the subcommittee was so tight that "we take no notes. Any notes that I take for the purpose of asking questions I tear up when we leave."

In the 1956 debate Saltonstall had observed: "The difficulty in connection with asking questions and obtaining information is that we might obtain information which I personally would rather not have, unless it was essential for me as a member of Congress to have it."

Fulbright commented, "The Senator from Georgia has stated that he has no interest in knowing about many of these things. This is not so with the Committee on Foreign Relations, because we have a different interest. We are not interested only in prosecuting a war or building a big military establishment, which is a legitimate interest of the senator's committee. We are not trying to infringe on that at all. We are interested in foreign relations . . .

"If we perform any function of value, it is advice and consent under the Constitution. How can we give any advice that is worth anything, if we are not informed as to what is going on and if we do not have information on which to base a judgment?"

Fulbright's efforts were to no avail. By a vote of 61 to 28 the Senate sided with Russell. Actually, the issue had been decided in the cloakroom well before. There it had been quietly pointed out that Senator Morse was likely to be one of the two Democrats assigned to the intelligence committee under Fulbright's proposal. Morse ranked fourth among Democrats on the Foreign Relations Committee, but Senator John J. Sparkman of Alabama, the No. 2 man, was then thought to be in danger of losing his seat in the fall election, and Mike Mansfield of Montana, the No. 3 man, was considered too busy as Majority Leader to serve. Morse, the most outspoken Senate critic of Vietnam policy, was viewed by most of his colleagues as an unpredictable man who should not be entrusted with delicate secrets in time of war. An advance head count indicated that sixty percent of those who voted against the Fulbright resolution actually favored it but could not bring themselves to accept Morse.

Apparently Russell realized that sentiment was building against him and decided it was necessary to head off a future challenge that might strip him of the chairmanship of the CIA subcommittee. When the new Congress convened in January 1967, he invited Fulbright, Mansfield and Bourke Hickenlooper of Iowa, ranking Republican on the Foreign Relations Committee, to sit with the subcommittee informally. However, Russell's concession clearly fell short of establishing any meaningful supervision of the CIA.

From the agency's inception in 1947, Congress has virtually

abdicated its responsibility to act as a check on the vast, hidden power of the invisible government. A thoroughgoing reform was needed, including creation of a broadly based Joint Committee on Intelligence and tangible evidence that the watchdogs intended to take their assignment seriously. Yet, there was no sign that the men who run Congress were even aware of the gravity of the problem.

The complacency was matched in the executive branch. The President reacted to the NSA scandal by resorting to the hoary bureaucratic practice of setting up a committee (one on which the head of the CIA sat as a judge of his own case). Predictably, the jury returned with a verdict of not guilty and recommendations containing a loophole through which new evils could emerge. The shadowy Special Group, which in the name of "national security" had permitted the CIA to intrude into domestic affairs in the first place, was to continue to protect the public interest.

The NSA incident amply demonstrated to the American people that the dividing line between the public and private domain had been dangerously crossed. It had also revealed that the Special Group and the CIA had violated the spirit, if not the letter, of the law under which the CIA was established. In such compromising circumstances, and at a time when the government's credibility was increasingly suspect, it was not likely that the public would long remain satisfied with a papering over of the problem.

Having once been permitted to intrude into domestic affairs and to corrupt the private sector, what assurance was there that the CIA would not do so again? Having failed in the past to recognize the moral and practical implications of certain CIA operations at home and abroad, what guarantee was there that the Special Group would be alert to future dangers?

It is an honored American tradition that when an institution fails, it is replaced. It is time, at least, to replace the obsolete machinery for control of the CIA. It is time to establish a visible and credible guardian of intelligence, one that will reassure the American people that the necessary secret instruments of its government are servants, not masters, of the national will.

A revolution is not a dinner party, or writing an essay,
or painting a picture, or doing embroidery
. . . a revolution is an insurrection, an act of violence.

—Mao Tse-tung

v communist china

Communist China's leading spy master is a stubborn, near-sighted old man, a rich landlord's son with an implacable hostility toward the values of his ancestors and toward the United States. His name is K'ang Sheng, and although nothing can be considered permanent about a China in chaos, Western experts agree that he emerged during Mao Tse-tung's "Great Proletarian Cultural Revolution" as overlord of Chinese intelligence. A thin-faced man with thick, round glasses, a pencil-line mustache and a menacing half-smile, he was catapulted into Peking's upper hierarchy in August 1966, rising from twenty-fifth to fifth place in the Politburo of the Chinese Communist party.

Like Mao Tse-tung's wife, former actress Chiang Ch'ing, who took a leading role in the cultural revolution, K'ang's wife, Tsao Yi-ou, became an important political figure during the rampages of the Red Guards.

K'ang was born in 1899 in Shantung Province at Chucheng, a small town forty miles west of the port city of Tsingtao, halfway between Peking and Shanghai. He was given the name Chao Yun at birth but rejected it in early manhood, apparently in revolt against his father and his bourgeois upbringing.

K'ang was educated at local schools and Shanghai University, where he joined a Communist youth group in his early twenties. He became a member of the Communist party in 1925 and went to work as a labor organizer in Shanghai. He is believed to have been brought into party intelligence and security work in the wake of Chiang Kai-shek's anti-Communist purge in April 1927.

K'ang was elected to the Central Committee of the Chinese Communist party at its Sixth Congress in Moscow the next year but remained underground in Shanghai, operating from a "secret house" in the French concession. There, somewhat buffered by French immunity from Chiang's Kuomintang, K'ang provided a haven for Communists on the run.

He was relieved of his Shanghai duties in 1933 and sent to Moscow to study Soviet intelligence, security and police techniques. He remained in Russia for four years, serving as the Chinese Communist party representative to the Comintern, acquiring a good knowledge of Russian and a bit of English and German. He was also published for the first—and virtually the last—time * as co-author of "Revolutionary China Today," a booklet foreshadowing the party's return to the united-front approach that had been abandoned in the split with Chiang in 1927.

In 1937 K'ang was called back to the Chinese Communist capital at Yenan'Shensi near the Mongolian border. He was immediately assigned to intelligence work and by 1939 apparently had become director of the Social Affairs Department, the long-standing euphemism for the party's central organ for security and intelligence. He held the post until 1946, when he was succeeded by Li K'o-nung,

---

* In 1949, shortly after the Communist takeover of the mainland, he appeared in print once again with a tough-minded, though relatively undogmatic article in *Red Flag* entitled "Communist Party Membership."

an old co-conspirator from Shanghai days who remained as head of the department until his death in 1962.

For eight years after World War II as the Communists seized and consolidated power in China, K'ang operated in almost total obscurity—even the fact that he had married and fathered two children did not become known until the mid-1950's. But he was clearly a power behind the scenes. When the Communists asserted nationwide control in 1949, he was named a member of the Central People's Government Council, the most important organ of the government prior to the reorganization of 1954. A *Who's Who* published in Shanghai in 1950 listed him as a member of the Politburo, the party's ruling group, but he may have been admitted secretly as early as 1943. By December 1954, in any event, he was officially identified as a member. The following March he took an active part in the national party conference that purged a number of high-ranking figures—an indication of his growing power.

Since 1955, K'ang has received extensive publicity in Communist China's controlled press, particularly in his role as a leading policy maker for higher education and as one of the principal links with the international Communist movement. He led a delegation to East Germany in 1956 for the Third Congress of Socialist Party Unity and accompanied Prime Minister Chou En-lai to Moscow for the Twenty-first Soviet Communist Party Congress in 1959.

He returned to Moscow the following February as head of the Chinese delegation to the meeting of the Warsaw Pact nations; there he fired the first direct salvo in the Sino-Soviet dispute. The Chinese had previously couched their criticism of Moscow in veiled language and arcane Marxist dialectic, but K'ang left nothing to conjecture. His speech made it unmistakably clear that Peking vigorously disagreed with Soviet policies toward the West, particularly on disarmament, and intended to pursue an independent line.

K'ang embellished his remarks in a score of important party meetings at home and abroad over the next few years. He emerged from the welter of polemics with a reputation as a tenacious advocate of an extremely tough line toward the West, particularly the United

States. He also proved himself an unwavering devotee of Mao,* a factor which doubtless accounts for his elevation to the party Secretariat in 1962 and his meteoric rise during the Cultural Revolution of 1966.†

As No. 5 man in China, K'ang is probably the highest-ranking intelligence chief in the world. His power is also enhanced by the nature of the Chinese intelligence system which, modeled closely after that of the Soviet Union, places him in charge of both internal security and foreign intelligence, i.e., the secret police and the espionage apparatus. In American terms, he is both Director of Central Intelligence and head of the FBI.

K'ang's overall control is enforced through the Social Affairs Department. Headquartered at 15 Bow String Alley in Peking, it keeps watch over the loyalty of party members and co-ordinates the intelligence activities of other party and government agencies.

Domestic security is delegated to the Ministry of Public Affairs, which also has responsibility for Hong Kong, Macao and Formosa in addition to the mainland. It employs approximately 250,000 members of the armed popular police, roughly one for every 2,500 citizens. The police, in turn, organize "voluntary committees" of housewives and other private citizens at the local level, providing the ministry with an all-pervasive network of informers and street wardens.

Since 1959 the ministry has been headed by Hsieh Fu-chih, a tough, much-decorated political commissar in the fight against the Japanese and Chiang. A year younger than K'ang, he was elevated to the Politburo during the Cultural Revolution and was given prominent position at public rallies, apparently to demonstrate Mao's determination to turn the security screws even tighter.

Foreign intelligence operations are delegated by the Social Affairs Department to two other central organs of the Politburo—the

---

* K'ang is mentioned twice, with approval, in Mao's *Selected Works*.

† The authors are indebted to Donald Klein of Columbia University's East Asian Institute for much of this biographical information. Mr. Klein, in collaboration with Mrs. Anne B. Clark, is compiling a biographical study of the Chinese Communist leadership.

United Front Workers Department and the International Liaison Department.

The United Front Workers Department serves a dual purpose. At home it provides a democratic façade for the party's dictatorship by enlisting the support of non-Communist experts and sympathizers. Abroad it acts as the principal link with the fifteen million ethnic Chinese who are permanent residents of other countries. It seeks to align the overseas Chinese in support of Peking's propaganda and diplomacy, to entice them into espionage, and occasionally, as in Malaya in the 1950's, to organize them for military insurgency.

The United Front also encourages talented or prestigious members of the overseas Chinese community to return to the mainland. Its two prize catches have been Ch'ien Hsueh-shen, a U.S.-trained engineer who developed China's first nuclear missile, and General Li Tsung-jen, former Vice-President of Nationalist China.

Ch'ien, son of a prosperous Shanghai businessman, came to the United States in 1935 at the age of twenty-five after attending Chiao-tung University. He took his master's degree in aeronautical engineering at the Massachusetts Institute of Technology and received his Ph.D., magna cum laude, at the California Institute of Technology.

During World War II, Ch'ien served in Washington as director of the rocket section of the United States National Defense Scientific Board, a position in which he had access to top-secret information. Just prior to V-E Day he was given the rank of Air Force colonel and sent to Germany as the head of a mission of scientists investigating Nazi advances in rocketry. He was also assigned to the top-secret scientific panel which produced a major report on the nature of future wars, *New Horizons—Science as the Key to Air Supremacy*.

At the end of the war Ch'ien returned to Caltech as an associate professor and eventually chief research analyst at the Jet Propulsion Laboratory. He took part in the first government-sponsored rocket research at Caltech and was subsequently named Goddard Professor of Jet Propulsion.

Ch'ien visited pre-Communist China in 1946, where he was first offered the presidency of his alma mater and then vetoed as too young by the Minister of Education. He returned to the United States within the year, then sought to go back to China permanently in 1950, after the Communist takeover. He was intercepted by the FBI, which had been alerted by his attempt to send 1,800 pounds of books ahead of him.

A hearing by the Immigration and Naturalization Service led to an order that he be deported as a Communist (two Los Angeles police detectives testified that he had joined the party in 1939). But the order was held up in Washington on the grounds that he would carry with him classified information "inimical to the best interests of the United States."

Finally, in 1955, when it was judged that his knowledge had become dated, he was permitted to return to China. There he was named to the Academy of Sciences and placed in charge of China's nuclear research program with special responsibility for missile development.* His work culminated on October 27, 1966, in the successful launching of China's first nuclear weapon carried by a guided missile.

The defection of General Li was technically less harmful but in some ways more embarrassing. Li had left China in 1950 after serving two years as Acting President of the Nationalist regime following Chiang's flight to Formosa. Refusing to join the Generalissimo in exile, he went to the United States.

Several years before his return to China in 1965, according to Nationalist Chinese intelligence, two Chinese Communist agents took up residence near his house at 77 New Street, Englewood Hills, New Jersey. Ingratiating themselves over a long period of time, they reportedly persuaded Li that he and his ailing wife would receive better treatment at home.

Shortly after his arrival in Peking by way of Switzerland, the seventy-four-year-old general held a news conference in which he alleged that in 1955 "a U.S. Republican bigwig" had tried to enlist him in a plot against Chiang. "He thought," Li said, "that I must have

---

* In 1958, after declaring its intention to do so at one of the periodic meetings with U.S. officials in Warsaw, Peking wrote to several Chinese scientists in the United States, asking them to return to the homeland. Some of them did.

some forces lying low in Taiwan since I had been Acting President and had commanded an army, and that I could arrange a coup . . . the United States would immediately land forces in Taiwan and overthrow Mr. Chiang Kai-shek and take over control on the pretext of his inability to maintain order, so that I could come into power."

Li's allegations paralleled an unconfirmed report that had circulated in the pro-Chiang China lobby in Washington during the first Administration of President Eisenhower. According to the rumor, Li had been hired by the CIA to eliminate Chiang. Several supporters of Chiang, including Styles Bridges, the influential Republican senator from New Hampshire, became so alarmed that they demanded reassurance from Frank Wisner, then the CIA's deputy director for plans.

In any event, by 1965 General Li was no longer of much political interest to Washington and there was no official attempt to interfere with his departure from the United States. On the other hand, Peking seized on his defection as a major ideological triumph and he must have been received eagerly by the Chinese intelligence community.

Shortly after his return, in the normal process of debriefing, Li must almost certainly have encountered an old enemy of civil-war days, Tsou Ta-p'eng, a veteran intelligence operator. It is general Chinese Communist practice to place the same official in two or more branches of the party and the government, using him as a control point in the fragmented bureaucratic machinery. Within the overlapping intelligence jurisdiction of the United Front, International Liaison and Social Affairs departments, Tsou appears to be that man.

Born in Manchuria in 1900, he has spent his entire adult life in Chinese Communist intelligence. He served in the Social Affairs Department under K'ang Sheng and Li K'o-nung during the Sino-Japanese war, rising to the rank of secretary-general. Later he carried out a series of intelligence assignments under various covers—mayor of Changchun in Manchuria, director of the Information Administration Bureau, and director of the Liaison Department of the People's Revolutionary Military Council.

In February 1958, when the proliferating intelligence functions of the Foreign Ministry were reorganized under a new front, the

Commission for Cultural Relations with Foreign Countries, Tsou was named a founding member. The next month he became vice-chairman of the commission and a year later, in April, he assumed a position on the Chinese People's Association for Cultural Relations with Foreign Countries, a "nongovernmental" organization that had been founded in 1954 and just reorganized. In June 1961 Tsou became vice-chairman of that group as well.

Thus, he was now placed at the very center of all three sections of the intelligence apparatus—the party, the government and the people's organization. From such a vantage point Tsou was in position to oversee the whole range of China's foreign intelligence operation and to make sure that it conformed to Mao's and K'ang's notions of violent change.

Mao and his old companions in arms literally projected their revolutionary experience at home onto the world scene. They saw a single, inevitable process of change: the "countryside" (underdeveloped nations) surrounding and destroying the "cities" (North America and Europe). Beyond normal intelligence gathering, the primary function of a Chinese agent is to speed that process, to create the conditions for radical change in the established order. As Mao decreed, the international revolution was to be advanced by any means, "bloody and bloodless, violent and peaceful, military and economic."

Since the "cities" will fall once the "countryside" has been mobilized, Peking has devoted most of its attention to the countries of Asia, Africa and Latin America. The Russians have been content to woo the newly independent nations in the hope that a natural socialist transformation would eventually steer them into the Communist camp. But the Chinese have refused to accept nationalist uprisings as more than a stopgap solution, insisting that there must be another wave of international revolution to smash all remnants of the traditional order.

In its dealings with the world, Peking has availed itself of all the conventional deceptions of the art of intelligence. Where it has normal relations, it uses its embassy to provide diplomatic cover for espionage.* Where it is unable to operate an embassy, it seeks to establish either a trade mission to act as a front for clandestine activity, or a bureau of Hsinhua (the New China News Agency), which was largely designed for this purpose. Where neither is possible, it tries to gain admission for visiting delegations which can perform the intelligence function for a short period and possibly lay the groundwork for a more enduring arrangement.

For example, at the end of the Korean War, Peking succeeded in sending representatives of the Chinese Red Cross Society to Japan to work out the repatriation of Japanese in China. The ostensible head of the mission was a woman, but the real leader was her deputy, Liao Ch'eng-chih, a diplomat of long experience and later ambassador to Burma. Liao successfully negotiated the repatriation and in the process established a quasi-official Chinese presence which has provided a continuing legal base for intelligence and espionage. To gather intelligence about Japan, Peking was previously forced to rely heavily upon Communist North Korea, which maintains close ties with the 570,000 Koreans in Japan. Of these, Japanese intelligence has estimated, fifty percent support North Korea, thirty percent South Korea, and twenty percent are neutral.

The North Korean regime operates through an outfit known popularly as Chosoren—the General Association of Korean Residents in Japan. North Korea pours large amounts of black (clandestine) money into Japan through Chosoren and reaps a big intelligence harvest in return; Japanese intelligence has traced an inflow of $38,-800,000 since 1957.

Radio Pyongyang in North Korea transmits coded intelligence instructions to agents in Japan as part of elaborate "station identification" numbers. Information flows back by way of repatriated Koreans. Since December 1959 the Japanese have permitted more than eighty-five thousand Koreans to return to their homeland. Often they hide intelligence messages among their personal possessions and it is impossible to intercept all of these without smashing every piece of

---

* As of 1967, Peking was represented in fifty countries. It maintained military attachés in at least half of them.

furniture and every household item. Japanese intelligence is convinced that in this manner North Korea pulls in a wealth of information about Japanese technology and the United States military establishment in Japan. And at least when Pyongyang and Peking have been on good terms, it clearly has made its way to China.

The flow of intelligence to Peking is surer and more direct from Southeast Asia, where more than ninety percent of the overseas Chinese live. Dominating the small-business economies of most of the Southeast Asian countries, the Chinese are by no means exclusively or predominantly pro-Peking. But their tendency is to hedge their bets. A picture of Chiang Kai-shek may hang in front of the shop but Mao Tse-tung's is likely to be in the back.

Peking's espionage establishment, like that of the other major powers, is intent upon acquiring as much intelligence as possible about other nations. But what distinguishes it is the emphasis it places on fomenting violent revolution whenever it can, particularly in the "third world."

A bitter struggle was waged in Malaya between 1948 and 1960 before the government managed to suppress a Vietnam-type insurgency mounted by the Malayan Communist party, which was composed almost entirely of ethnic Chinese. Finally forced underground, the movement continued to prosper in Chinese schools and at Nan-yang University in predominantly Chinese Singapore. And on Sarawak, Malaysia's primitive provincial outpost on the island of Borneo, a Chinese clandestine Communist organization was uncovered in the early 1960's, preparing for a Maoist-style uprising. In 1963 the government cracked down and began to isolate the troublesome Sarawak Chinese in "resettlement villages." In Singapore it arrested student leaders and the heads of the Communist-front opposition party, which controlled thirty local labor unions. But Peking's apparatus had by no means been suppressed. In 1964 open riots were fomented in Singapore between Malays and Chinese. And the following year Sim Siew Lim, a Chinese intelligence agent who had slipped into the city from Shanghai in 1960, was arrested along with twenty others on charges of plotting the assassination of Singapore government leaders.

Farther south, in Indonesia, Peking appeared on the verge of a complete takeover prior to the abortive Communist coup of September 20, 1965, that backfired and cost Sukarno his power. The pro-Peking Indonesian Communist party (PKI), financed by money extracted from the local Chinese business community, had been rapidly growing in strength, and Djakarta had become a base for Maoist insurgency movements in Malaysia and the Philippines. A PKI intelligence school had been established in the southern Philippines in an attempt to resurrect the Huk movement, which had been crushed by Ramon Magsaysay in the early 1950's, and the Chinese were attempting to set up two other remote guerrilla training centers.

With the advent of anti-Communist military rule in Djakarta and the suppression of the PKI, the various Chinese Communist front organizations in Indonesia withdrew to Peking. In January 1966 the New China News Agency announced that the Malayan National Liberation League, formerly a part of the Malayan Independence Movement in Djakarta, had set up a mission in Peking, joining the National Liberation Front of South Vietnam and the Thailand Patriotic Front.

The Thai front had been founded early in 1965 with a vow "to drive the U.S. imperialists out of Thailand and overthrow the traitorous, fascist and dictatorial Bangkok government." Because the bulk of the Thai population was relatively well off and loyal to the king, Chinese agents concentrated on the three million ethnic Chinese, Vietnamese, Laotians and hill tribesmen along the neglected, impoverished northwestern frontier. Agitators, trained in China at Kunming and Nanning, headquarters for the Chinese People's Minorities Program, circulated among Thailand's Lahu tribe, passing word of the coming of a new "messiah" anticipated in the local religion. Shortly thereafter a Chinese-indoctrinated "messiah" reportedly appeared, claiming possession of the "magic hammer, magic rope and magic knife," which, by Lahu tradition, could kill all enemies even if they numbered "as many as the sesame seeds in three baskets."

Propaganda for the various fronts was broadcast by the Voice of the Thai People, a clandestine radio station located in North Vietnam or South China. An important base for the activity directed against Thailand was the Chinese embassy in Vientiane, capital of neighboring Laos.

In Burma, Peking's intelligence operations centered in the White Flag, an outlawed Communist movement that had been waging an armed insurgency since 1949. Although Peking officially supported Rangoon's policy of nonalignment, it hardly bothered to conceal its connections with the White Flag. Leaders of the insurgency were granted political asylum in China, and Radio Peking openly broadcast greetings to the movement on its fifteenth anniversary, in October 1964.

Although Southeast Asia has been the prime target of Chinese intelligence, its hand has also shown elsewhere in Asia. In Nepal a Chinese technical expert, Huang Yung-sheng, who defected to the West in April 1964, said a Chinese road-building project there was a front for an effort to "subvert the Nepalese government and Communize the country." He asserted that the construction team included five hundred Chinese soldiers in civilian guise and that arms for pro-Peking agents were concealed in road-building material. Huang's charges led to the departure of the Chinese ambassador and the military attaché, Colonel Kan Mai, who had also reportedly been seen in Tibet and India just before the Chinese invaded.

In Ceylon the Chinese embassy was active in the unsuccessful effort to re-elect Madame Sirimavo Bandaranaike as Prime Minister in 1965. After the election the new government threatened to take action against any embassy that had a staff "far in excess of what is required for the performance of legitimate functions"—an obvious reference to both the Chinese and the Russians, who were vying for ascendancy in Ceylon's Communist party.

By the mid-1960's Ceylon was, besides Mongolia and India, the only place in Asia where the pro-Moscow wing was dominant and still actively engaged in promoting revolution, Russian style. In the rest of Asia, and in Australia as well, the KGB had become so bogged down in counterintelligence operations against the Chinese that its subversive activities had practically come to a standstill.

In the Middle East the situation was reversed. The Chinese embassy in Damascus, Syria, was Peking's headquarters in the Arab world. Its chief task was to neutralize Soviet influence and encourage the formation of pro-Peking Communist splinter groups. Peking had unusually large embassies in the area and established a string of "bookshops" and "trading companies" to support its underground and provide cover for its agents. It also sought to ingratiate itself through a front group called the China Islamic Association (CIA) but met with little success everywhere (except in Yemen), not only because of its unfortunate choice of initials but because hand-picked CIA "pilgrims" failed to pay their respects at appropriate mosques.

Similarly, in Egypt, the political center of the Arab world, the Chinese apparatus was frustrated when the pro-Peking Arab Communist party was implicated in a plot to assassinate President Gamal Abdel Nasser in December 1965. The Chinese ambassador hurriedly left the country after an investigation was launched into links between the embassy and the conspirators. He was followed by the head of the New China News Agency, who was accused of financing the operation.

Ironically, Cairo had been the beachhead for Peking's original effort to penetrate Africa; Nasser's United Arab Republic was the first African nation to recognize Communist China. In the early 1960's the Chinese began to move into West Africa and the newly independent nations south of the Sahara.*

Premier Chou En-lai bluntly declared at Mogadiscio, Somalia, in February 1964, "An excellent revolutionary situation exists in Africa today." China sent its most experienced diplomats to Africa and transported large delegations of Africans to China (225 groups in 1964 alone). It also set up guerrilla warfare academies at the Nanking and Wuhan academies of military science and gave instruction there to recruits from Algeria, Angola, Botswana, the Cameroons, the

---

* At Peking's high-water mark early in 1965, it was recognized by eighteen African countries. By 1966 only fourteen countries maintained diplomatic relations with Peking; seventeen with Nationalist China; and eight with neither.

two Congos, Guinea, Kenya, Malawi, Mozambique, Niger, Nigeria, Portuguese Guinea, Rhodesia, Rwanda and South Africa.

Peking Radio broadcast 112 hours a week to Africa in English, French, Arabic, Hausa, Swahili, Italian and Portuguese (in addition to the Cantonese and Kuo-yü dialect programs for the overseas Chinese on the Indian Ocean islands of Mauritius, Madagascar and Réunion). Peking also flooded the bookstores with glossy, subsidized publications, and dispatched hundreds of agents in the guise of diplomats, journalists, agricultural advisers, technical experts and artists.

In the Sudan in 1964 the Chinese embassy was implicated in the passing of arms and money to stir up riots, which led to the downfall of the military government.

In Malawi in 1965 the Chinese ambassador to neighboring Tanzania was cited as "the steering hand" in a plot to overthrow the government. In Zambia the same year four council members of the United Trades' Union Congress were fired for taking bribes from the Chinese mission to foment strikes. In June 1965 the Chinese were denounced by the Kenya government for secretly shipping arms through the country and for bankrolling a network of agents. In March the following year a member of the Chinese embassy was expelled.

In the Central African Republic in January 1966 a new military regime discovered a cache of arms and ammunition bearing "foreign markings." Relations with Peking were promptly severed and thirty Chinese, some of whom had entered the country illegally, were ousted along with the embassy staff and representatives of the New China News Agency.

During the same month the Chinese were also ejected from Dahomey, losing their base of operations for nearby Togo, Upper Volta, Niger and Nigeria, which had refused them diplomatic recognition.

Kwame Nkrumah was overthrown while visiting Peking in February 1966. The new military government in Ghana accused the self-styled "Redeemer" of having established—with Chinese assistance—a network of six spy schools for the subversion of other

African countries. A guerrilla warfare manual, cribbing copiously from Mao and bearing Nkrumah's by-line on the title page, was found in the Redeemer's safe. Relations with Peking were severed and 430 Chinese were expelled, including intelligence officers and guerrilla warfare instructors.

The strong reaction against Communist China that followed Nkrumah's downfall had been foreshadowed in Burundi a year earlier when diplomatic recognition was withdrawn from Peking and the Chinese mission ordered out of the country. The reason was the assassination of Premier Pierre Ngendandumwe and the defection of Tung Chi-p'eng, a twenty-four-year-old assistant cultural attaché. Tung said the Chinese had used Burundi as a staging area for Gaston Soumialot's unsuccessful revolt against the central government of the neighboring Democratic Republic of the Congo, the former Belgian colony. He quoted Mao to the effect that " 'Burundi is the way to the Congo and when the Congo falls the whole of Africa will fall.' "

Headquarters for the Congo operation was the Chinese embassy in Brazzaville in the former French Congo, just to the west of the Democratic Republic of the Congo. Colonel Kan Mai, fresh from Nepal, served as "first secretary" while running two training camps for the Congolese rebels at Gamboma and Impfondo, north of the capital. With the acquiescence of the friendly Brazzaville government, Kan Mai provided money and arms for Pierre Mulele, who had received eighteen months of guerrilla training in Peking, and for Christophe Gbenye. But the operation withered away in 1966 after a rapprochement between the two Congos.

Kan Mai had been assisted by an extraordinary journalist named Kao Liang, chief African correspondent for the New China News Agency. Kao's name is the same as that of a tough grain cereal of northern China, a self-reliant plant, durable in heat or cold, adaptable to a variety of soils, and the base of a potent liquor. And in his many assignments for Peking, Kao has proved himself a man of comparable qualities.

Taking up residence in Dar es Salaam, the capital of Tanzania, in 1961, Kao carried his intrigues the length and breadth of Africa. In Dar he lived much too well for a newspaperman. His house and his car were too big, his parties too frequent and his bankroll too large. In short, his lavish ways exposed his cover, as similar habits have sometimes betrayed CIA men, but it seemed to trouble him not at all. In fact, he openly asserted more importance than that of an NCNA correspondent and once checked into a hotel in Burundi as the "Chinese ambassador."

Kao was the prime mover in the pro-Peking coup in Zanzibar in 1964, passing out money and arms to the insurgents, including Sheik Abdul Rahman Muhammed (Sheik Babu), a former NCNA "correspondent" who emerged as Foreign Minister. Kao was also active in Mauritius (he was expelled in 1964), Réunion and Kenya, and made a practice of attending all independence celebrations, whether or not invited, with a big roll of money.

Earlier Kao performed his intelligence assignments under NCNA cover in India (expelled in 1960), Nepal and at the 1961 Geneva Conference on Laos. He was clearly an unusual journalist but not an unusual NCNA journalist, for since its inception the agency has been operating as a conduit for intelligence and a cover for espionage. NCNA began as the Red China News Agency in 1932, but the "New" was substituted for the "Red" in 1937 when Japan invaded China and the Communists formed a united front with the Nationalists. It now maintains headquarters in a walled-off, heavily guarded building in Peking, directing correspondents and stringers in more than sixty countries.*

---

* In 1966 there were offices in Burma, Cambodia, Ceylon, Hong Kong, Japan, Laos, Macao, Mongolia, Nepal, North Korea, North Vietnam and Pakistan in Asia; Algeria, Congo-Brazzaville, Ethiopia, Ghana, Guinea, Mali, Senegal, Somalia, Sudan, Tanzania, Tunisia, the United Arab Republic and Zambia in Africa; Afghanistan, Iraq, Kuwait, Syria and Yemen in the Middle East; Britain, France, Sweden (also for Denmark, Norway and Finland), Switzerland and West Germany in western Europe; Albania, East Germany, Hungary, Poland, Rumania, the Soviet Union and Yugoslavia in eastern Europe; and Canada, Chile, Cuba and Mexico in North and Latin America.

NCNA is believed to have more than a hundred men in Hong Kong but they are rarely seen at press conferences, news events or even journalistic

Much of NCNA's work involves the simple collection of unclassified documents—newspapers, magazines, books, technical journals. Within its resources, Peking is as assiduous in the collection of overt intelligence as any other major power. But the main thrust of NCNA's activities is of a diplomatic or intelligence nature, as can be seen from the operations of its busier correspondents.

Wang Te-ming, an army major in the Korean War and later an NCNA correspondent in Burma, served as the agency's representative in Kenya in the early 1960's. He lived in the embassy compound and carried a diplomatic passport, although he asserted the rights of a journalist to exempt himself from the normal travel restrictions imposed on the representatives of foreign governments. He effected liaison with all the important leftwing personalities in Kenya, passed out large sums of money, and was implicated in the summer of 1965 in an abortive leftwing effort to seize the headquarters of the ruling Kenyan African National Union. Two weeks later, on July 22, 1965, he was declared a prohibited immigrant and given twenty-four hours to leave Kenya.

Yang Hsiao-nung, NCNA director in France and Switzerland, was a Chinese intelligence agent in Europe and personally transported a large sum of black money into the Congo in 1960. The same year Ma Chia-chün, former first secretary at the Chinese embassy in Rangoon, became Yang's assistant in the Paris office. He undertook Chinese consular duties prior to establishment of diplomatic relations with France, and in 1962 was transferred to the embassy in London.

Chiao Kuan-hua, former NCNA representative in Hong Kong, became assistant to the Chinese Minister of Foreign Affairs in 1954 and Deputy Foreign Minister in 1964.

Tseng T'ao negotiated diplomatic relations between China and Cuba while serving as director of the Havana bureau of NCNA in 1960. Later he also negotiated diplomatic relations with Algeria and became Communist China's first ambassador there.

---

meeting places. NCNA was not represented in Czechoslovakia. Its first bureau was established in Prague in 1948 but was closed by the Czechs in 1963 for biased reporting.

Li Yen-nien served simultaneously in 1963 as NCNA correspondent and director of the commercial information office of the Chinese Import and Export Corporation in Chile, and as head of a commercial delegation to Uruguay.

Wang Wei-chen and Chü Ch'ing-tung, NCNA correspondents in Brazil, were arrested on April 3, 1964, together with two interpreters and five members of the Chinese Trade Promotion Office. They were charged with espionage and subversion by the military junta which had just overthrown President João Goulart. All nine were found guilty by a military court and sentenced to ten years in prison. They were expelled from Brazil the following April.

Lacking a diplomatic base anywhere in Latin America outside of Cuba, Peking has made extensive use of commercial cover as an alternative. In addition to Brazil, the Chinese have established trade relations with Argentina, Chile, Mexico, Uruguay and Venezuela. The commercial advantage has accrued almost exclusively to the Latin Americans, reflecting Peking's principal interest in achieving a foothold for other purposes.

Peking has also attempted to insinuate itself within the overseas Chinese community in Latin America, numbering about 220,000 and concentrated principally in Peru, Cuba, Costa Rica and Mexico. In addition, Peking has been unusually active in promoting "cultural" exchanges. Thousands of Latin American doctors, lawyers, scientists, painters and journalists have gone to China and more than two dozen formal Chinese delegations have paid return visits.

Many of the delegations are ill-disguised fronts for propaganda or espionage. In 1963 a trade mission to Mexico City was led by Chang Kuang-tuo, described in the local press as "an expert agitator and ideologist of revolutionary war." In 1964 an acrobatic troupe visiting Mexico was escorted by Hsin Fu, deputy director of the Politburo's propaganda department.

A special school was set up in Peking in 1960 to train Latin American Communists in subversion and violence. Recruits have come from Colombia, Cuba, Ecuador and Peru. Chinese agents have been active in the Communist movements of the hemisphere. Pro-

Peking parties have been established in Brazil, Peru, Colombia and Bolivia, and splinter groups have emerged in Argentina, Chile, Ecuador, Guatemala and Uruguay.

China has relied very heavily upon Cuba as a staging area for these operations in Latin America. But Fidel Castro made it clear in 1966 that his hospitality was wearing thin. In a speech on March 13 he attacked Mao as senile and barbarous, accused the Chinese of "launching an imperialist-type campaign against Cuba," and threatened to break off diplomatic relations.

Peking has had even greater difficulties in establishing a solid footing in Europe. Prior to the open split with Moscow, the Chinese operated out of their embassy in Prague, well situated on the border between eastern and western Europe. But when the Czechs clamped down in 1963, the Chinese were forced to transfer their espionage headquarters to the embassy in Switzerland.

Today it is the center of Peking's spy operations in Europe. The Chinese maintain a diplomatic establishment of more than two hundred persons at the Berne embassy. A sizable portion is attached to an embassy school which trains the Chinese diplomatic corps in the niceties of Western etiquette and protocol. But it is obvious that the embassy is also being used for less academic purposes. In June 1965 the Swiss government warned the Chinese ambassador, Li Ching-ch'üan, that it would no longer tolerate his "irregular activities," which included the financing and direction of agents of the pro-Peking French Federation of Marxist-Leninist Circles.* The following February an embassy secretary and a Nationalist Chinese official were expelled from Switzerland as alleged members of an international ring transmitting information about Nationalist China to Peking.

Peking also operates in Europe from its base in Albania, its lone ally in the Communist bloc, and through the pro-Chinese Belgian

---

* The Chinese also maintain close ties with the Committee for Recognition of People's China in Greece, the Association of Marxist-Leninists in Austria, the Marxist-Leninist Center of The Netherlands, and the League of Marxist-Leninist Youth in Italy.

Communist party, headed by Jacques Grippa. Grippa, who was prominently displayed on the official podium in Peking at the start of the Cultural Revolution in August 1966, reputedly receives a bankroll of $100,000 a year from China.

Much of Peking's energy in Europe seems to be expended on counterintelligence and efforts to guard against defection. The most revealing incident to date occurred in The Netherlands in the summer of 1966.

Prins Mauritslaan is a street of drab row houses in The Hague, about seven minutes by car from the center of town. Number 17 is a three-story yellow brick house on the corner. On the afternoon of Saturday, July 16, a neighbor observed a man lying on the sidewalk in front of No. 17, moaning in pain. He telephoned the police but by the time they arrived the sidewalk was clear. The injured man, forty-two-year-old Hsu Tzu-tsai, had been carried into the house, which served as the rented residence of the third secretary of Communist China's diplomatic mission. Hsu was a houseguest, together with eight other Chinese delegates to the Nineteenth Annual Assembly of the International Institute of Welding, which was concluding its meeting that day in nearby Delft.

At first the occupants of No. 17 refused to let the police enter, but after some discussion one officer and an ambulance attendant were admitted. Hsu was put into the ambulance, and accompanied by two Chinese, was driven to the Red Cross Hospital, a minute or two away. He was examined and x-rayed, the pictures showing a fractured skull, broken ribs and a spinal injury.

While Hsu was in the x-ray room, the Chinese made a telephone call. Shortly afterward a sedan with diplomatic tags pulled up in front of the hospital with three or four men inside. Two of the Chinese discussed Hsu's condition with the examining physician in the presence of two Dutch detectives. The Chinese said they wanted to take Hsu out of the hospital. The doctor refused.

While the discussion was going on, three of the other Chinese entered the x-ray room and laid Hsu on a stretcher. A nurse, returning with the x-rays, saw Hsu being taken to the elevator. She handed the plates to the Chinese and told them to take Hsu to the emergency room. Instead, they carried him to the car and put him in the back seat. Then they drove to No. 7 Adriaan Goekooplaan, the office of the Chinese chargé d'affaires, where the eight other delegates had been assembled.

That night the chargé, Li En-ch'iu, was summoned to the Dutch Foreign Ministry. Officials protested the removal of Hsu from the hospital as a violation of the law and requested that he be returned.

"When in spite of the *démarches* undertaken," the Foreign Ministry declared in a communiqué of July 19, "the patient was not returned to a hospital, the chargé d'affaires was again summoned to the ministry on July 18th, where he stated that the victim had died in his office in the afternoon of July 17. The facts already known are so serious that they have caused the government to declare the chargé d'affaires *persona non grata* and to request him to leave the country within twenty-four hours."

A Foreign Ministry spokesman said the chargé, who left with his wife for Peking that afternoon, did not deny that Hsu had been removed by the Chinese from the hospital. His position was that the Chinese had brought him there for a medical opinion, and having got it, took him back for the best care they could give him.

How and why had Hsu died?

He and the other technicians had come into contact with a number of Americans at the Welding Assembly. There were about eight hundred delegates there, a number of them civilian and military employees of the United States government.

The New China News Agency said: "Secret U.S. agents, with the connivance of the Dutch government, used every sordid means to induce, illegally and repeatedly, members of the Chinese delegation to desert and betray their own country . . . Hsu, incited by U.S. agents, jumped down from the building where he was lodged, in an attempt to run away, and injured himself."

The Dutch police conjectured that Hsu jumped or fell in an

attempt to defect, or after being falsely accused of wanting to. A neighbor told the police that when Hsu was lying on the sidewalk, a third-story window was open but some minutes later it was closed. Hsu might have been trying to reach the roof, which would have given him access to other houses in the row.

From the moment the Dutch government learned of Hsu's death, it demanded custody of his body as well as the right to interrogate the eight other delegates. The Chinese refused both requests but devised a face-saving procedure for disposal of the body. They called in an undertaker, who turned it over briefly to a police medical examiner for an autopsy, which showed that Hsu had fallen from a "considerable height." The undertaker then cremated the body and handed back the remains to the Chinese, who, still insisting that they had never formally relinquished possession, shipped the ashes to China.

The Chinese would not budge in their refusal to let the eight technicians be interrogated, apparently because of fear that an effort would be made to induce them to defect. For five months the technicians languished inside No. 7 Adriaan Goekooplaan, never once emerging onto the street. A twenty-five-man police detachment set up a twenty-four-hour guard, and reporters and television cameramen camped outside. Sightseeing buses brought tourists to gawk, and a number of youths squatted on the street, strumming guitars and singing songs.

Finally, on December 29, the impasse yielded to compromise. Three officials of the Dutch Foreign and Justice ministries, accompanied by an interpreter, were permitted to see the technicians at No. 7. It was a visit of about an hour and a half—far too short for intensive questioning through an interpreter, but long enough to satisfy Dutch propriety.

For its part, the Chinese diplomatic office in The Hague insisted that the Dutch had not been allowed to conduct an "illegal interrogation" and that the initiative for the meeting came from the technicians. It expressed the technicians' "friendly feeling" for the Dutch people—but not the Dutch government—and repeated the earlier accusation that Hsu had been approached by American agents. A

Yugoslav propaganda broadcast said they were CIA men.

The next day the Chinese technicians flew home via Moscow, each of them wearing a lapel pin with a profile impression of Mao.* Before boarding the plane in Amsterdam, they formed a circle and recited one of Mao's teachings: " 'To pick up a rock only to let it drop on your own feet is the way of fools. Reactionaries are certainly that sort of fool.' "

With that they clenched their fists, shouted "Long live Chairman Mao!" and turned their backs on Holland.

Peking's intelligence activities in the United States are limited largely to the massive collection of unclassified material. Peking will buy virtually any book, magazine, newspaper or technical journal it can lay its hands on. It acquires them openly through U.S. publishers and distributors, or indirectly from a variety of sources: ethnic Chinese residing in the United States, New China News Agency offices in Ottawa and Mexico City, friendly Europeans traveling in the United States, and seemingly innocent individuals and mail-order houses in Hong Kong and Europe.

A publisher in Washington, for example, once received a letter bearing the return address "W-8, Berlin, Germany." It was sent from the Communist-controlled Eastern Sector of the city but the writer, a Chinese agent, implied otherwise: "As I live in Berlin and wish to get the newest technical papers of the American Rocket Society, I sincerely hope that you would help and send them to me regularly . . . I shall pay for this, and I believe you will offer me a suitable price."

Over a number of months the writer, using a pseudonym, had succeeded in acquiring a mass of maps, blueprints, scientific documents and other valuable data from business firms, industrial plants, universities, publishing houses and technical societies.

Another Chinese agent, who had adopted an Anglo-Saxon-

---

* Communist China immediately lifted its ban on the departure from Peking of Gerrit J. Jongejans, the Dutch chargé d'affaires. Jongejans had been declared *persona non grata* but had been held as a hostage for the safe departure of the Chinese technicians from The Netherlands.

sounding name, was discovered receiving a heavy volume of printed matter from the United States through the General Delivery window of a post office in a western European city.

The collection of overt intelligence is co-ordinated by the Chinese through Post Office Box 88 in Peking, which serves as the mail drop for Guozi Shudian (International Bookstore) and Waiwen Shudian (Foreign Language Bookstore).*

FBI Director J. Edgar Hoover has declared activity of this sort to be of major concern. In testimony to a House appropriations subcommittee on March 4, 1965, he said, "Communist China represents one of the gravest long-range security threats and the FBI is continuing to devote close attention to coverage of possible Chinese Communist agents and sympathizers in the United States. There is every likelihood that Chinese Communist intelligence activities in this country will increase in the next few years, particularly if Communist China is recognized by the United Nations and is thereby able to establish a diplomatic mission in this country."

In his annual testimony to the subcommittee the following year, on February 10, 1966, Hoover said, "The security problem presented by Red China has assumed larger proportions. Our work load has more than doubled during the past several months. Red China has made concerted efforts to acquire unclassified technical data shipped from this country for their libraries and government agencies. Because of their lack of basic research, it is only logical to assume that they will resort to other means, such as espionage, to obtain information they cannot get publicly."

However, as of the start of 1967, Chinese espionage within the United States did not come near matching Soviet operations, since Communist China had no diplomatic base in America. This was reflected in the fact that as of that date, there had been no arrests by the FBI of any Chinese Communist espionage agents in the United States. Presumably, however, the government worries about a number

---

* These and other outlets also attempt to pour Chinese literature into the United States. Americans who pick up Radio Peking on shortwave and send in the standard acknowledgment cards receive a packet of Chinese propaganda in the return mail.

of the forty-nine ethnic Chinese employed by the United Nations Secretariat. Most of the Chinese were originally accredited to the UN through Nationalist China, but some of them have traveled to the mainland during their biennial home leaves.

The overwhelmingly loyal Chinese-American community * appeared virtually immune to Peking's persuasions, although there have been isolated instances of Communist sympathy. The Petrel Club, a group of young Chinese-Americans in San Francisco, was implicated in Chinese Communist front activity during the 1950's prior to a crackdown by the Immigration and Naturalization Service.

The *China Daily News,* a newspaper founded in New York in 1949, is generally regarded by Chinese-Americans as pro-Peking. In 1955 the paper paid a $25,000 fine and its late editor, Eugene Moy, was given a one-year prison term for violation of the Trading with the Enemy Act. The paper had printed advertisements for Chinese Communist banks that were seeking to induce Chinese in the United States to send money to the mainland.

Such activity, however, is limited and there is no evidence so far that Peking has been able to establish a base of any significance within the Chinese community. Nevertheless, a special training school on Chinese espionage was established by the FBI in 1966, mainly as a hedge against the day when Peking gains recognition in the UN and, with it, diplomatic cover for intelligence operations.

Just as the United States and Europe have proved difficult targets for Chinese espionage, the "third world" has increasingly become an elusive arena too. The excesses of the Cultural Revolution rapidly dried up a natural reservoir of sympathy toward Peking in Africa and South America. Revolutionaries, previously attracted by China's militancy, began to harbor second thoughts. Chided for having closer relations with "imperialist" Britain than "socialist" China, Dr. Hastings Banda, the Prime Minister of Malawi, retorted, "I am less afraid of Queen Elizabeth II than I am of the Kubla Khan in

---

* As of the 1960 census, there were 237,292 ethnic Chinese in the United States, centered mainly in New York, Chicago, Los Angeles and San Francisco.

Peking." Even within the extreme left wing, a previously fertile source of Chinese intelligence agents, disaffection was rampant. In its first issue of 1967 the far-left *African Statesmen* warned that Peking's influence in Africa would evaporate unless it climbed down from its "pinnacle of self-deception to deeply study and understand Africa's problem."

The comment reflected a general failing of Chinese intelligence. The ultimate test of any intelligence system is how well it describes and analyzes the world scene for its national leadership. Peking's conception of the forces at work outside China—particularly in the United States and the Soviet Union—was so warped that it could only reflect a radical failure of the intelligence process. Much of this could be attributed to Mao's dogmatism and his decision to rule by terror. All intelligence systems are susceptible to the temptation of telling their leaders what they want to hear. China's system is the most susceptible of all.

Yet, fanaticism is not without its strengths, and Peking's setbacks in the world may only inspire its espionage establishment to even greater effort and violence. Despite repeated failures of diplomacy and intelligence, there has been no sign that Peking has lost its conviction of ultimate triumph.

"There is a Chinese saying," Mao reminded the Red Guards. " 'Either the East Wind prevails over the West Wind or the West Wind prevails over the East Wind.' I believe it is characteristic of the situation today that the East Wind is prevailing over the West Wind."

In enterprise of martial kind,
When there was any fighting,
He led his regiment from behind—
He found it less exciting.
But when away his regiment ran,
His place was at the fore, O—
That celebrated,
Cultivated,
Underrated
Nobleman,
The Duke of Plaza-Toro!

(*All*)
In the first and foremost flight, ha, ha!
You always found that knight, ha, ha!
That celebrated,
Cultivated,
Underrated
Nobleman,
The Duke of Plaza-Toro!

VI the "illegals"

The Gondoliers, or the King of Barataria, was first presented on December 7, 1889, at the Savoy Theatre in London by Richard D'Oyly Carte. Sir William S. Gilbert and Sir Arthur Sullivan wrote it toward the end of their twenty-year collaboration, and with its gay Venetian setting, it was an immediate success.

In the opera the celebrated Duke of Plaza-Toro, a Spanish grandee, arrives in Venice with his lovely daughter, Casilda, and they become involved with a group of raffish gondoliers. There is a farcical subplot and much baby-switching, but the inevitable aged nursemaid straightens out the mixed identities, and all ends well.

On May 18, 1962, eight hundred persons had gathered in the auditorium of the Mergenthaler Vocational High School in Baltimore to see the Gilbert and Sullivan classic. The performance they watched, at $1.50 per person, was perhaps not as glittering as that which had graced the stage of the Savoy, but for an amateur group, the Comic Opera Company of Baltimore was putting on a creditable show.

The troupe had rehearsed three months for this opening night of a two-night run, and what they lacked in professionalism, they made up for in spirit. Moreover, the costumes were colorful. The Venetian gondoliers wore red-and-white striped sailors' shirts, open at the neck, wide red sashes around their waists, light-blue knee britches, and to top it off, stocking caps with long tassels and pompons.

The last man on the left in the chorus line, like the other gondoliers, engaged in a little light dancing to accompany his song. He was a tenor, a short, stocky and compact man with thinning sandy hair.

It may be that he particularly appreciated the Gilbert and Sullivan plot with its switched identities, since the name he used, leading all the others in alphabetical order on the printed program, was not his own. Indeed, even the audience in Mergenthaler Vocational High School might have enjoyed the light opera more had they realized that the end man in the chorus who was skipping to and fro for their amusement was a Russian spy, a trained professional agent of the GRU, the Soviet military intelligence.

He had been born in Russia forty-three years before, two years after the Revolution, in the Georgian city of Tiflis, and the path that brought him to the footlights of a Baltimore high school stage was as circuitous as the nature of his work.

Robert Keistutis Baltch—that was the name he was using—belonged to that small group of men, the cream of the Soviet espionage elite: the "illegals." He was skilled at his work, as he had to be, for he had been chosen for a hazardous field of duty, the United States. A Soviet spy caught in England faces no more than a prison term; in America the risks are higher. Somewhere along the line in their training, Soviet intelligence agents are undoubtedly required to read Section 794, subdivision (a) of Title 18 of the United States Code, which provides, among other possibilities, that spies "shall be punished by death."

The colorful costume of a gondolier was, therefore, only one of the bizarre and incongruous aspects of Baltch's existence. His assignment in the United States was, at that point, to build up his cover by leading a life of painstaking normalcy. He was to become an ordinary American, a joiner, with a job, hobbies, friends and a wife.

He had managed all of these things. Baltch lived with his wife, Joy Ann, in an apartment at 3515 Greenmount Avenue. She was an intelligent woman in her early thirties, with a strong facial bone structure that made her look attractive, in a plain sort of way. He taught French at the Berlitz School and she was a hairdresser at Pierre's Beauty Salon. Her customers liked the quiet, reserved woman who seemed to have a German accent.

The couple lived frugally, in keeping with their modest combined income, and they had a family membership in Blue Cross. Baltch had earned a "safe driver" award and was a member of the YMCA; since he was a good citizen, he had just paid the Internal Revenue Service an additional $224.07. His wife was a properly licensed cosmetologist in the State of Maryland, and like her husband, she had a social security card.

There was nothing out of the ordinary about them, except that on weekends they would drive to a rented cabin in the woods in Dulaney Valley, north of Baltimore, where Baltch would tune in Radio Moscow on his Hallicrafter shortwave set, listen for his call letters at the precise time and at the exact frequency listed in his radio schedule, and write down coded instructions from the Center.

Except for the fact that they had no children, they were, superficially at least, as typical a couple as might be found anywhere in America. It was the GRU, however, which had arranged that they should meet and marry, and this they had done three years earlier, in New York.

As a study in how Soviet "illegals" operate in the United States, their case is intriguing, if only for the reason that while a great deal has been learned about them, a great deal has not. For example, one of the facts that is not known, outside the "illegal" section of the GRU in Moscow, is precisely how and when they entered this country. But the likelihood, based on past, known cases of Soviet "illegals," is that they came in on forged U.S. passports from either Canada or Mexico. The probability is that they did so late in the year 1958.

Whatever names they used then were probably quickly discarded along with the passports. Early in 1959 they appeared in New York City. He took a sublet at 413 West Forty-eighth Street and she moved into an apartment at 105 Riverside Drive under the name of Joy Ann Garber.

He made his first move to build his cover in March of that year when he appeared at the offices of the Berlitz School as Robert K. Baltch, seeking a job as an instructor. It was the earliest trace of him that has been found in the United States. He claimed that he was an American raised in Canada and France, that since 1952 he and his father had run a real estate business, and that he gave private French lessons on the side. Since the Berlitz School does not normally have reason to suspect that GRU agents might be among its applicants for employment, and since Baltch was fluent in French, he was hired and went to work at the Rockefeller Center branch the following month.

It was perfectly natural in New York for a forty-year-old bachelor with a new job to meet and court a girl, and on April 16 Robert K. Baltch and Joy Ann Garber appeared at the clerk's office in the ornate Municipal Building across the street from City Hall and took out a license to be married. The next step was to find a clergyman or a judge.

As late as half a century ago, the profession of marriage broker was a common one in Europe, and there are enough first- and second-generation Americans in New York so that the tradition of the old country has not entirely died out. One of those who maintained the custom was a dark-haired man with dark eyes named Sam Pauline who had inherited the business from his father. It was prominently advertised in the classified pages of the Manhattan telephone book, and if the ad was not designed to attract the carriage trade, Pauline's service was nevertheless perfectly respectable—and centrally located. There in the Yellow Pages Baltch found what he was looking for:

PAULINE'S MATRIMONIAL BUREAU
Est. 40 Yrs. = Marriage Broker
Sincere, Confidential Service
Single, Widowed, Divorced People
ALL AGES & RELIGIONS
Introduced to Ideal Life Partners
COUPLES WITH OWN LICENSES MARRIED IMMEDIATELY
Opp. Macy's = Room 908
110 West 34 N.Y.C. . . . . . LAkwna 4–0024

Since Baltch had already found his Ideal Life Partner, it was the third line from the bottom that attracted his eye. He called Sam Pauline, who, true to the promise of his advertisement, assured Baltch that he would arrange for a minister to marry the couple on April 20, after the required waiting period. The minister would be Sam's friend the Reverend Glenn Argoe.

On the appointed day, at 11:30 A.M., the two GRU agents arrived holding hands at the marriage broker's office across the street from Macy's. To Sam Pauline they looked like a typical couple: "They were giggly and seemed in love."

Very possibly Baltch and his bride were taken aback when they saw the gray-haired minister, for it was an unforeseen touch straight out of Graham Greene. The Reverend Glenn Argoe was a woman. A motherly, middle-aged lady with glasses, she looked as if she ought to be spooning out potato salad at a Baptist church supper back in Canton, Ohio, her hometown. But somewhere along the line she had left the Midwest for mysticism, and she now presided over the Spiritual Science Mother Church, Inc., an occult house of worship located in a room on the tenth floor of the ancient Carnegie Hall Studios building at Fifty-sixth Street and Seventh Avenue. On Wednesday nights it offered "New Age Light Teachings by Cosmic Masters," and the Reverend Glenn Argoe lived in a world of x-ray vision, flying saucers, ESP and automatic writing. Down the hall on the same floor was an actor's workshop, and it was not always possible to tell whether some of the people who entered the portals of the Mother

Church had been sent to practice the Method or were actually seeking spiritual guidance. But the Reverend Glenn Argoe was a kindly, gentle woman, and she offered genuine comfort to those bereft souls who sought her out.

To marry the young couple standing before her in Sam Pauline's office, she performed what she liked to call her "occult mystical service."

"Dearly beloved," she began, "we are gathered here in the sight of God and an invisible host of witnesses, to join this man and woman together in the bonds of holy matrimony, signifying to us the mystical union of man with his Creator . . . love is a sacred fire which must not be burned to idols . . . Robert, wilt thou have this woman to be thy wedded wife? Joy Ann, wilt thou have this man . . . ?"

The two Soviet spies gave their assent. Then, joined by Sam Pauline and the two building employees he had pulled in from the hall as witnesses, they bowed their heads as the minister concluded:

"Let us pray. Dear Father, bless these two children, hold them in thy love, direct them in thy light, fill them with thy love, and for this descending, answer to our prayer. We thank thee. Amen, amen, amen."

Hand in hand, Mr. and Mrs. Robert K. Baltch left the office. As they walked out into Thirty-fourth Street to be swallowed up by the crowds of shoppers in Herald Square, they had every reason to be happy. They had safely entered the United States and completed the first phase of their assignment in espionage.

They were not, however, the only GRU "illegal" agents in Manhattan in April 1959. In the same month a short man of about fifty, with a thick, difficult-to-place European accent moved into a ground-floor apartment on West Eighty-fourth Street, just off Central Park. He wore steel-rimmed glasses, which gave him a cold appearance, and he kept very much to himself. His name was Kaarlo Rudolph Tuomi. There we must leave him for now.

The Glavnoye Razvedyvatelnoye Upravlenie sends "illegals" to this country in "singles" or "doubles" (in the parlance of U.S. counterintelligence agents in charge of finding them). "Doubles" are a male and female who live together as man and wife. It solves the problem of sex, since it is safer than if either were to seek a partner elsewhere.

Although much about Soviet "illegals" remains shadowy and uncertain, there is some evidence that the women agents may be instructed to seek jobs as beauticians, manicurists or domestics, or similar positions where a foreign accent and lack of a previous employment record will not prove a great obstacle. To some extent this could narrow the fields in which the FBI might seek them out.

Shortly after the wedding, Joy Ann Baltch enrolled in the Banford Academy of Beauty Culture, Inc., an educational institution at 165 West Forty-sixth Street, off Times Square. She was graduated with honors on March 18, 1960, and on April 16 * she applied to the Division of Licenses of the State of New York for a permit to practice hairdressing. She put down her date of birth as "May 16 1930 Springfield Mass.," as she had in taking out the marriage license the year before. By that time she and her husband had moved, and she listed her address as "450 139th St." This was not entirely correct, since they were living at 450 East 139th Street in the Mott Haven section of the Bronx.

During the spring or early summer of that national election year the Baltches must have moved from New York, for in July, the month that John F. Kennedy was nominated for President in Los Angeles, Mrs. Baltch wrote to the New York State license division in Albany and asked that the notice of her examination as a beautician and cosmetologist be forwarded to 2100 Mount Royal Terrace in Baltimore. She was forced to leave this trail marker behind because she had not yet been called for her exam at the time she left New York with her husband.

---

* Curiously, this was precisely a year to the day after the couple had taken out their marriage license at the Municipal Building. It suggests that her instructions from the GRU were to wait a year before she applied for her hairdresser's license and that these instructions were followed literally.

In late September she was summoned back to New York, and took her written state exam at the City Center; a few days later, on October 3, she was back to take the second half, the practical exam. She passed both—she had completed a thousand hours of training at Banford—and her license was issued later in October.

During this period, several "legal" members of the spy ring of which the Baltches were a part began arriving in New York. On August 16 Alexei Ivanovich Galkin, forty-two-year-old agent of the GRU, arrived in Manhattan to take up his cover duties as first secretary of the Byelorussian Mission to the United Nations. He and his wife, Nadezhda Sergeevna, knew New York, for he had been stationed there from 1951 to 1956 as an employee of the UN Secretariat.

On October 10, a week after Joy Ann Baltch passed her exam, a dark-haired Soviet diplomat arrived in New York to be a personnel officer at the UN. Ivan Dmitrievich Egorov, a graduate of Leningrad State University, was at thirty-nine a highly placed officer of the GRU who had operated previously in Ottawa and New Delhi. With the help of his wife, Alexandra Ivanovna, who later followed him to New York, Egorov was the Baltches' "illegal support officer" in the United States. Without ever meeting them directly, it was his task to provide them with such assistance as they might need to operate in America. It was a symbiotic relationship, much like that of the pilot fish to the shark.

The Egorovs and Galkin were joined a year later by Petr Egorovich Maslennikov, a third Russian diplomat who was part of the GRU net in the United States. His cover job was that of first secretary of the Soviet Mission to the UN.

In the meantime the Baltches had settled into Baltimore. She went to work in the beauty salon at Thirty-third and Charles streets, and he, after his job in New York, had no difficulty in becoming an instructor at the Berlitz School in Baltimore.

Baltch told a number of acquaintances that he was writing a book about a new method of teaching French which he claimed to have devised. The text was illustrated by a series of photographs showing the proper position of the lips for pronouncing the words phonetically. Joy Ann had posed for some of these pictures, but so had others, including an obliging lady professor of French at Goucher College. She was a customer of Joy Ann's and had met Baltch through her.

By the spring of 1961, within a year of moving to Baltimore, the Baltches were well established in their new surroundings, with a carefully developed background in New York that would check out should anyone bother to look into it.

One day in mid-May of that spring, the telephone rang in a suburban house at 107 Hillyer Street in East Orange, New Jersey. The couple who lived there rented out a room for extra income, and since they had placed an ad in the Newark *News,* they were expecting some calls. The lady of the house answered, and from the sound of the coins dropping in the pay phone, she assumed that the man responding to her advertisement was probably calling from New York, across the river.

He was well-spoken, although he had a thick foreign accent. He said he found the city "too crowded" and too busy, and he wanted to get out into the suburbs. East Orange is in Essex County, and although it is part of the urban sprawl of metropolitan New York, it does have some grass and trees, and the caller's desire to move there to get out of the city seemed natural enough.

The new roomer moved in immediately, on May 15, and proved to be a perfect gentleman. He worked in a shipyard on the New York waterfront—at least that's what he said—and he left every morning on an early commuter train for the city.

He kept to himself, and did his own cooking. He had a stamp collection, he seemed to be interested in baseball and he was seldom without his camera. He took his clothes to the neighborhood Laundromat and he would hang them out to dry in the backyard at Hillyer Street. Sometimes when he was hanging out the wash he chatted with his landlady about life or the weather. But he revealed little of himself. He was five foot five, with dark-brown hair, and he wore steel-rimmed glasses. He had told his landlady his name was Kaarlo Tuomi, and he was listed that way in the Essex County telephone book for 1962.

Kaarlo Rudolph Tuomi remains a mysterious figure in the shadowland of espionage, for where he walked, he left only the lightest of footprints. As in Reino Hayhanen's and Gordon Lonsdale's backgrounds, there are traces of Finland in Tuomi's; he may well have been born in the United States and taken back to Finland at an early age. In any event, the man calling himself Kaarlo Tuomi was a trained Soviet agent; his assignments in America had been planned directly with Galkin, Maslennikov and other officials of the GRU in a hotel room on Lenin Street in the city of Kirov and at the GRU school on Dorogomilovskaya Bolshaya Street in Moscow.

His was something of an espionage odyssey, for over the years his work had taken him to France, Belgium, Finland and Denmark, to Montreal and Vancouver, Canada, and now to the United States, where he had ranged as far west as Milwaukee and Chicago, Minnesota and Michigan, collecting defense secrets for the GRU.

Unlike the Baltches, who were still engaged in building up their protective cover in ever-thicker layers, Tuomi was actively collecting information. When he took the commuter train into New York from East Orange each day, he would indeed go to work "in the shipyards." But this phase of his work consisted of frequenting bars and restaurants and talking with servicemen near the Brooklyn Navy Yard, the Brooklyn Army Terminal, the submarine base in New London and the naval shipyard at Groton, Connecticut. He passed on his information to Maslennikov, Galkin, Egorov and three other "legal" GRU agents by means of a series of "dead drops" located at a stone wall in Yonkers, just over the New York City line, and in other hideaways in the Bronx and Queens. For its drop points, the GRU generally favored railroad overpasses and elevated subway lines in deserted areas.

Tuomi had moved from Manhattan to Jackson Heights and finally to East Orange. Somewhere along the line the FBI had picked up his traces and turned him into a double agent—the most danger-ous game in the world. If the GRU had discovered this, it would surely have killed him, if not while he was hanging out his wash in East Orange, certainly at one of the lonely drop points in the Bronx or Queens.

To guard against the possibility that an agent will be "turned" by the counterintelligence forces of the target country in which he is working, the GRU seldom permits one "illegal" to know the identities of other "illegals" in the same *apparat*. There is no reason, therefore, to assume that Tuomi knew the cover names, identities or where-abouts of the Baltches. But through Tuomi the FBI had penetrated the Soviet ring, and the Baltches were already in grave danger.

They did not know it, and continued to live their prosaic life in Baltimore. Baltch mentioned to a friend at Berlitz that he was inter-ested in studying voice. Early in 1962 the friend introduced Baltch to Alan L. Jemison, a twenty-four-year-old church organist. Baltch made an excellent impression on Jemison, the more so because he gave him $25 in advance for the voice lessons. It seemed at the time an enormous sum to the young musician, who was supporting a wife and three children.

Jemison found his new pupil quick to grasp the essentials, but very tense. "Look, you've got to relax," he told him. Sometimes Jemison would even take Baltch by the shoulders and shake him a bit in an effort to loosen him up, but to no avail. After they had got to know each other, Baltch asked him one day, "How could I break into TV?" Jemison said he had no contacts in that field and discouraged his pupil from pursuing a television career.

To Jemison, Baltch had a "noticeable accent" and was clearly a foreigner. Baltch explained that by saying he was a French Canadian. Jemison also thought there was a certain "foxiness" in his manner, which was a recurrent note in the reactions of those who came to know him.

Jemison was musical director of the Comic Opera Company of Baltimore and it struck him that this happy-go-lucky organization of friendly, beer-drinking amateurs might help his tense pupil to relax. And so, in April, Baltch became a card-carrying member of the light-opera troupe. After the performance of *The Gondoliers* he demonstrated a folk dance at the cast party (he said it was French-Canadian). But then Baltch dropped out of the opera company and Jemison's orbit.

During this period, probably as part of a GRU safety procedure, the Baltches were constantly changing residences in Baltimore. Since they arrived they had already moved once, to Parkwyrth Avenue, and in March 1962 they moved to Greenmount Avenue. They only stayed there until July, when they moved again, to 9423 Ridgely Avenue. At the same time they gave up their cabin in the valley, and Baltch applied—unsuccessfully—for extra work as a French translator at the Martin Company, a defense plant in Baltimore.

In the fall of 1962 events began to move rapidly on a broad front. On September 23 Tuomi met with Galkin and Maslennikov at the Greystone Railroad Station in Yonkers. In Moscow the following month the KGB closed in on Oleg Penkovsky, the GRU colonel secretly spying for the West. The GRU then began recalling agents from all over the world whose position they feared might have been endangered by Penkovsky. But no alarum went out to the Baltches; their cover was considered secure. Instead of being summoned home, they received orders to proceed to what was their ultimate target in the United States. On November 6 they obeyed these orders. With their worldly possessions packed in suitcases and boxes piled in the back of their 1953 Studebaker, the Baltches drove south—to Washington.

It is peculiar that the GRU chose the name of Joy Ann Garber for the agent who materialized in New York in 1958–59. And the use of that name must have puzzled the FBI a great deal when the Baltches were finally discovered some four years later. For on the face of it, the choice of that name appeared to be a slip on the part of the GRU.

Spies are seldom arrested when first uncovered, in the hope that if they are watched, other spies will be found. In the case of the Baltches it was of utmost importance to find out as well who they really were. To do this the FBI organized dozens, perhaps even hundreds of agents to try to solve what must have been one of the most intriguing puzzles in the annals of espionage. The search was carried on in several cities and states and, ultimately, in several countries.

In the twentieth century, in the democracies as well as in police states, the individual is in the clutches of the bureaucracy from birth to death. As he progresses he leaves behind him a sea of paper along the way, most of it meaningless. Much of espionage and counterespionage consists of the dull and often unrewarding task of wading through records, studying them to discover some significance. In the case at hand, there were by now two documents of interest on file in New York: a hairdresser license application, in which "Joy A. Baltch" had given her birth date as "May 16 1930 Springfield Mass." and a marriage license in which "Joy Ann Garber" had given the same information.

In checking their name card files, the FBI agents found the name Joy Ann Garber already listed, albeit innocently. It was there because a man named Ossip Garber, convicted in 1939 of conspiracy to violate United States passport laws, had a daughter, Joy Ann, aged eight at the time.

Ossip Garber was born in Russia in 1889. He came to America in 1906, married a girl named Sonia Marder nine years later and was naturalized in 1923. By profession he was a photographer and lived in Springfield, Massachusetts. It was there that a daughter, Joy Ann, was born, on May 16, 1930. Three years later the family moved to New York City.

In November 1937 a couple named Mr. and Mrs. Adolph Arnold Rubens, traveling from New York on forged U.S. passports as "the Donald L. Robinsons," arrived in Moscow—and disappeared. What happened to them was never satisfactorily explained, nor was Rubens' true identity disclosed. But it was established that the couple and several other Americans had managed to obtain forged U.S.

passports of good quality. And in the subsequent investigation of the Rubens-Robinson case, Ossip Garber, then a photographer in the Bronx, was arrested. In March 1939 an indictment handed down by a federal grand jury alleged that before "Robinson" had sailed away to the Soviet Union, he had appeared twice in Garber's photo studio.

In all, nine persons were indicted as members of the passport-forging ring. Garber was convicted on May 2, 1939, and sentenced to two years. Federal investigators said that the passports had been used by Communist agents to travel abroad. At the trial the U.S. attorney had not mentioned the Soviet Union, but he contended that the passports had been used by "agents of a foreign state engaged in espionage activities . . . in this country." He had charged that the defendants acted not for money but "because of their sympathies with the political aims of the foreign state."

Ossip Garber served part of his sentence, was released in 1940 and died in 1951. What had happened to his little girl? Joy Ann Garber had gone to Hunter College, and on December 28, 1950, married Robert Seskin, an Air Force veteran and graduate of the City College of New York who was an engineer for a Bronx corporation. They moved to Norwalk, Connecticut, where Mrs. Seskin became a teacher in the Norwalk public school system. She was granted maternity leave and left her job after giving birth to a daughter, Ora, in 1956.

The Seskins were living at 6 Wayfaring Road in Norwalk when the FBI located them. It hardly seemed likely that the suburban mother, schoolteacher and housewife could be leading a double life in another city as Joy Ann Garber, hairdresser and GRU agent, but for the moment the FBI did not want to approach Mrs. Seskin to ask.

The Joy Ann Garber whom the Reverend Glenn Argoe had joined in wedlock with Robert K. Baltch, had, in taking out her marriage certificate, listed her father's name as Ossip and her mother's as Sonia. She had also presented what proved to be a copy of the real birth certificate of the housewife living in Norwalk. So there was clearly either one woman leading two lives or two women claiming to be the same person.

The pattern proved similar for Baltch. The FBI located a second Robert Keistutis Baltch, whose occupation seemed as far removed from espionage as that of Mrs. Seskin. He was a Roman Catholic priest, the assistant pastor of St. Casimir's Church in Amsterdam, New York, a Mohawk Valley industrial town that manufactures carpets, linseed oil and brooms.

In taking out his marriage license in 1959 Robert K. Baltch, Berlitz instructor, had listed his birthdate as February 17, 1924, Dormont, Pennsylvania, which is where the priest was born on that date. Both the priest's father, Anthony, and his mother, Julia, were born in Lithuania. His father came to America in 1900 and his mother in 1913, and both became naturalized citizens. But in 1933 they returned to the old country, taking their young son with them. The boy attended high school and a seminary in Lithuania. The war came; the Baltches tried to get out but could not because the Soviet Union had gobbled up Lithuania and the other Baltic states in 1940. After the war the Baltch family—the parents, Robert and his sister—went to the American embassy in Moscow and obtained U.S. passports. But the Lithuanian government held their passports for five months before granting exit visas. Finally, in March 1947, the family was able to fly to Berlin. They sailed for America from Bremen, and at age twenty-three, Robert K. Baltch was repatriated to his native land. He continued his studies and became an ordained priest; his sister, Aldona, became a doctor.

Aside from the obvious fact that Roman Catholic priests are not permitted to marry, there were other major discrepancies between the two Robert K. Baltches. The priest was six feet tall, brown-haired and slender. The other Baltch was five foot seven and sandy-haired. The priest had recently applied for a passport, and his picture on the application did not match the surveillance photographs the FBI had taken of his namesake.

Similarly, a Hunter College yearbook photo of Joy Ann Garber, the Norwalk housewife, did not match the picture attached to the application for the hairdresser license in New York State. The hairdresser form had been filled out by hand. A sample of Mrs. Seskin's handwriting, obtained from public records, was compared with it. The two did not match.

The only possible conclusion was that two Soviet agents, posing as Mr. and Mrs. Robert K. Baltch, had stolen the identities of two Americans, the Connecticut housewife and the Catholic priest in Amsterdam.

Why had the GRU picked these identities? Possibly a GRU case officer in Moscow, checking through case files for likely cover identities, noticed that Ossip Garber, the photographer convicted of passport conspiracy in the Rubens-Robinson affair, had a daughter, Joy Ann, who would be about the right age for the woman agent they had in mind to send to America in 1958. The risks involved in choosing the identity of Ossip's daughter, the GRU may have reasoned, would be outweighed by the convenience of it all. A good deal was already known about Ossip Garber's background, much of it having come out publicly during his arrest and trial.

The Russians had an even better opportunity to learn whatever it needed to know about the real Baltch family. Not only had they lived in Lithuania, but the Soviets had been in a position to abstract the data on Robert K. Baltch while the Lithuanian government was holding his passport. In both cases, the ease of acquiring cover information must have seemed worth the infinitesimal risk that in a country of 190,000,000 persons the two GRU agents would encounter their namesakes.

The FBI did not at that time approach Mrs. Seskin or the priest, on the chance that in some unforeseen fashion this might tip off the GRU Baltches. As it turned out, Mrs. Seskin and Father Baltch were completely unaware that Soviet intelligence had stolen their identities.

In Washington the Baltches moved into the Woodbine apartments at 2839 Twenty-seventh Street, a Northwest residential area close to the Sheraton Park Hotel, near Cathedral and Connecticut avenues. Baltch was hired by George Washington University to teach evening classes in French. At the same time he enrolled as a student in a once-a-week course in intermediate German at Georgetown University. Mrs. Baltch answered a newspaper ad and obtained work at Ann Dalton Hair Designs in Cleveland House, only four blocks from their apartment.

She proved a discreet employee, never volunteering information nor asking questions. However, she told one inquiring customer that both her parents were killed in the war in Germany, and another that her mother alone was killed in an air raid. She also talked of having been born in the United States but educated in Hamburg.

The Baltches led a quiet domestic life and made few friends, none close. They went to the movies and joined the local library. Baltch took out a District of Columbia driver's license; he also bought a pair of contact lenses.

One of Baltch's pupils in the beginning French classes at George Washington was Dr. George Cornelius Ruhle, a sixty-three-year-old international specialist for the Interior Department's National Park Service. He noted that the instructor did not write his name on the blackboard the first day, as was customary, and it was a long time before Dr. Ruhle got to know his name. Most of the students simply called him "Professor."

Dr. Ruhle belonged to the Cosmos Club, and he invited Baltch to join him there for lunch one day. Ruhle, who had traveled extensively in his work, suddenly said to his luncheon partner, "You don't strike me as French. What nationality are you?" Baltch, totally at ease, replied that he was born in Switzerland but had lived "all my life in the United States." The question might have secretly disturbed Baltch, but he must have enjoyed being a spy and dining with a government official at an exclusive social club in the capital.

In his other role as a student of German at Georgetown, Baltch could not help getting to know some of his classmates—there were only four people in the Saturday morning class taught by Professor Kurt Jankowsky.

The others were Cornelia Maria Fehner, a bibliographer for the United States Information Agency and a former State Department librarian in Warsaw and The Hague; Sister Marie Blanche, a nun who was studying physics; and Nancy Jane Dixon, a pretty, vivacious New England girl who worked for the National Science Foundation. Miss Dixon had become interested in German while on a trip to Switzerland in the summer of 1962, and in the fall she had enrolled in the course at Georgetown. She became quite friendly with Baltch, and they would chat during coffee breaks in the three-hour class.

On one occasion Professor Jankowsky asked the students to submit papers describing their jobs; Miss Dixon chose to attack the grayness of government work. After class Baltch asked her just what sort of work she did. "Research analyst," she replied.

"What's that?" Baltch asked. Miss Dixon said it had to do with the retraining of high school mathematics teachers, a subject in which Baltch evidenced no further interest. From time to time Baltch would question her as to how to get tickets to the Arena Stage or how to do other things that, Miss Dixon realized later, most people could manage without asking. But Baltch said he was a professor and this personality quirk did not seem out of character at the time.

Twice during the school year the class got together socially. Before the first party at Jankowsky's apartment in Arlington late in 1962, Baltch expressed great hesitation about bringing his wife, describing her as timid and shy. But the other students insisted and so he brought Joy Ann, together with the flowers that he had been delegated to find for the party. Nancy Jane Dixon was puzzled at Baltch's advance description of his wife. She found Mrs. Baltch to be good-looking; far from shy, she chattered on about meats and roasts and other domestic subjects. Jankowsky played Indian music and became embroiled in a long literary discussion in which Baltch made it clear he did not like modern poetry.

The second party, toward the end of the spring term, was held at Miss Fehner's apartment in Washington. The guests were almost the same, except that a Catholic priest, Father Joseph Stubenbort, came instead of the nun, whom he had replaced in the class. It was a relaxed Sunday evening, and the wine and conversation were good. During the party Baltch presented his hostess with a lovely book of color photographs of Germany. It was passed around the room, ending up open on Mrs. Baltch's lap. Nancy Jane Dixon, to whom Mrs. Baltch seemed distinctly German, looked up just then to notice "tears rolling down her face." They lasted only a moment but made a deep impression on Miss Dixon, who thought, "Oh gosh, she must be homesick."

After the party Miss Dixon offered the guests a ride home. Mrs. Baltch seemed nervous about it and declined, but her husband insisted, and the couple argued about it as they went downstairs to the street. Miss Dixon's 1959 two-door green Opel still had Connecticut plates, for she had not yet gotten around to changing them for District of Columbia tags. As they came near the car Mrs. Baltch said to her husband, "Bob—let's not." She may have feared that by driving them home, Miss Dixon would learn where they lived, or it may have been the sight of the Connecticut plates. It was a coincidence that before coming to Washington, Miss Dixon had taught in the public school system of Norwalk, Connecticut, at the same time as the real Joy Ann Garber. From 1955 to 1958 Miss Dixon had been a teacher at Nathan Hale Junior High School, which, as all of its children knew, had been named for a spy. (Miss Dixon does not recall ever meeting Joy Ann Garber Seskin, and does not remember having mentioned her life in Norwalk to Joy Ann Garber Baltch, although she may have.)

The Baltches finally joined Miss Dixon and the priest in the car. It was an odd foursome that drove through Northwest Washington that evening: two GRU agents; a teacher from Norwalk, like the real Joy Ann Garber; and a Catholic priest, like the real Robert Baltch.

On Rock Creek Parkway, Miss Dixon took several wrong turns. In retrospect she wondered what would have happened if she had been arrested while driving, after several glasses of wine, with the wrong license plates and a carload of Russian spies.

Throughout this period Baltch, the Georgetown German scholar and part-time French professor, remained in touch with the Center.

As in Baltimore, he did so by shortwave radio. He had strung a wire in the hall outside his apartment in the Woodbine, and the aerial was attached to his Hallicrafter. Twice a month, according to a precise schedule, Baltch would listen for his call sign—usually 859, although occasionally it was 327 or 642. On January 9 and 27 his code came crackling over the shortwave band on 13120 kilocycles at 8:30 A.M. Washington time. The days of the month and sometimes the wavelengths varied in subsequent months—in February, for example, he listened on the eleventh and twenty-sixth—but the pattern remained basically the same.

On Sunday, April 28, 1963, Baltch made the first of three important trips that clearly linked him to the GRU network in New York. Accompanied by his wife, Baltch took a morning train to New York. They then traveled by subway to Queens and walked a short way to the Long Island Rail Road bridge on Woodside Avenue between Thirty-seventh and Thirty-eighth avenues. Together they walked under the bridge, left and returned, both times spending about five minutes looking it over.

On Saturday, May 25, Baltch alone took the afternoon train to New York. The FBI had the Long Island Rail Road bridge under surveillance. At 8:10 P.M. Ivan Egorov, who was known to be a GRU officer at the UN, and his wife, Alexandra, walked under the bridge. He attached a magnetic container to a steel girder, left and returned two hours later. Finding the container undisturbed, Egorov removed it. As he and his wife departed, Baltch came down the street from the opposite direction. He had just missed the connection. When he found nothing under the bridge, he wandered around for a time in the neighborhood, returned and then came back again at 6:30 the next morning. Finally he gave up and returned to Washington.

On June 6 Tuomi left a magnetic container at another GRU "dead drop" in Queens, on Astoria Boulevard. Inside was information on rocket-launching sites in the United States, obtained at the request of his superiors, but presumably first screened by the FBI. Later the same day Egorov picked up the container. Nine days afterward Baltch took his third trip to New York. Wearing a green

Tyrolean hat and a dark raincoat, he left the Woodbine in Washington, boarded the afternoon train and at 7:40 P.M. showed up near the railroad bridge in Woodside. An hour later the Egorovs strolled under the bridge, left a package and walked off. Shortly thereafter Baltch, removing the package, cleared the drop. He took a piece of chalk from his pocket, ground it into the pavement and left.

At 11 P.M. the Egorovs returned in a Chevrolet and stopped beneath the bridge. Mrs. Egorov got out and leaned over the girder, her chest heaving as if she was sick. Her husband took her by the shoulders as though to console her, checked the drop and saw that the container was gone. They got back in the car and left.

Soon after this last trip to New York, the Baltches showed signs of getting ready to leave Washington. They sold the Studebaker, collected empty boxes from neighborhood stores and started packing. The FBI decided to step in.

On the evening of July 2 Baltch answered the knock on the door of his apartment. He and his wife offered no resistance to their arrest or the search of their apartment. They claimed they were packing to go on vacation in New England.

But inside a false-bottomed nightstand there was evidence that they were probably planning to travel farther than that. The nightstand contained three envelopes. The first two held fifty $20 bills each, for a total of $2,000, and the third two beautifully forged U.S. passports. Another $2,160 was found inside an overshoe in a closet, and $164 more in a plastic pouch.

Hidden with the envelopes was a red silk bag with gold drawstrings containing a gold-metal compact wrapped in paper. Written on the wrapping paper was Baltch's radio schedule, giving the dates and hours when he listened to Moscow (in Greenwich Mean Time), his call numbers and assigned kilocycles. Baltch explained away the Hallicrafter shortwave set by saying he liked to listen to European broadcasts.

The compact itself contained a cellulose one-time pad of the type used by Soviet intelligence the world over.* As was standard, half the

---

* These are always small. Baltch's pad was 1¼ by 1½ inches and ⅝ inch thick.

pages had five-digit groups printed in red, the other half were in black.

A linen closet in the apartment contained extensive photographic equipment, including an enlarger and the inevitable Exakta camera. The FBI also found developers for invisible ink, packaged to resemble aspirin and milk of magnesia tablets, and several address books, one of them with scribbled, cryptic references to addresses in France.

The Egorovs were arrested in their apartment at 144–15 Forty-first Avenue in Flushing, Queens. Both claimed to have diplomatic passports, which they did not. Mrs. Egorov, short and tough-looking, wrapped her arms around the leg of a heavy upholstered chair and refused to leave. She had to be pried loose and carried out by the FBI men.

Attorney General Robert F. Kennedy and FBI Director J. Edgar Hoover, in announcing the arrests, said the four had conspired to transmit to the Soviet Union information relating to "United States rocket-launching sites . . . military and Navy installations, troop movements, shipping and military waterfront facilities."

Alan Jemison, the young musician who had been Baltch's voice coach, learned of the arrest that night. "I came home dead tired, turned on the eleven P.M. news—and for Chrissakes they were hauling him away!" Jemison had mixed emotions when he realized his friend was a spy, and he "turned cold inside" when the thought occurred that Baltch might be executed. Jemison stared at the set, thinking over his relationship with Baltch, and it was then that something struck him: "I finally realized why he was so tense."

Other acquaintances heard the news in different ways. Nancy Jane Dixon was riding to work on a bus when she caught sight of a headline in the Washington *Post* that the person next to her was reading. The people in the picture looked familiar. "May I see that?" she asked.

The Baltches were moved to New York, held without bail, and on July 15 indicted with the Egorovs by a federal grand jury in

Brooklyn. Since it is always difficult to prove that a substantive act of spying has taken place, the Department of Justice often prefers to bring charges of *conspiracy* to violate the espionage statutes. The Baltches and Egorovs were so charged. The penalty can be the same as for a substantive violation: imprisonment or death. Galkin and Maslennikov were named as co-conspirators in the case, but not as defendants, for they had left the United States early in May, and in any event they had diplomatic immunity.

A conspiracy has been likened to the links in a chain, since each member does not have to commit the same offense in order to be joined in guilt to the others. In this case the links were these: in September 1962 Tuomi had met with Maslennikov and Galkin at the Greystone Station in Yonkers; on June 6 the next year Tuomi had left information in a magnetic container for Egorov; Egorov in turn had left a package for Baltch on June 15, and with it Baltch had rejoined his wife in Washington.

The probability is that what Baltch finally plucked from under the bridge in Woodside was the cash and the two forged passports and that these would have been used by the Baltches to leave the country. A great deal of time and money had been spent on getting them in position in Washington and only the GRU can say why they were recalled. It is possible that some minute evidence of surveillance or of danger had alarmed one member or another of the ring.

At any rate, the passports were fascinating. They had pictures of the Baltches, but were made out in the names of James Oliver Jackson and his supposed wife Bertha Rosalie Jackson, with a Silver Spring, Maryland, address. The passports were completely fabricated, for the Soviet craftsman who made them had not started with real American passport blanks. A great deal of care had been exercised not only in the details of their manufacture but in the selection of the names that they bore.

Both passports were dated May 23, 1961, and their numbers were in sequence. The one with Baltch's picture and the name James Oliver Jackson was B388384. It turned out that an American named James Oliver Jackson had been issued a passport with that number on that date.

The real James Oliver Jackson was a six-foot, blond forty-three-year-old track coach of 2018 Cedar Crest Drive in Abilene, Texas. He went to Australia for the 1956 Olympics and in May 1961 applied for a new passport in order to coach a U.S. track-and-field team at international meets in the Soviet Union, Poland, Germany and England. He traveled for six weeks that summer, and somewhere along the line the GRU must have seen or photographed his passport.

At GRU headquarters in Moscow someone with a very sharp eye for detail must also have noticed another document that came across his desk, giving the passport data of a Lutherville, Maryland, advertising man who lived just north of Baltimore and not far from the weekend cabin which the Baltches had rented. His name was Harry Lee Jackson, and his passport had also been issued in May 1961.

As it happened, the applications of the track coach in Abilene and the advertising man in Maryland were processed in the State Department passport division on the same day, and because they were probably handled in roughly alphabetical order, as would be normal, Harry Lee Jackson's passport was stamped B388385, the next number in sequence after the one issued to the track coach.

Harry Lee Jackson visited western Europe in July 1961 and presumably that is where Russian intelligence got a look at his passport. The alert official at GRU headquarters on the Arbatskaya Ploshchad must have seen that two passports were issued in sequence on the same day to persons named Jackson, in widely separate parts of the country. By altering the Harry Lee Jackson passport data, the Russians produced one in the name of Bertha Rosalie Jackson, and this was dispatched to Joy Ann Garber Baltch in Washington, 4,900 miles away, via a railroad bridge in Queens.

The next problem for the government, and a complex one, was to try to establish the true identities of the man and woman arrested in Washington. The Baltches' apartment had yielded up a box of pills from a Paris druggist, at 20 Rue d'Aumale, which is a small street on the Right Bank, near the Gare St. Lazare. Baltch was fluent in French and there was the address book, found in the apartment, with fragments of French addresses. Why Baltch took it to America with him, in violation of every rule of espionage, can only be attributed to the fact that spies, being human, err.

One of the entries was a girl's first name, listed this way: "Laurette, 98 Rue Jean . . . [illegible word] Villejuif."

At the request of the FBI, the Direction de la Surveillance du Territoire * undertook the search for Laurette. The French police were able to establish that from 1941 to 1951 a young French girl named Alice Laure Eikenberry had lived at 98 Rue Jean Jaurès in Villejuif, a suburb at the southern edge of Paris. She was known to her friends by her nickname Laurette. Mlle. Eikenberry had long since moved from Villejuif. She was located, however, at 32 Avenue de Grigny in Morsang-sur-Orge, a village in the Seine-et-Oise department south of Paris. She was married, and her name was now Alice Laure Ventis.

When the DST showed her a photograph of Baltch she said immediately, "Why, that's Alexandre Sokolov." They had met at a dance in Paris in 1946 when she was seventeen, and she remembered him very well. He was a pleasant young man, and he had told her that he was a professor of English.

With Laurette's identification, the DST located a rather full dossier on Alexandre Sokolov in their files, for he had come to their attention as a French citizen of pro-Soviet leanings. Alexandre Sokolov was born in Tiflis on February 26, 1919, son of Vincent and Nadine Orlova Sokolov. His father came from Vladivostok and his mother was born in Nizhni Novgorod † on the Volga. Soon after Alexandre's birth the family left Russia and made its way to Turkey, where a second son, Igor, was born in Constantinople in August 1920. By 1922 the Sokolovs had moved to France, where they were blessed with two more children: Michel, born on December 2, 1923, and finally a girl, Marie, born two years later. Like his father, Alexan-

---

* The DST is responsible for internal security and corresponds to the FBI. It should not be confused with the Service de Documentation Extérieure et de Contre-espionnage, the SDECE, which parallels the CIA.

† The city was renamed Gorki in 1932, for the writer, who was born there.

dre became a naturalized French citizen. He was raised in France, studied at the lycée and at the Sorbonne, where he earned certificates in psychology and in the English and French languages and literature. He lived in the Paris suburb of Courbevoie, and as he had correctly informed Laurette, he had received his license to teach English.

He had other, political interests. He joined the youth section of the Union of Soviet Citizens, registered as a member of the Communist party and was active in pro-Russian circles in Paris. He served in the French army during World War II, but in 1947, the year after he had met Laurette and scribbled her name in his address book, he asked to renounce his French citizenship. He was permitted to do so and obtained a Soviet passport. Two years later he left France, ostensibly on his way to the Soviet Union via East Germany. In fact, as the trail was later retraced, he had gone to Potsdam, East Germany, where he was employed by the Soviet army until 1953. When he returned to Russia that year, he took with him an East German wife, probably the woman who appeared in New York five years later as Joy Ann Garber and whom he married, for the second time, in Sam Pauline's office. This is thought to be the case, for the woman arrested in Washington as Joy Ann Baltch did seem to have a German background, but neither the FBI, nor the DST, nor the West Germans were able to establish her true identity.

Around the time Alexandre Sokolov left France, the rest of the family had also returned to the Soviet Union, with the exception of Michel. At the age of ten, two years after his father died in 1931, Michel had been sent to live with a lady in England. He grew up there, served in the British navy during the war, became a naturalized citizen, and in 1952 married a girl named Sheila Grant. He added her last name to his, and by 1963 he was a prosperous farmer living as Michel Sokolov-Grant. The British authorities tracked him down and interviewed him, and more details of the Sokolov family's background were sketched in.

All of this took time, and in the meanwhile the machinery of the United States federal courts had, slowly, begun to move. When the four GRU agents were arrested, the Soviet government had protested on behalf of the Egorovs, but said nothing at all about the Baltches. In Washington, Soviet chargé d'affaires Georgi M. Kornienko called at the State Department, claiming that the Egorovs had diplomatic status and had been arrested illegally, but the State Department rejected the protest.

On July 22 the Baltches and the Egorovs pleaded not guilty in federal court in Brooklyn. The Egorovs seemed to have funds to retain counsel, but the Baltches said they did not, and Judge Jacob Mishler appointed Edward Brodsky, a young former assistant U.S. attorney with a razor-sharp mind, to defend them. Although only thirty-three, Brodsky had already made his mark in the legal profession. After graduating from New York University Law School, he had joined the Justice Department in Washington as an attorney in the special unit created by the Eisenhower Administration to fight organized crime. He helped prosecute a number of the mobsters who had gathered at Apalachin, New York, then returned to New York in 1959 and as an assistant U.S. attorney in the Southern District successfully prosecuted mobster Joe Valachi on a narcotics charge. It was during the course of this trial that Valachi started to "sing" to federal agents about the Cosa Nostra.

Having served the government, Brodsky could call upon his understanding of its workings in defending his clients. This he did, and in a persevering manner, for it was his court-appointed task to defend the Soviet "illegals" from a possible penalty of death.

His opponent, U.S. attorney Joseph P. Hoey, a courtroom veteran, was just as determined. In contrast to Brodsky, who was thin and rather scholarly in appearance, Hoey was a bluff, affable, white-haired Irishman, the son of a contractor who built churches. If he was not as youthful and nimble as Brodsky, he was nevertheless a careful, experienced prosecutor who knew his business.

In mid-August, during the pretrial maneuvering, Brodsky asked the court to order the government to provide a bill of particulars spelling out the espionage charges; he also demanded the home addresses of those who were to be government witnesses, and he suggested that the government had eavesdropped on the Baltches in the Woodbine. It was some months before the government's answering briefs were filed, and in the interim there was a spectacular development in the case.

To understand what happened, it must be recalled that 1963 was a curious year with respect to U.S.-Soviet relations, which were being conducted on two levels. On the one hand, the secret espionage war between the two great powers burst out into the open in an unprecedented series of major spy cases all over the globe. On another level, Moscow and Washington drew closer together than at any time since the end of World War II. On the spy front, in Moscow the Russians had sentenced Colonel Oleg Penkovsky to death in May, and his British courier, Greville Wynne, to prison; in Stockholm Swedish air force colonel Stig Wennerström was arrested on June 20 as a long-time Soviet spy; in London on July 1—the day before the Baltches were arrested—the British announced that Kim Philby was a Soviet agent who had fled behind the Iron Curtain; and in Washington, Soviet diplomat Gennadiy Sevastyanov was expelled for trying to recruit a Russian-born employee of the CIA.

Other currents were stirring on the diplomatic level. In April, in Geneva, the Soviet Union accepted the United States proposal to establish a "hot line" communications link between the two countries; in June President Kennedy announced in his American University speech that talks would start on a nuclear test-ban treaty. Moscow and Washington reached quick agreement by July 25 and the historic pact was signed in Moscow on August 5.

Against this backdrop the State Department moved to clear away some of the Cold War underbrush. No gesture could be made involving the Baltches, for the Russians would not concede that they were their agents, but the Egorovs were another matter.

Two high U.S. officials paid an unpublicized call on Deputy Attorney General Nicholas Katzenbach. Ambassador Llewellyn E. Thompson, Jr., top State Department Soviet expert, and Leonard C. Meeker, department counsel, came to seek Justice Department approval of a deal with the Russians. They proposed that the Egorovs be traded for two Americans, Marvin W. Makinen, twenty-four, of

Ashburnham, Massachusetts, and the Reverend Walter Ciszek, fifty-eight, a Jesuit priest from Shenandoah, Pennsylvania, who had been held by the Russians since 1940. Makinen, a Fulbright scholar at the Free University of West Berlin, had been arrested in Kiev on July 27, 1961, and convicted of photographing Soviet defense installations for U.S. military intelligence while on an automobile trip through Russia. He had confessed to spying and was sentenced to eight years.*

Thompson and Meeker argued persuasively that a trade would soften relations with Moscow, and that there were certain foreign policy benefits to be reaped. However, Katzenbach was cool to the idea of a trade. He contended that since Makinen was not a professional intelligence agent and the Egorovs were, Washington would gain less than Moscow.

Katzenbach had not flatly opposed a trade, but he nevertheless professed surprise when the State Department officials came back early in October and announced to him that the deal had been arranged. He then had to explain to Attorney General Robert F. Kennedy what he felt was at least a misunderstanding inside the government.

None of this was public knowledge, but on October 11 Hoey went before Federal Judge Joseph C. Zavatt and asked that the charges against the Egorovs be dismissed so that they could be sent back to Russia in a spy exchange. Egorov, sitting in court, smiled broadly at the news. His wife appeared puzzled, and he leaned over to explain to her.

"Two for two?" Judge Zavatt asked the U.S. attorney.

"Yes," replied Hoey.

At 6 P.M. the same day, the Russians arrived at Idlewild Airport in the custody of federal marshals. They had to wait almost five hours when mechanical trouble delayed their SAS flight to Copenhagen. They were accompanied on the flight by Alexei Vlasov, the third

---

* When James B. Donovan, the remarkable American attorney for Rudolf Abel, went to Berlin in February 1962 to negotiate the master spy's exchange for U-2 pilot Francis Gary Powers, he also brought back what he termed "assurance by the Soviet government that if better relations should develop as a result of what has transpired, clemency will be granted to Makinen."

secretary of the Soviet UN mission, who said he was returning home on "vacation." In Copenhagen the Egorovs boarded an Aeroflot plane for Moscow. At dawn the next day Makinen and Father Ciszek arrived at Idlewild on a BOAC flight. During the night they had unknowingly passed the eastbound plane carrying the Egorovs home.

The spy exchange was publicly reported, but backstage, two people on opposite sides of the case were privately annoyed. Edward Brodsky did not learn that the Egorovs had left until his wife, Cynthia, turned on the radio, heard a news broadcast that they were on the plane and telephoned her husband. Had he known he would have asked that the Egorovs be held and called as witnesses, which he could not have done so long as they were defendants.

In Washington, J. Walter Yaegley, Assistant Attorney General in charge of the Internal Security Division of the Justice Department, was equally miffed, but for different reasons. He felt that it was a bad trade and would weaken the government's case against the Baltches, who were now left as the lone defendants. There were long conferences within the Justice Department on whether to reindict the Baltches under the new circumstances. Brodsky was approached by the Justice Department and asked whether he would enter into a deal to plead the Baltches guilty to a minor charge of entering the country illegally. They would then be convicted and shipped home. Although this sort of secret bargaining goes on frequently between the government and defense attorneys, the public is generally unaware of it. Ultimately agreement could not be reached, and the government decided to obtain a superseding indictment of the Baltches, who were still being held.

In France by this time, the DST had interviewed Laurette Ventis, and in England, M.I.5 had located Michel Sokolov-Grant, so that when the Baltches were reindicted on December 17, he was identified by his true name of Alexandre Sokolov.*

Brodsky was told at one point that the government had tried to

---

* Because the government had quite a handful of names to deal with, the indictment, to be precise, read: "ALEXANDRE SOKOLOV, also known as Robert Keistutis Baltch, Robert Baltch, and James Oliver Jackson; and JANE DOE, also known as Joy Ann Garber, Joy Ann Baltch, Joy A. Baltch and Bertha Rosalie Jackson."

trade the Baltches, too, for certain Americans held in the Soviet Union, but that the Russians had refused, claiming they had no idea of who the Baltches were.

The ramifications of the case seemed endless. Also, the federal courts move slowly, and not until Monday, September 28, 1964, did the trial begin in the United States Courthouse in Brooklyn before Judge John F. Dooling, Jr. Earlier in the month Robert Kennedy had resigned to run for the Senate, and Katzenbach was now Acting Attorney General and, as such, the top Washington official in overall charge of the case.

As the trial opened, it was disclosed that the government's star witness against the Baltches would be Kaarlo Rudolph Tuomi, Soviet "illegal" and double agent for the FBI. Brodsky renewed his demand for the abode of all government witnesses under a 1795 statute that had not been invoked before in an espionage case. His motion caused a flurry, because it meant the disclosure to the defense of the home addresses of FBI agents and of Tuomi. Tuomi had been whisked from East Orange under government protection on the day of the arrests, and he was now living in a hotel under the name of John J. O'Toole, which was actually the name of the FBI man assigned to protect him. The press focused on Brodsky's demand for addresses, and much was made of it, but in fact it was of little importance to what happened.

More significant was Brodsky's pressure on the eavesdropping issue. The attorney had charged more than a year before that the government had listened in on his clients in their Washington apartment. He had made the charge because he believed that the affidavit, submitted by an FBI agent to obtain a search warrant, was so detailed in its description of the ciphers, false documents and passports that might be found in the Baltches' apartment as to suggest advance knowledge. Hoey's assistant, Joseph J. Marcheso, replied in two affidavits that the eavesdropping allegation was a "mere fishing expedition" unsupported by "a scintilla of evidence."

On the opening day of the trial in federal court, Brodsky raised the question again before Judge Dooling and Hoey assured the court that "we weren't stationed there and we did not have a microphone in the apartment." The legal sparring continued on Tuesday. Dooling ordered Tuomi's address placed in a sealed envelope and given to Brodsky. The dull process of selecting a jury began; by Thursday night, after each side had exhausted its total of forty-four challenges, ten men and a woman had been picked.

But in Washington there was consternation behind the scenes when Katzenbach learned through Hoey and Yaegley that there had, after all, been a microphone in the wall of the Baltches' apartment in the Woodbine. Who had failed to tell this to whom is not something that can be determined with certainty. From 1940 to 1965, the Solicitor General told the United States Supreme Court in 1966, the FBI had blanket authority to use electronic eavesdropping devices in national security and certain other cases; it needed approval of the Attorney General only in wiretapping cases.* The FBI would thus have acted within its authority in bugging the Baltches' apartment. The courts, however, have held that the government must prove that it obtained no leads or evidence in this manner, and the Supreme Court has ruled that if the government enters a room to plant a microphone, it has violated constitutional rights against trespass.

In a heated meeting with Yaegley, Katzenbach argued that the case against the Baltches thus had been tainted by the microphone (which had been placed while his predecessor Robert Kennedy was Attorney General), and he ordered the prosecution dropped for this reason. He also ordered Hoey to correct the record that stood in the federal court in Brooklyn.

On Friday, October 1, as this upheaval was taking place behind the scenes, the court convened as usual at 10 A.M., and the twelfth juror, a man, was selected. Dooling ordered the jury sworn and declared a lunch recess until 2:30 P.M. As far as anyone knew at that

---

* On June 30, 1965, President Johnson ordered curbs on bugging by federal agencies and directed that wiretapping be limited to "national security" cases with specific authorization of the Attorney General. In December 1966 the issue broke out into a major political skirmish between Robert Kennedy and J. Edgar Hoover. The FBI Director charged that use of microphones "obviously increased at Mr. Kennedy's insistence" while he was Attorney General. Robert Kennedy replied that Hoover was "misinformed." Each released documents to support his position.

point, the actual trial was to begin after lunch. But it became obvious that something was going on when the court reconvened. There were whispered conferences among lawyers, the judge failed to show up on time, and the Baltches were led from the courtroom and then back in again. Finally, at 3:04 P.M., Hoey, his face flushed, rose to remind the court that he had assured it on Monday that "we did not have a microphone in the apartment." He added, "The government would like to clarify its answer, your Honor, of last Monday. I made further inquiry of the Department of Justice and have ascertained that the building in question was used for more than identifying the defendants' address. I would like to point out that there was no evidence or leads obtained from that situation; that there was a microphone placed in the apartment of the Baltches prior to their entry into the apartment, and it had been removed prior to July second, 1963, when they were apprehended on this charge."

His voice dispirited, Hoey then declared, "Your Honor, I have been instructed by the Attorney General, in the interest of national security of the United States of America, to offer no testimony whatsoever in regard to . . . the only acts within the conspiracy . . . which can in any way connect the two defendants, Alexandre Sokolov and Jane Doe, with this international conspiracy. For that reason, your Honor, in the interest of national security . . . the government moves to dismiss the indictment against both of these defendants."

For Baltch, the words were an almost unbelievable reprieve, a weird and unexpected ending to the story. He reached for the hand of his wife. The two spies suddenly sensed freedom instead of a long prison term or possible death sentence.

Judge Dooling is a slim, dark-haired man of great presence on the bench. He dismissed the indictment and then he turned to the baffled jurors with these words:

"Your first sense of this must be a mixture of mystification and of the futility of our week's work together. Neither you nor I can know with what complexities our government has had to deal . . . we can and do know this, and know it afresh today and with a new sense of its meaning: This case does not go forward because the defendants are, under our Constitution, entitled to a public trial, to be informed of the accusation against them and confronted with the witnesses against them. The interest of our national security, it has been concluded, precludes that. The consequence is not a secret trial, nor a trial on shapeless charges, nor a trial without the production of witnesses, but on the contrary a dismissal of the case because a constitutional trial cannot in this case be guaranteed to the defendants because the national security interest forbids it.

"We can take pride in the majesty of spirit that disdains to deviate one iota from principle in order to obtain a particular objective. We can count ourselves honored to witness this dignified act of constitutional government.

"This is government as free men would have it."

Dooling is a brilliant jurist and his statement was eloquent, no less so for the fact that it did not apply to the case at hand. For even by the broadest interpretation of the term "national security," it was not the reason why the prosecution was dropped. Katzenbach had ordered the government to withdraw for the sole reason that he felt the microphone would not only be an embarrassment but would make it difficult to win the case.

Yet, Dooling's words were not without larger meaning. Defending Soviet spies, as James B. Donovan found out in the Abel case, is not a popular business, and it is one of the strengths of the American system of justice that they *are* defended, often by brilliant men. Donovan lost the Abel case by one vote in the United States Supreme Court, and Brodsky's strategy won freedom for the Baltches. From the point of view of the American system, it is well that even Soviet spies, who are enemies of that system and are attempting to inflict harm upon it, are afforded its legal and constitutional protections.

On the other hand, from the security point of view, what is important about Soviet spies is that they be caught, and this the FBI did. It found them, it watched them, it unraveled their various identities and even learned Baltch's real background. Whether a spy, once caught, is imprisoned, or sent home, or traded, is probably a good deal less important than catching him and putting an end to his spying. The O. Henry ending to the Baltch case was scarcely a triumph for the GRU, whose ring was broken and whose agents were exposed.

Alexandre Sokolov and his wife were turned over to the immigration authorities, since they had not entered the United States legally. At a hearing in Manhattan a week later they stood before Ira Fieldsteel, an immigration officer, and faced a fourteenth-floor window through which they could see the Statue of Liberty in New York Harbor. They declined to give their names or answer any questions (under the Fifth Amendment) but asked to be deported to Czechoslovakia.

At 9:52 P.M. on October 15, Air India flight 108, destination Prague, took off from Kennedy International Airport. Aboard were the woman who called herself Joy Ann Baltch, and Alexandre Sokolov of Tiflis, Istanbul, Paris, Potsdam, Moscow, New York, Baltimore and Washington, also known as Robert K. Baltch and James Oliver Jackson, language instructor, part-time song-and-dance man, and Russian spy. On the apron, a small knot of government officials watched as the aircraft grew smaller and smaller, finally to become swallowed up in the darkness to the east.

They're here now, in America.
Their agents are all over the world.

—Vice-President Richard M. Nixon,
Davenport, Iowa, October 28, 1960

VII the city of magic

On the night of March 12, 1956, Dr. Jesus Maria de Galindez, a
scholarly Spanish Basque and foe of Generalissimo Rafael L. Trujillo
lectured to his class at Columbia University, had a cup of coffee with
some students, waved good-bye and disappeared into the subway,
forever.

There was every reason to believe that he had been kidnaped
and killed on Trujillo's orders. The resultant shock was widespread,
for Americans did not like to think that the long arm of a murderous
Dominican dictator could reach out into New York City.

The shock was even more acute among Dr. Galindez' neighbors
at 30 Fifth Avenue, a seventeen-story red brick apartment building
where he was known as a quiet and dignified tenant. He had been
living in 15-F, a four-and-a-half-room apartment overlooking lower
Fifth Avenue, which is a particularly lovely part of New York. Three
blocks to the south is Washington Square, with its gray stone arch

reminiscent of the Arc de Triomphe in Paris. The substantial apartment houses in the area impart an aura of respectability to Greenwich
Village, and it is possible to live in them in middle-class comfort with
just a touch of Bohemianism, for the arty shops of Eighth Street are
right around the corner.

Galindez' neighbors were not, of course, certain that he was
dead. But apartments in New York, and in the Village, are always
hard to find, and, not to be ghoulish about it, the residents of 30 Fifth
Avenue, after a decent interval, could not help thinking that the
desirable Galindez apartment might now be available. And so in June,
less than twelve weeks after the disappearance of Dr. Galindez,
another tenant, Dr. John Gilmore, moved upstairs from 11-B, in the
rear of the building, to the nicer apartment of the missing scholar.

Dr. John Gilmore was one of New York's most prominent
medical illustrators and a successful author who could well afford the
better location. His first check for the $257.50-a-month rent on his
new apartment was dated June 18, 1956; the issue of *Life* magazine
of that very date contained illustrations by him for an article on
President Eisenhower's ileitis operation. Page 52 showed a photograph of press secretary James C. Hagerty briefing newsmen while
Major General Leonard Heaton, commandant of Walter Reed Hospital, explained the operation on a blackboard by drawing a chalk
diagram of Eisenhower's intestines. Below the photograph were three
detailed medical drawings "by Dr. John Gilmore" explaining the
surgery for the layman.

It was, in a way, surprising that Dr. Gilmore chose to move into
the vacant apartment of a man who was at the center of a highly
publicized international mystery, one that had brought the press, the
police, the FBI and the CIA streaming into 15-F.* One might think
that Dr. John Gilmore would have been the last person to want to

---

* On May 29, 1957, the State Department said in a note to the Dominican Republic that "sufficient evidence had now been uncovered to indicate" that
a missing American pilot, Gerald Lester Murphy, acting with certain other
Dominican and American nationals, "may have been connected with the
disappearance of Dr. Galindez." There was considerable evidence that Murphy
had flown the drugged scholar from Amityville, Long Island, to the torture

attract such attention to himself, since, as it later turned out, he was a spy for the Soviet Union, an agent of the GRU.

Moreover, he was already under investigation for his suspected espionage activities. In April 1956, the month after Galindez vanished, Gilmore appeared at the Los Angeles office of Fairchild Aerial Surveys, Inc., and asked to buy high-altitude photographs of that city. He flashed a business card that read: "USA in Pictures, John Gilmore, Ph.D., Art Director, 30 Fifth Avenue, New York 11, N.Y." He said he wanted to use the photographs in guidebooks he was publishing of various U.S. cities, including Philadelphia, Chicago, New York and Los Angeles. He purchased a $12.50 aerial photomap of the Los Angeles area, covering two thousand square miles and taking in the California coastline. He returned the next day, ordered two enlarged maps of the coastal area and asked that he be sent additional aerial photographs of industrial plants for "review by the editorial board."

The FBI learned of his visit to Fairchild, and although the photomaps he had purchased were not classified, the incident seemed suspicious enough to warrant further inquiry. He lived at 30 Fifth Avenue, as his business card indicated. Only five foot two, he was stocky and jowly, with brown graying hair and dark horned-rimmed glasses that gave him a trustworthy, professional air. A friendly and gregarious man, Gilmore was a long-time resident of the Village. He had a girl friend, Ruth Davis. He walked his brown-and-white wire-haired terrier in Washington Square. His hobby was Oriental art, and he set aside Saturdays for art auctions. He was a great movie fan and would sometimes see two, three or four movies in one day. He also

---

chambers of the Dominican Republic. In July, Trujillo, who was known as the Benefactor, hired Morris L. Ernst, a celebrated New York civil rights attorney, and William H. Munson, an ex-judge, to investigate the disappearance of Galindez for a minimum fee of $100,000. After ten months Ernst revealed that he could find no evidence to connect either his client, Trujillo, or Murphy with the disappearance of Galindez. Ernst thought "the entire story" was "a canard" trumped up by Trujillo's enemies, and charged that Galindez had collected more than $1,000,000 as representative of the Basque government in exile, an anti-Franco movement. Although Ernst did not publicly say so, there seems little doubt but that Galindez had been receiving funds from the CIA. His disappearance has not been solved, and the United States, after its note of May 29, 1957, developed a peculiar lack of interest in the case.

had a consuming fear of death, and for that reason would never go to funerals.

There was no question that he was a well-known medical illustrator, an excellent artist who had been employed by a number of reputable textbook firms and large pharmaceutical houses. He seemed to have prepared a medical exhibit for the American Medical Association convention in New York in 1953 (which may be the only time a Soviet spy has worked for the staunchly conservative AMA). He was also an authority on sex, having co-authored with Samuel A. Lewin two illustrated books entitled *Sex Without Fear,** first published in 1950, and *Sex After Forty,* published by the Medical Research Press and distributed by Grosset and Dunlap in 1952.

Gilmore's life seemed above suspicion, but as the investigation developed, certain disturbing facts began to emerge: he had no Ph.D.—in fact, no college degree at all—and little or no formal education. He certainly had no right to call himself "Doctor." Around 1949 he had been in contact with the Soviet Mission to the United Nations. He had been collecting aerial photographs all over the country. And his real name was not John Gilmore.

None of these things was a crime, but the FBI decided to approach him directly to see if more could be learned. On November 26, 1956, five months after he had moved into apartment 15-F, Gilmore was interviewed there by two special agents, George A. Dimler and Lawrence McWilliams.

He readily admitted that his real name was Willie Hirsch and that he was born in Kassel, Germany, on January 6, 1908, the son of Adolph and Emma Wickersheimer Hirsch. The family moved to Munich when he was fourteen and he was sent to America to live with his aunt Frieda Chamberlain in Philadelphia.†

---

* *Sex Without Fear* can be read at the Library of Congress only in the rare-book room. A revised edition, with a foreword by Sarah K. Greenberg, was published by Medical Research Press in 1962. *Sex After Forty* ("A revealing and helpful book! . . . Seventeen inspiring chapters") was advertised at $4.95 in the *New York Times Book Review* as recently as February 26, 1967.

† After the interview the FBI was able to establish that Willie Hirsch had entered the United States aboard the S.S. *Resolute* on August 31, 1923. Because

A couple of years later, Hirsch told the FBI agents, he became a merchant seaman on oil tankers, working occasionally as a hospital orderly between trips. Once, when shipping out, he found he did not have enough money to reclaim a bag which contained his discharge slip from his last voyage, so a friend provided him with the slip of a John Gilmore; he had signed on that way and used the name since. Illness beached him at the Marine Hospital on Staten Island in 1929. He became an orderly there and did some medical drawings.

He met Dorothy Baker, a Russian-born girl active in leftwing causes, and they were married in 1932, when she was twenty-six. He gave his name as John Gilmore, his age as thirty-two and his birthplace as Philadelphia. With his wife he became active in an organization called Friends of the Soviet Union, and was hired as art editor for its magazine, *Soviet Russia Today*. In 1936 the magazine sent him to Moscow, ostensibly to get better pictures for its pages, and Hirsch illegally took out a U.S. passport in the name of his cousin, Sidney Joseph Chamberlain, the son of his aunt Frieda. (He visited his mother in Munich on the way.) But after his return he left the magazine because of a disagreement. He concentrated on a career as a medical illustrator, while Dorothy got a job at the Worker's Book Shop in Manhattan.

Hirsch said he had never become a citizen. During World War II he registered for the draft, again under the name of his cousin (who was dead), but was never called. (He freely admitted the passport and draft violations, probably because he knew the statute of limitations for those offenses had long since run out.)

---

he was a minor he was detained for five days but then admitted, and as far as the records showed, sent to live with an uncle in New Orleans. Immigration files recorded the uncle's name as M. I. Sontheimer, 2118 Teniston Street, New Orleans. This was checked and it was found that in 1923 an Isaac Sontheimer had lived at 2118 Peniston, not Teniston, and that he was an embalmer. Now, more than thirty years later, the FBI interviewed Isaac's grandson, Maurice Sontheimer, who ran Tharp-Sontheimer-Tharp, Inc., a funeral home. He said he had never heard of Willie Hirsch and that his grandfather had died in 1923, the year the S.S. *Resolute* arrived at Pier 18, New York, which may explain why Willie eventually ended up with Aunt Frieda in Philadelphia. But if he *had* lived for a time in New Orleans with his uncle, the embalmer, it might explain his later marked aversion to funerals.

After the war he and his wife separated, although they remained good friends, and he moved into an upper Village apartment house at 117 West Thirteenth Street. While living there, he met Ruth Davis, an ex-WAC and divorcee from Brooklyn who had served during the war in India and China with the United States Army Air Corps as an aerial photographer. She was twenty-seven when they met, the daughter of Barnet and Jennie Bernstein Davis, immigrants from eastern Europe. She had married a man named Jerome Baum, and they had a daughter, Susie, but the marriage broke up. She saw a lot of Hirsch and they became extremely close; when he had a heart attack it was Ruth Davis who nursed him back to health. Afterward they started working on a book together. It was to be called *New York, City of Magic*. It would contain aerial photographs.

As the investigation progressed, it became clear that if Dr. Gilmore-Hirsch was a spy he was an unusual one, for he was a by-line writer for *Collier's* and the *Saturday Evening Post* and had sold drawings to *Life*.

Among other details the investigation turned up an article entitled "A New Treatment for Kidney Stones." Under the by-line "John Gilmore and Eric Northrup," it appeared on page 30 of the January 17, 1953, issue of the *Saturday Evening Post*. Accompanying the article was a blood-red picture of a medical mockup, credited to Gilmore, showing three kidneys in cross-section. The article extolled the virtues of hyaluronidase, a wonder drug brewed from bulls' testes which was said to help prevent formation of kidney stones. Three physicians had experimented with the drug along these lines, and one, Dr. Arthur J. Butt, was located in Pensacola, Florida. He confirmed that he had worked with Gilmore to promote the story of hyaluronidase.*

Two years later, when Eisenhower had his heart attack at Den-

---

* Marketed under several brand names, it is normally used as a "spreading factor" to carry and spread other drugs that have been injected into tissues, although it has also been employed in the treatment of kidney stones.

ver, *Life*'s article on the President's coronary was accompanied by four large color illustrations. These depicted a human heart on the mend twelve hours, four days, six weeks and three months after an attack. The credits showed the drawings were by "John Gilmore."

A Soviet spy promoting kidney cures, writing for the slick magazines and illustrating an article about the President's heart attack? It seemed unlikely, but the FBI decided to keep Hirsch under periodic surveillance, a task made easier by his frequent walks in Washington Square with his dog. In March 1957 the FBI summoned Hirsch to its New York field office for a second interview. It added little to the mosaic except the fact that Hirsch and his wife, Dorothy—to whom he was still legally wed—had been filing joint federal income tax returns under the names Sidney and Dorothy Gilmore Chamberlain.

The questioning by the FBI had no apparent effect on Hirsch's activities. Either he was supremely confident that he had flummoxed the FBI or he was under enormous pressure from the GRU, for a little more than a year later, in July 1958, while passing through Chicago, he telephoned an old friend, William D. McCuaig. "Do you want to make some real money?" he asked. Hirsch explained that he had "friends overseas" who would provide the money and that he was hiring agents all over the country. Hirsch had turned to McCuaig, an employee of the Cook County Board of Social Welfare, because he had known him for some twenty years and, mistakenly, thought he could be recruited to spy. They first met in 1933 or 1934 when Hirsch went to Chicago to attend a medical convention. They had been mutual friends of Dorothy Baker's; in fact, McCuaig, who had worked in New York for a time, had dated her before she became Mrs. John Gilmore. In 1950 he exchanged Christmas cards with Hirsch (whom he knew as Gilmore). McCuaig knew enough about the Gilmores to assume that the "friends overseas" were the Russians. He thought over the telephone call and went to the FBI.

It was a busy time for Hirsch. On July 22 his divorce became final and on August 8 he married Ruth Davis in Connecticut. (The day before, a Soviet official attached to the UN became a father for the third time, and his pride in his baby girl, who was named Marina, was soon to come to the attention of the federal government.)

In October, Hirsch placed another call to McCuaig and said he would be coming out to see him. He arrived in Chicago on October 24 and had dinner with McCuaig at the Tropical Hut Restaurant. Afterward, at McCuaig's residence, Hirsch said he had learned from his overseas friends that the international situation was becoming acute; McCuaig would do well to align himself with the winning side. Throwing caution aside, Hirsch said he had worked for the Soviets for a long time and had been well rewarded. A top Soviet operator was coming to Chicago to see McCuaig the next day; he was a charming man and McCuaig would like him. Hirsch could promise no salary, but there would be a generous expense account. McCuaig, who had assumed the delicate role of double agent for the FBI, reported back to the government on this and all other conversations.

The next afternoon McCuaig got a telephone call from Hirsch, and they later met in the lobby of the Sherman House Hotel. Hirsch then disappeared across La Salle Street to a Walgreen's drugstore, returning with a short, slick-haired, swarthy man whom he introduced as Peter. The three drove to a bar at Damen and Madison, where Peter tested the social worker by asking how he felt about the Hungarian revolt and about the Soviet Union in general. Apparently satisfied, Peter then asked McCuaig to obtain a map of the Chicago area showing Nike sites and other military installations. He also asked for a list of local industries manufacturing strategic materials, for the names of any friends who worked in defense plants, and for as many aerial and ground photographs of defense installations around Chicago as could be acquired.

The Soviet agent directed McCuaig to submit reports in his own handwriting (which the Russians favor to compromise an agent and keep him in line) and he told him that he might be sent on trips to Mexico and other parts of Latin America. Future meetings would be in New York. In the late afternoon the three men adjourned to Riccardo's Restaurant and Gallery, a popular after-theater spot in Chicago displaying the works of local artists.

On the way Peter expansively and foolishly told McCuaig that he was a Soviet national who lived in New York, that he had spent some time at the UN, had formerly lived in England, and had one son and two daughters—the youngest girl only two months old. After dinner at Riccardo's, Peter made a date to meet McCuaig alone at 10 A.M. the next day at the same Walgreen's.

As it happened, the next day was the last Sunday of the month and Chicago switched early in the morning from daylight to standard time. McCuaig, pondering this, decided to arrive at the drugstore an hour early, at 9 A.M. standard time, in case the Russian had neglected to set his watch back. Soviet intelligence apparently is lax in training its agents on the peculiarities of American time changes, for Peter showed up an hour early. He and McCuaig walked to Holloway's Cafeteria for breakfast, then drove in the social worker's car via the Outer Drive to Chesterton, Indiana, and back, talking along the way. Peter said that Gilmore was no longer to be considered McCuaig's espionage contact, although he was free to see him socially. The Russian warned that the work might be dangerous. But McCuaig should not hesitate to make suggestions if he had better ideas on how to operate. The money would be more than adequate.

The Soviet agent then said that McCuaig should call him "Peter Stephens" if an occasion arose where he had to be introduced to anyone. Then, borrowing an old envelope from McCuaig, he printed the name "Peter Stephens" and, under it, the word "Gipsy" —selected, he explained, because at one point McCuaig had jokingly remarked that Peter resembled a "Slavic gypsy." In turn, McCuaig suggested that his own code name be "Duncan."

Peter gave McCuaig $200 in cash and instructions for their next meeting. As they drove along the tollway, he took a marked Pennsylvania Railroad timetable from his pocket. He studied it, and then told McCuaig to board the Broadway Limited leaving Chicago for New York at 6 P.M. on November 21. He was to book a roomette, get off at Newark at 9:15 A.M. and enter the station coffee shop. There he would see "Peter Stephens" sipping coffee at the counter. McCuaig would sit down next to him and place the photographs and other material, wrapped in brown delicatessen paper, between them. They would shake hands, chat briefly, and McCuaig would depart, neglecting to take the packet. During the conversation over coffee, Peter would let him know where they were to meet the next day in New York. This was the end of Peter's instructions, and by then the two men had driven and talked for four hours. Back in Chicago, Peter got out of the car and left.

McCuaig had already passed on to the FBI the personal information that Peter had disclosed about himself, and it turned out to be accurate, for there was a Soviet UN official in New York with a two-month-old baby daughter. With that key piece of information, plus the physical description provided by McCuaig, the FBI concluded that Peter must be Igor Yakovlevich Melekh, forty-five, chief of the Russian translation section of the UN's Office of Conference Services. Melekh, born in Leningrad, had been stationed in London during World War II as the Soviet naval attaché (his hobby was collecting books on English history). His wife, Irina Konstantinova, was born in Rostov-on-Don in 1925. They had a daughter, Nataliya, in 1951, and a son, Mikhail, in 1954. He entered the United States on June 10, 1955, lived with his family at 333 West Eighty-sixth Street and maintained a summer home in Rye, New York. A second daughter, Marina, had been born two months before, on August 7, 1958. In Chicago the FBI showed photographs of Melekh to McCuaig. He identified him as Peter Stephens.

But early in November, before McCuaig was to take the Broadway Limited to Gilmore's City of Magic, he received an unexpected telephone call at the Green Door Book Shop, where he worked part time. It was Willie Hirsch. "Don't do anything," he said, "until you get further instructions."

This was a confusing turn of events, since it had been made clear to McCuaig that he was to receive no further directions from Hirsch. The FBI advised McCuaig to keep the date at the coffee shop in Newark in any event.

He did. Arriving on time, he checked his luggage and entered the coffee shop in the station. No Melekh. He then went to the Savarin Restaurant and saw him sitting at the counter. Perhaps these things work smoothly only in the movies, for McCuaig found that the seats on both sides of Melekh were occupied. Improvising, he sat down opposite him and they nodded slightly to each other. While McCuaig watched, Melekh started chatting with a man sitting next to him. Was he trying to get the man to move so they could follow the script? McCuaig never found out, and at any rate, the man did not budge. Melekh got up, paid his check and walked out. McCuaig did the same and followed the GRU agent down a stairway, where Melekh greeted him effusively.

McCuaig said he was glad they had made contact because he was not sure he should have come at all. "Why?" Melekh asked hastily. McCuaig told him of the call from Gilmore. Melekh, stunned, asked him to repeat what he had said. He did. Almost speechless, Melekh asked McCuaig to meet him later. He told him to take the BMT Jamaica line and be waiting at the Cleveland station in Brooklyn at 9 P.M. If for any reason Melekh could not make it, he promised to be at the subway station the following night. Obviously, Melekh had to do some checking on what had possessed Hirsch to gum up the arrangements.

In the meantime FBI men on the scene at the Pennsylvania Station in Newark spotted yet another Soviet agent in the waiting room. He was Kirill S. Doronkin, a film editor in the public information department of the UN Secretariat. Doronkin had no doubt been assigned by Melekh as a countersurveillance agent. It is not unusual for a second Soviet intelligence officer to be on hand to see if he can detect evidence of counterespionage activity.

Doronkin had entered the United States two years before and he, too, had been seeking aerial photographs of the Chicago area through channels entirely different from Melekh's. Doronkin had recruited a Canadian who turned double agent (like McCuaig), and co-operated with the Mounted Police. Only a week before, on November 15, the Canadian had kept a date at a parking lot in Scarsdale, New York. A Russian whose name he did not know was there to receive the aerial photographs of Chicago. It turned out to be Doronkin, accompanied by his wife.

Melekh and Doronkin left the Newark railroad station together. Melekh failed to meet McCuaig that night in Brooklyn but came the next evening. Together they walked the streets of Brooklyn for almost an hour. Melekh obviously had been unable to find Hirsch, for he asked McCuaig where the call to Chicago had come from. McCuaig said he did not know, but the operator had asked for "seventy cents more, please," if that was any help.

Complimenting McCuaig for keeping his head and coming to Newark as scheduled, Melekh told him to go ahead with his assignment and prepare the map and photographs. He added that he would send three books to Chicago as a signal for McCuaig to come to New York the third Saturday in January, which would be the seventeenth. Two books would mean to come with the pictures but to memorize the details marked on the map, and one book would mean to come with whatever he had on the Saturday following the date the book was received.

McCuaig objected. Playing his part, he pointed out to Melekh that books would not fit in his mail slot and could easily be stolen from the vestibule of his home. Instead, he suggested that Melekh send letters containing picture post cards. This was agreed upon. Melekh then produced a subway map and showed McCuaig the site of their next meeting: McCuaig would take the IRT subway to Main Street in Flushing, Queens. From there he would walk to Fong's Chop Suey Restaurant on Main Street. At 1 P.M. he would take a table, order lunch and wait. If Melekh failed to appear, McCuaig was to leave, return at 3 P.M. and follow the same procedure. It was a part made for Peter Sellers: one could picture McCuaig bloated with a second Chinese meal of Foo Young, Subgum Chow Mein and lichee nuts, patiently waiting for the Soviet spy. But the resilient double agent voiced no protest. Melekh gave him $200 wrapped in a newspaper, and the two men parted.

On January 17, 1959, McCuaig returned to New York, arriving at the restaurant rendezvous in Queens at 12:55 P.M. Its correct name proved to be the Fong Lan Chinese American Restaurant, but since this sounded close enough to Fong's Chop Suey Restaurant,

McCuaig entered. Melekh was already there, sitting in a booth that commanded a view of the entrance and street. He was the only customer in the place, which made him rather conspicuous, but this was not inconsistent with the faint overtones of comedy that ran through all of Melekh's espionage arrangements. He was going by the book, but some unexpected element always seemed to crop up to strike a discordant note.

They ordered lunch, and Melekh said he had seen Dr. Gilmore and questioned him about the phone call. Melekh brushed it off as a minor misunderstanding. McCuaig then produced the films; he said he had brought 100 exposures, including ground photos he had taken himself of defense installations. In truth, these were "feed" materials prepared by the FBI and cleared first with the Pentagon in order to be relatively harmless to security. Among them were shots of Nike sites around Chicago, and a map keyed to the photographs.

Melekh then issued new instructions. McCuaig was to come to New York on March 14, and go to Woolworth's on Allerton Avenue in the Bronx at 1 P.M. They would meet and talk in the five-and-dime store. Melekh gave McCuaig $500 in cash and emotionally told him how well he had done, how much the Russians were depending on him and how richly he would be rewarded.*

But Melekh failed to show up at the Woolworth's in March, and the likely explanation is that on January 15 the United States Mission to the UN delivered an unpublished note to the Secretary-General asking that Kirill Doronkin be dismissed for clandestine activities. News of this action soon reached Doronkin. When the GRU realized that Doronkin's intelligence work had been discovered, it must have feared that his presence in Newark on November 22 could have contaminated the Hirsch-Melekh-McCuaig operation. The danger

---

* This is fairly standard procedure. Harry Gold, the atom spy, was told he had been secretly awarded the Order of Lenin, entitling him to free trolley rides in Moscow for life. Colonel Wennerström, who felt his merits had not been recognized by the Swedish air force, was told by his Soviet controllers that he had been promoted to the rank of major general in the GRU. They assigned to him the impressive code name "Eagle" and assured him that large sums of money were accumulating in his name in a bank account in Moscow which he could draw upon, some day.

was probably not learned in time to stop the meeting at Fong Lan's. Doronkin's UN contract was up in March and it was not renewed. He left the United States on March 11, three days before the scheduled meeting at Woolworth's.

All contact by the Russians with McCuaig was broken off, although Hirsch's activities during the rest of 1959 took on a strange, Kafkaesque quality. He would go to Second Avenue at Sixty-eighth Street in Manhattan on successive Fridays, looking for contacts that never came.

In 1960 a series of events took place that were to turn the Hirsch-Melekh case into a watershed in the espionage history of the Cold War. They began on May 1, when Francis Gary Powers, a CIA pilot, was downed in a U-2 over Sverdlovsk, deep inside the Soviet Union. The Eisenhower Administration first denied, then admitted the reconnaissance flights, then threatened to continue and finally promised to end them. The Paris summit meeting blew up on May 16 in the wake of the U-2 furor, and the episode for the first time awakened millions of Americans and others to the magnitude of spying in the modern world.

The Eisenhower Administration tried to fight back by pointing out that the Russians engaged in espionage, too, and on a wide scale. To get this message across, a large-scale counterattack was launched. On May 18, while Premier Khrushchev was violently denouncing Eisenhower at a memorable press conference in Paris, Vice-President Richard M. Nixon took the unusual step of disclosing a case of Soviet espionage in the United States. Speaking in Syracuse and Buffalo, New York, Nixon said that on September 18, 1959, on the very day that Khrushchev, a "master of espionage," was addressing the UN in New York, two Russians were caught attempting to get classified information from an American.* Senator Albert Gore, the Tennessee

---

* According to published reports, Nixon indicated that the Russians had been nabbed in Springfield, Illinois. Later his press secretary corrected this and said Nixon had meant Springfield, Massachusetts; further, the Russians had not been arrested, but one had quietly been ousted from the United States in January. The case involved an attempt by Soviet intelligence to obtain United States cryptographic information.

Democrat, assailed Nixon for "giving forth about the arrest of Russian spies . . . in a campaign speech."

The effort to balance the U-2 incident by exposing examples of Soviet espionage continued. Late in May, Henry Cabot Lodge, American ambassador to the UN, displayed a carved replica of the great seal of the United States that had been presented to Ambassador Harriman in Moscow in 1945. The seal had adorned the office of four U.S. ambassadors to Moscow before it was discovered in 1952 to contain an electronic bug that broadcast conversations to listening Soviet intelligence.

But such was the impact of the U-2 affair that the United States remained on the defensive that summer. The continuing countereffort to publicize Soviet espionage activity was overshadowed when, on July 1, a United States Air Force RB-47 reconnaissance plane with a crew of six, flying from England on an "electromagnetic research" mission, was shot down by a Soviet fighter plane over the Barents Sea. The Soviet government claimed the aircraft had violated the Soviet border, but Washington said it was never any closer "than about thirty miles." Obviously Khrushchev, pressing his psychological advantage resulting from the U-2 uproar, had used it as an excuse deliberately and coldly to shoot down the RB-47. He apparently hoped thereby to discourage U.S. "ferret" flights along Soviet borders, missions which are designed to test and pinpoint Soviet radar and electronic defenses. Ten days went by before Moscow conceded that it was holding the two surviving crew members, Captain Freeman B. Olmstead, of Elmira, New York, the co-pilot, and Captain John R. McKone, of Tonganoxie, Kansas, the navigator, both of whom had parachuted to safety. The Russians also disclosed they had the body of the pilot, Major Willard G. Palm, of Oak Park, Illinois. (They finally returned his body, and Major Palm was buried in Arlington National Cemetery.) But Moscow rejected strong United States demands that the two fliers be released immediately. They were imprisoned in Lubianka, held for trial as spies and interrogated constantly by the KGB. Eisenhower's invitation to visit the Soviet Union had been canceled by Khrushchev when the Paris summit exploded, and the chill and near-break in relations between the President and the Premier made the early release of the RB-47 fliers seem unlikely.

In Los Angeles in July, Kennedy and Johnson were nominated by the Democrats, and later in the month, in Chicago, the Republicans chose Nixon and Lodge. Espionage became an inevitable issue in the presidential campaign; Nixon hammered repeatedly at Kennedy's politically vulnerable suggestion that Eisenhower might have apologized to Khrushchev over the U-2 episode to save the summit meeting. On August 19 a Soviet court convicted Francis Gary Powers of spying and gave him a ten-year sentence. In September, Khrushchev arrived in the United States for the second visit in as many years, but this time he was confined to Manhattan while he attended the UN General Assembly. On October 12, enraged at a speech by a Philippine delegate, Khrushchev removed a brown loafer from his right foot, waved the shoe, pounded it on his desk and adopted a mock pitcher's stance as though threatening to throw it at the rostrum. He also held impromptu news conferences, and on one occasion the Associated Press photographed him in front of the Soviet UN mission, grinning and waving to the crowd. Half hidden behind the Premier's upraised right arm, but recognizable in the picture, was Igor Melekh.

On October 27, twelve days before the presidential election, Attorney General William P. Rogers announced the arrests of Melekh and Willie Hirsch by the FBI on espionage charges. A year and nine months had gone by since their last overt act. The delay may very possibly have occurred in the hope that Hirsch and Melekh would lead the government to still other GRU spies in the United States. At the time of the announcement Rogers, a trusted friend of Nixon's, was acting as his closest political adviser; he was aboard the Vice-President's plane during much of the last two whirlwind weeks of the campaign. News of the arrest of two major Russian spies on the eve of the election was not likely to harm the Nixon campaign, since the Vice-President had emphasized that he could be tougher and cooler in dealing with the Russians than his inexperienced opponent.*

* Whatever the reasons for the timing of the arrests, Nixon was quick to seize upon the case for political advantage. In Davenport, Iowa, the next day, he said, "I know the men in the Kremlin. I have seen their hard faces. I have

Melekh was arrested by the FBI at his apartment on West Eighty-sixth Street while a birthday party was in progress for his son, Mikhail. The meticulous list of what was taken from the GRU agent's apartment became part of the court record, and while most of the items that were catalogued resembled the innocent debris of anyone's life, some of them did not. For instance, mixed in with "color slides of Parrot Jungle, Florida" and "one blue plastic spoon" was a description of a slip of paper on which were scribbled references to "the US Program in controlled fusion" and a $25 "International Missile and Spacecraft Guide." Duly catalogued as well were a discount card in Melekh's name from "Sam Goody, World's Largest Record and Audio Dealer" and "2 tickets to Carnegie Hall Concert on October 28, 1960," which Melekh did not get to use.

At the same moment that Melekh was arrested on the West Side of Manhattan, Willie Hirsch was seized at 30 Fifth Avenue. Hidden in a box of medical slides in his apartment was a slip of white paper suggesting that Hirsch had been working on naval as well as aerial assignments. The note was signed simply "M," which may or may not have stood for Melekh. It said:

"Here are the questions I referred to in my note. Description of new means and methods of locating and combating submarines, and documents relating to the organization of antisubmarine defense of coasts, bases, ports, and ships on their way in sea and at anchor.

"Of primary importance are:

"1. Description of long range multiple throwing A/S weapon, the MK 31.

"2. Hydro-acoustic devices, the QCB type.

"3. Radio hydro-acoustic buoys.

"4. Manual 'Comar Pac ASW Hunter' (Killer Panther).

"Keep all materials you get until you hear from us in the usual

had Khrushchev shake his fist in my face and talk about his missiles. I know that he is ruthless, fanatical, cold, and that he has only one aim—and that is to conquer the world . . . as long as you have adversaries like that, they're going to make trouble for us. They're going to make trouble all over the world. You saw it if you picked up your papers today. They picked up a couple of Communist spies in New York. They're here now, in America. Their agents are all over the world, and they will continue to be. They will continue to stir up trouble."

way. May I ask you and your friends to have all these questions in mind all the time because of their importance. This is the main task for your group. Advise E and W to use all their connections for this purpose, and acquire new ones.

"Wish you success. M."

Hirsch professed to know nothing about the note. Both men had been arrested on warrants issued earlier in the day in Chicago, after a federal grand jury there indicted them for conspiracy to spy. The indictment named Doronkin as a co-conspirator but not as a defendant, since he had left the country. Melekh and Hirsch faced prison sentences of up to twenty-five years if convicted.*

Arraigned in federal court in Manhattan, they were held in $50,000 bail each. Platon D. Morozov, a Soviet representative to the UN, called on Secretary-General Dag Hammarskjöld to intercede in obtaining the "immediate release" of Melekh (he said nothing about Hirsch), and blamed Melekh's arrest, oddly, on CIA Director Allen Dulles. Valerian A. Zorin, chief of the Soviet delegation, also protested to Hammarskjöld, and called Melekh's arrest "scandalous." A week later Federal Judge Edward Weinfeld released Melekh on bail after his wife, Irina, emptied a brown leather briefcase containing $50,000 in cash, which Melekh's attorney, William Kleinman, said she had obtained as a "loan" from the Soviet embassy. The court confined Melekh to Manhattan, and his wife promised to inform the government "at once" if he tried to slip out of the country, an arrangement to which the U.S. attorney agreed with understandable reluctance. On the day after Kennedy was elected President, Melekh's lawyers argued in federal court that he should not be sent to trial in Chicago because he had diplomatic immunity, but the court found he did not and the case and the defendants were moved to Illinois. There Judge Edwin A. Robson reduced Hirsch's bail by half, but he could not raise it and remained in jail. Meanwhile Melekh had hired Edward Bennett Williams, one of the nation's more celebrated trial

---

* Unlike the Baltches, Hirsch and Melekh could not have been sentenced to death, since they were indicted under a milder section of the espionage laws.

lawyers, and Williams filed a flurry of motions seeking dismissal of the case and demanding the identity of the person in Chicago (McCuaig's name had not been revealed in the indictment) whom Melekh had allegedly paid. These motions were answered by the government on January 13, 1961, but the public paid little attention to the legal maneuvering in the spy case in Chicago, because in Washington John F. Kennedy was about to be inaugurated as President amid great drifts of snow and the excitement and glitter of the New Frontier.

For the past six months, however, there had been continual efforts to gain the release of the RB-47 fliers, and if one had been plotting the two cases on a graph, the line marked Melekh-Hirsch was about to cross the one marked Olmstead-McKone. Llewellyn Thompson, the patient, shrewd U.S. ambassador in Moscow, had been trying to persuade the Soviet Premier to let them go. But Khrushchev told Thompson (just as he told President Kennedy's press secretary, Pierre Salinger, two years later) that he had no intention of releasing the fliers during the election campaign, because he did not want to help Nixon.

In his book, *With Kennedy,* Salinger wrote that when he saw Khrushchev in May 1962 at his *dacha* near Moscow, the Soviet Premier claimed that Nixon, through a high-ranking Republican intermediary, had tried to influence the 1960 presidential election; the intermediary had approached the Russians before the election with the request that the RB-47 fliers be released. Khrushchev is quoted by Salinger as having said, "We, of course, understood that Nixon wished to make political capital out of this for himself in advance of the elections . . . And this, of course, could have played a decisive role in the elections. That is why we decided to wait a while until Kennedy came to power . . ."

When he wrote about his conversation with the Soviet leader, Salinger did not name Nixon's alleged intermediary. But Khrushchev, according to the record of their conversation, had told Salinger that it was Henry Cabot Lodge, Nixon's running mate, who had tramped through the cornfields of Iowa with Khrushchev while serving as his personal guide during the Premier's 1959 visit to America. Khrushchev offered no details of Lodge's alleged pre-election approach on Nixon's behalf.* Salinger in all likelihood did not name Lodge because he was then actively serving as ambassador to Saigon.

Late in November of 1960, after the election, two emissaries of President-elect Kennedy moved into the picture. Walt Rostow and Jerome B. Wiesner, MIT professors who had served as members of the Kennedy brain trust, were in Moscow for the sixth Pugwash International Conference of Scientists and Scholars. Although both Kennedy emissaries later occupied high positions in the Administration,† they were technically in Moscow as private citizens and made this clear when they called on Vasily V. Kuznetsov, First Deputy Foreign Minister, who had once served briefly as a member of the Communist party presidium and had occupied a series of important diplomatic posts.

As a former major in the OSS, Rostow was not a newcomer to secret missions. His trip to Moscow had been cleared beforehand with Kennedy and with Allen Dulles, then Director of the CIA, which gave it quasi-official standing. When he returned to Washington, Rostow reported to Kennedy in a 4,600-word confidential *aide-mémoire:*

"After he had addressed us as 'guerrilla fighters for Kennedy,' if not public officials of his Administration, Kuznetsov then raised the question, 'What can we do to help the new Administration?' Wiesner's first statement was 'Do nothing,' which led to general laughter . . . We then proceeded to a list which had been previously discussed with Ambassador Thompson. We urged that the RB-47 pilots be returned without Kennedy's having to ask for them or bargain for them." The

---

* Lodge, who remained on as ambassador to the UN after his nomination as Vice-President, told the authors that while at the UN, "I, of course, did everything I could to bring about the freedom of the RB-47 fliers." But he said that after he resigned in September to campaign, "I never had any contact of any kind with a representative of the Soviet Union."

† Wiesner served as Kennedy's science adviser. Rostow, a White House and State Department official under Kennedy, stayed on to become President Johnson's assistant for national security and top White House policy maker for the war in Vietnam.

talk covered a wide range of other East-West problems, and "Kuznetsov replied by stating that the Soviet government regarded Senator Kennedy as a brave man and they honored him for his courage in expressing regret over the U-2 incident. They were sincerely anxious to be helpful to him in his new responsibilities."

In a conversation with yet another Soviet official Rostow outlined a timetable for action before Kennedy would agree to visit Russia: "Return of the RB-47 pilots," completion of a nuclear test-ban treaty, a Kennedy-Khrushchev meeting in New York to sign it, progress on disarmament, free elections throughout Germany and guaranteed Western access to Berlin.

With Khrushchev's shoe-pounding in mind, Rostow warned the Russians that if the Soviet Premier came to New York to sign the treaty, it would be preferred that "Mr. Khrushchev arrive with his top hat, wearing his shoes; that the formal signing take place; perhaps a quiet day of private conversation between the two men; and that Mr. Khrushchev then go home. Total elapsed time: three days maximum. The point made was that if a second visit to New York should occur, it should be melodramatically different in tone than the last." With or without top hat, Khrushchev never returned to New York. The test-ban treaty, when it did come to pass three years later, was signed in Moscow.

Ambassador Thompson continued his own, official negotiations to free the fliers, and two days after Kennedy's inauguration Thompson received word in Moscow that Olmstead and McKone would be released as a gesture of good will toward the new President, but the news would have to be announced simultaneously in both capitals. On January 25, 1961, at his first televised news conference as President, Kennedy dramatically announced that the airmen were being released as a result of conversations between Khrushchev and Thompson.*

---

* Eighteen hours in advance of Kennedy's announcement, the Washington bureau of the New York *Herald Tribune* had learned that the fliers were to be freed. Shortly before midnight David Wise, one of the authors, then the newspaper's White House correspondent, called Salinger for comment. He was told that the President considered the story inimical to the national interest, and that its premature publication might wreck the deal and endanger the lives of the fliers—who were still in Soviet hands at that hour. With authorization from

(He also reaffirmed Eisenhower's summit pledge not to send American aircraft over the Soviet Union.) The President was on hand to greet the fliers when they arrived at Andrews Air Force Base two days later for an emotional reunion with their wives.

Two weeks after the fliers had come home, the United Press carried a short, cryptic item from Moscow. The story said that according to "journalistic sources," Soviet newspapers were being flooded with letters, as yet unpublished, demanding that Igor Melekh be set free as a "fair exchange" for the RB-47 fliers. The same day that the dispatch was printed in some U.S. newspapers, a pretrial hearing of the Melekh-Hirsch case was mysteriously postponed by Federal Judge Robson in Chicago. Assistant U.S. attorney Albert F. Manion told the court he had been asked by Washington to seek the delay "in the best interests of justice." He did not elaborate.

In fact, the request had come from newly appointed Attorney General Robert Kennedy. What amounted to the first "spy trade" of the Cold War was under way, but the President and Robert Kennedy did not want to announce it that way. It was an unprecedented situation. Neither country had ever publicly engaged in such a trade before, and both sides were cautiously feeling their way. The international climate was such that the Kennedy Administration, only eight months after the summit blowup in Paris, did not feel it would be politic to link the two cases publicly. (But the precedent was being established for the openly acknowledged Powers-Abel trade a year later.)

On the surface it still appeared that Melekh and Hirsch were headed for trial—and jail. On March 20 Judge Robson overruled all defense motions except one: the name of the U.S. citizen whom Melekh had paid was "to be disclosed to the defendants two weeks prior to the date of the trial." This was entirely a legal skirmish, because the government had already stipulated that his name would

---

his paper, he agreed to hold up on the story. Kennedy praised the *Herald Tribune* for this action in a telegram sent by Salinger to publisher John Hay Whitney. In his book, Salinger wrote: "Olmstead and McKone might still be in Lubianka Prison if it hadn't been for the *Herald Tribune*'s willingness to kill the story in the national interest."

be "fully disclosed" at the trial (the government's case rested chiefly on McCuaig's testimony), and, of course, Hirsch and Melekh already knew his identity.

But there was no trial. Four days later, on March 24, Manion appeared before Judge Robson with a request from Attorney General Kennedy that charges against the two men be dropped. A message from Robert Kennedy to Judge Robson said the request followed consultations between the State and Justice departments. It had been concluded that quashing the case, on condition that Melekh leave the country, "would best serve the national and foreign policy interests of the United States."

No one in the crowded courtroom appeared more startled than Judge Robson. In theory he could have disregarded the request from another branch of the government, but in practice he had little choice, because a federal judge cannot hold a trial if the government declines to prosecute. He dismissed the charges.

In Washington, Secretary of State Rusk announced that he had recommended in a letter to Robert Kennedy that the trial be dropped, in the belief that it would improve "our position as regards the protection of United States citizens in the Soviet Union." A State Department spokesman emphatically denied that there was any "deal" with the Russians, or that there was any connection at all with the release of the RB-47 fliers. As far as can be determined, there was no written agreement to trade the airmen for Melekh and Hirsch, but Robert Kennedy had agreed to drop the proceedings against the two GRU agents solely because of Soviet action on the RB-47 fliers.

William McCuaig was not required to testify in court, and the modest social worker never sought public recognition for his delicate and potentially dangerous work (McCuaig's double-agent activities have not been reported before). He had no training as a spy—nothing could be farther removed from the world and ideals of a social worker—but he served his government quietly and well in a difficult role that seems a necessary part of our age.

Igor Melekh left for home aboard the North German Lloyd liner *Bremen,* which sailed just after midnight on April 8 from Pier 88 in

Manhattan. Standing at the rail with his family, he took a last look at New York. In his arms, holding an Easter rabbit and a ball, was his pretty baby daughter, Marina, now twenty months—a pivotal if unlikely figure in a chain of international events involving Presidents and Premiers, Ministers, judges and the intelligence services of two world powers.

Willie Hirsch was freed from jail three days later, as immigration officials pondered his status. On April 21, President Kennedy was asked at his news conference whether the spy case had been dropped as "a part of a bargain for the RB-47 fliers."

"There was no connection," the President replied. "The dropping of the charges was made after an examination of the details of the case and of the national interest and it was felt that it would be useful to take the action we took. I am sorry I can't be more responsive . . ."

That there was no "overt" bargain was perhaps technically true, because the trade had been a tacit one, but Washington and Moscow knew there had been at least a de facto trade, even though that terminology had been avoided.

The following month the Immigration Service moved to deport Willie Hirsch and set a date for a hearing, but it was never held because he voluntarily agreed to leave. With his wife, Ruth Gilmore, and her daughter, Susie Baum Gilmore, he sailed for England at noon on July 21 from Hoboken, New Jersey, aboard the S.S. *Rotterdam* of the Holland-America Line. From London they had booked a BOAC flight to Prague, and after that—perhaps the GRU could say.

Ruth Gilmore later wrote to friends back in the United States that Willie Hirsch had died behind the Curtain. No more than that is known of the end of the story. Ruth Gilmore is a citizen and was not arrested with her husband; she is free to return to the United States. Should she do so, she would probably be asked some questions, which she might well choose not to answer, about the fate of the dynamic, jowly little man who abhorred death.

*These activities have their own rules
and methods of concealment
which seek to mislead and obscure.*

—**President Dwight D. Eisenhower,**
May 11, 1960

VIII the espionage revolution

The bright orange flash of an SA-2 missile lit up the sky over
Sverdlovsk on May Day 1960; the rocket fire sent the U-2 fluttering
to earth, probably brought down a pursuing Soviet jet fighter as
well,* and ushered in a new era in the history of espionage.

---

* After intensive questioning of Francis Gary Powers, the CIA concluded
that a Soviet plane had also been hit. When the U-2 pilot returned to the
United States in February 1962, he was whisked off to Ashford Farms, a
sixty-five-acre private CIA estate on the Choptank River in eastern Maryland,
where he was kept for twenty-four days. The mansion, near Oxford, was
protected with a heavy wire fence and guarded by German shepherd dogs.
Powers later testified to the Senate Armed Services Committee that when
Russian farm workers surrounded him after he parachuted to the ground, one
of them held up two fingers, as if to ask whether there were two pilots. "I told
him no, just shook my head no, and pointed to myself and held up one finger
telling him that I was alone. And then he pointed up in the air and I looked up
and saw what I think was a parachute, but I knew that I had no other
parachute on board the aircraft."
    The business of the two parachutes was never cleared up in Powers'

It brought a kind of instant sophistication to a world which, before then, had been only dimly aware of the clandestine underside to affairs of state. President Eisenhower shattered precedent when he assumed responsibility for the U-2 flight. But the explanation he gave in his memoirs is revealing:

"Francis Gary Powers was no individual traveler sneaking across borders between guards and living in concealed garrets in the land of a potential enemy; Powers had been apprehended thirteen hundred miles within Soviet territory, flying a piece of expensive machinery, equipped with the most intricate sets of cameras . . . In the diplomatic field it was routine practice to deny responsibility for an embarrassing occurrence when there is even a 1 per cent chance of being believed but when the world can entertain not the slightest doubt of the facts there is no point in trying to evade the issue." *

It was only a question of time, really, before the vast espionage establishments created since World War II would openly collide in a spectacular fashion, such as the U-2 affair. In its wake a whole new set of unwritten international rules of espionage emerged, as well as a new way of looking at spying on the part of both governments and people. Taken as a whole, it amounted to nothing less than an espionage revolution.

Accompanying the new public awareness of intelligence operations as a fact of international life was a huge increase in spy entertainment.

Early in 1961 *Life* printed a list of President Kennedy's ten favorite books. Ninth on the list was the name of Ian Fleming and *From Russia with Love*. It gave a tremendous push to the British author's books; the taste for James Bond seemed almost universal, appealing alike to teenie-boppers and college professors, commoners and kings. The U-2 incident had educated millions to the realities of

Senate testimony, but CIA experts had already formed the opinion that the Soviet anti-aircraft missile battery had, inadvertently, also shot down a Russian plane. Although the Russians routinely sent interceptors aloft, the high-altitude Lockheed spy plane flew well above their reach.

* Dwight D. Eisenhower, *The White House Years, Waging Peace: 1956–1961* (New York, Doubleday, 1965).

spying; Fleming and his imitators fed the public appetite for more. The spy story became the literature of the times. Not only in books but in television and motion pictures as well, the spy became the new, cool anti-hero of the mid-twentieth century.

Thus the enormous Bond cult was not unrelated to the real world of espionage. If the public accepted the reality of spying in the modern world, governments were not far behind in taking advantage of the new freedom.

The return of the RB-47 fliers and President Kennedy's release of Willie Hirsch and Igor Melekh was the first, cautious groping of both sides toward what rapidly became standard procedure. As unthinkable as it might have been in the previous decade, nations began publicly trading their spies in the 1960's. This also meant that nations were admitting for the first time that they *had* spies, for to trade a spy is to concede that he exists. But, as Eisenhower had said, there was now "no point in trying to evade the issue."

In May 1961, one month after Melekh had sailed home on the *Bremen,* James Donovan, New York attorney for Rudolf Abel, received a letter postmarked Leipzig and bearing the return address "Eisenacher Strasse, No. 22." It was signed "Hellen Abel," the purported wife of the convicted KGB colonel, then serving a thirty-year sentence in Atlanta Federal Penitentiary. The letter proposed a trade of Rudolf Abel for Francis Gary Powers.

More letters were exchanged between Donovan and "Hellen Abel"—letters actually ghostwritten by the CIA and the KGB. The correspondence eventually led to the successful trade of Powers for Abel, on February 10, 1962, in the early morning mist on Berlin's Glienicker Bridge. Simultaneously, at the Friedrichstrasse crossing, as part of the package negotiated by Donovan, the Russians released Frederic L. Pryor, twenty-eight, of Ann Arbor, Michigan, who had been arrested in East Berlin on August 25, 1961, as an espionage suspect. The son of a prominent Midwestern industrialist, Pryor had been seized less than a month after the arrest in Kiev of Marvin

Makinen, his fellow student at the Free University of Berlin (an academic institution frequented by CIA and United States military intelligence agents).

The Soviet government, later to glorify Russian spies in general and Abel in particular, was still moving gingerly at that early date. The Soviet public learned of the sensational exchange only through a letter printed in *Izvestia* on February 23, supposedly from Abel's family:

"Esteemed Comrade Editor! We, Helen and Lydia Abel, Rudolf Abel's wife and daughter, ask that our letter be published in your newspaper so that the whole public of the Soviet Union may know about the humane act of the Soviet government.

"Our husband and father, Rudolf Abel, while in the United States of America in 1957, was arrested without grounds upon the denunciation of a swindler and provocateur, accused of anti-state crimes for allegedly performing intelligence work for the Soviet Union and illegally sentenced to 30 years of hard labor.

"All our numerous appeals, including appeals to the President of the U.S.A. . . . failed. We then addressed ourselves to the Soviet government and established contact with the relatives of F. Powers, who was sentenced in the U.S.S.R.; they in turn addressed themselves to the U.S.S.R. government, with a request for his pardon . . .

"The Soviet authorities took a sympathetic view of these requests. As is known, F. Powers was released . . . With all our hearts, we thank the Soviet government and its head, N.S. Khrushchev, personally for this highly humane, magnanimous act."

Eleven months later, in December 1962, James Donovan brought the Bay of Pigs prisoners home for Christmas, in a trade not of spies, but of a whole brigade of men—survivors of the CIA's invasion of Cuba—for food and drugs.

On April 22, 1963, three CIA electronics technicians in Cuban jails were among a group of U.S. prisoners quietly traded for four pro-Castro Cubans in New York. Daniel L. Carswell (one of the CIA's top wiretap wizards), Eustace H. Danbrunt and Edmund K. Taransky had been convicted of tapping the wires of the Havana office of Hsinhua, the New China News Agency. On January 10, 1961, they were sentenced by a Cuban military court to ten years each. A pretty, blond American embassy secretary, Mrs. Majorie Lennox, was ordered out of Cuba in connection with the case. In the trade, Castro got back Francisco (The Hook) Molina, who was serving a twenty-years-to-life sentence for killing a nine-year-old Venezuelan girl while shooting up a New York restaurant on the occasion of Castro's UN visit in 1960; and three saboteurs, Roberto Santiesteban Casanova (an attaché at Castro's UN mission), Antonio Sueiro Cabrera and José Garcia Orellana, who had planned to blow up department stores in Manhattan and oil refineries in New Jersey. In all, twenty-seven Americans, some of doubtful citizenship, were let go by Castro in the exchange, but Washington's primary purpose was to free the three CIA agents.

In October, Ivan and Alexandra Egorov, fellow GRU agents of Alexandre Sokolov alias Robert Baltch, were traded for Makinen and Father Ciszek.

By April 22, 1964, when Gordon Lonsdale, the KGB "illegal" in Britain's Portland case, was swapped for Penkovsky's courier Greville Wynne at the Heerstrasse crossing point in West Berlin, spy exchanges, if not yet standard international practice, were no longer something new.

But diplomatic traditionalists, as well as many United States intelligence officials, looked askance at the trades, fearing that the Russians would indiscriminately seize innocent Americans and charge them with spying in order to trade them for Russians held in United States jails. To an extent these fears have come true: the Russians have gone to extraordinary lengths to attempt to win the freedom of a high-ranking KGB man convicted of espionage in the United States.

On the evening of Saint Patrick's Day 1962, SAS flight 911 from Copenhagen taxied to a halt at Idlewild International Airport in New York. One of the passengers who got off was a blond, burly Russian, a tough-looking man with a wide, Slavic face and expressionless gray eyes. He carried Soviet passport No. 001664. Perhaps he had once been a sailor, for he had two tattoos: on the inside of his right thumb the Russian letter *E,* and on his left forearm, a ship in a circle beneath the name *SEDOV.*

Igor Alexandrovich Ivanov, thirty-one, accompanied by his wife Nadezhda and his five-year-old daughter, had been sent from Moscow ostensibly to take up duties as a chauffeur for Amtorg, the Soviet trade agency at 355 Lexington Avenue in New York. With his family, Ivanov moved into the Hotel Greystone, at Broadway and Ninety-first Street; later they moved to a house in the Rockaways, a section of Queens.

Ivanov spoke some English, although poorly. He seemed to come and go as he pleased at Amtorg, enjoying much more latitude than would normally be expected of a chauffeur. He was an intelligent man, poised, alert and self-confident.

On April 21, 1963, Gleb A. Pavlov, a six-foot, thirty-nine-year-old attaché at the Soviet Mission to the UN, drove across the Hudson River to New Jersey with two passengers, Ivanov and Vladimir I. Olenev, another attaché at the mission. While Pavlov was parked in a restaurant lot in Closter, a Ford Falcon pulled up beside him. Pavlov got into this car, and when he left after a short conversation with the driver, he was carrying a light-tan attaché case.

The FBI had followed Pavlov to New Jersey, and from the license plates of the Falcon, its owner was identified the next morning as John W. Butenko, a thirty-seven-year-old electrical engineer employed in an extremely sensitive position by the International Electric Corporation, a subsidiary of the giant International Telephone and Telegraph Corporation. The son of Ukrainian-born parents, he lived with his elderly, crippled and widowered father in Orange, New Jersey. He was a bachelor and a loner whose hobby was playing the stock market, in which he had about $30,000 invested. He had been an honor student at Rutgers, and had held a number of jobs with major electronics firms before going to work in 1960 for International Electric at Paramus, New Jersey. He was the $14,700-a-year control administrator of the highly secret Project 465L, a massive, computerized communications system designed for the sole use of the Strategic Air Command of the United States Air Force.

In the nuclear-missile age, when the United States might have to react to an enemy attack in minutes, the Air Force felt there was need of a computer system that would, in seconds, memorize, analyze and transmit data to SAC headquarters, giving top commanders information on the status of all SAC forces. This the 465L was designed to do. It provided the high-speed communications equipment to pour data into SAC headquarters at the astonishing rate of three thousand words per minute. More important, it translated the data into huge seven-color electronic wall displays—the sort of supersophisticated war-room charts that man has achieved in the twentieth century, the better to program Armageddon.

According to the subsequent testimony of one Air Force expert, Major Henry Eugene Davis, 465L could communicate, if need be, "SAC alert messages . . . that would send SAC aircraft crews to their aircraft, [to] get airborne and prepared to go to war," messages that "would cause the missile crews to begin their missile countdown preparing for missile launch in the event of war."

As control administrator of 465L with a top-secret clearance, Butenko had complete knowledge of the complex communications system, and his job entailed frequent trips around the country to SAC bases to plan its installation. In short, he knew it all.

The nerve center of SAC was a delicate and important enough target to merit the KGB's attentions. Let the GRU collect aerial photographs of Chicago—this was far bigger game. To go after it, the Russians had dispatched a team of experienced KGB operators to New York. First to arrive, in 1960, was Pavlov (probably the case agent in charge), followed by Olenev in 1961, by Ivanov in 1962, and, on May 29, 1963, by Yuri Romashin, a sleek, athletic-looking man whose cover title was third secretary of the Soviet UN mission.

After Butenko's rendezvous in April a series of clandestine meetings followed in May, September and October of 1963 between Butenko and the Russians against a dreary backdrop of the roadside hamburger stands (The Golden Key Kafe), suburban shopping centers, highways and gas stations of Bergen County. It was an appropriately rootless, Fellini-like setting for the alienated young defense engineer's actions.

All told, five meetings were observed during 1963 between Butenko and various of the four KGB men, and each of these involved much jumping in and out of cars, switching of briefcases, and complicated evasive driving designed to throw off surveillance.

The fifth meeting took place on October 29 in the railroad-station parking lot at Englewood. Butenko arrived there just before 8 P.M. Ivanov and Pavlov drove up and parked behind him. The two cars started to pull out of the lot, with Ivanov leading the way, when the FBI moved in and blocked them. Romashin was picked up by the FBI as he lingered on foot nearby; in all likelihood he was the team's countersurveillance man.

On the rear seat of the Russians' ancient green Ford was a brown attaché case containing two restricted International Electric documents dealing with the SAC communications project. A third, six-page document headed "451st Strategic Missile Wing" included a drawing of an ICBM base, showing a launch silo, a propellent terminal and missile fuel tanks, and a drawing of a Titan missile. Also recovered was a map of Ellsworth Air Force Base, South Dakota, and a document headed "HQ 821st Combat Support Group, SAC, Ellsworth AFB, S.D."

The outwardly unimpressive Ford proved to be a sort of KGB mobile unit, equipped with the most sophisticated Soviet electronic and photographic devices yet uncovered in a spy case in the United States. In one of the opening scenes of *Goldfinger,* the villainous protagonist cheats at cards by means of a tiny radio receiver disguised as a hearing aid. From a hotel room a young lady, scantily dressed but equipped with powerful binoculars, broadcasts instructions to Goldfinger about his opponent's cards when James Bond arrives to distract her. The FBI found that Romashin was wearing what appeared to be a hearing aid, attached to a pink electrical cord with a jack at one end. It could be plugged into the receiving end of a miniature transmitter-receiver system, like Goldfinger's, which the KGB men had with them when they were arrested. The system consisted of two slim, gunmetal-gray portable radio units, each about the size and shape of a paperback book. The receiver had an antenna, small clips to attach the device to clothing, and a numbered dial marked 0, 1, 2 and 3. The 0 was the "off" position. If the dial was moved to 1, the receiver would vibrate to alert the KGB man to any incoming message. He could then turn to one of the other numbered channels for an audio message.

The companion transmitter operated on 63 megacycles and was powered by rechargeable nickel cadmium cells. The miniaturized equipment had a range of from three blocks to two miles. Both units were of KGB manufacture.*

On the floor of the KGB car were two supermarket shopping bags. In one was a highly sophisticated document-copying camera, rather like a slim attaché case in its general size and shape, only 2⅛ inches thick. Mounted on it was a cartridge containing forty feet of film, enough to copy four hundred documents. The camera could operate on a 12-volt battery, but it could also be powered by the car's cigarette lighter. For this, the KGB had designed a converter, a small metal box with an outlet that the camera could be plugged into and a wire lead at the other end that fit into the car's dashboard lighter.

In the other shopping bag was a clock radio with a secret compartment, containing still another document-copying camera, a 3- by 4-inch miniature version in the shape of a cigarette case. It operated on three small batteries.

When apprehended, Romashin was, bizarrely, wearing his pajamas under his clothing. Because he had diplomatic immunity, he could not be held, and with Pavlov and Olenev, the other two members of the UN mission, he was ordered out of the country by the

---

* The case demonstrated that today's spies really do use Bond-like gadgets. One of Ian Fleming's great admirers was CIA Director Allen Dulles, who was first introduced to his books by Jacqueline Kennedy. Dulles became fascinated with the radio "homing" device which Bond installed in an enemy's car so that he could track it across the Alps. He ordered CIA's laboratories to see if they could come up with such a device. The report came back that it was not practical; when the person being followed reached an urban area, there was too much interference with the signal.

State Department the next day. But Ivanov, because his cover was Amtorg, enjoyed no such immunity, and he and Butenko were arrested and indicted by a federal grand jury for conspiracy to commit espionage.

The lengthy trial opened at Newark a year later, in October 1964, and Ivanov listened through plastic earphones to the simultaneous Russian translation of interpreters provided by the State Department. During the trial Butenko testified that he had visited the Soviet embassy around 1953 to ask about relatives in the Soviet Union; he also said he had been approached in 1963 by a man known to him as George Lesnikov who offered to provide news of these relatives. Butenko claimed his meetings with Soviet officials at Bergen County hamburger stands were for this purpose. "I did not intend to indulge in espionage," he said.

The jury did not believe him, and on December 2 found both Butenko and Ivanov guilty. Ivanov told the court his arrest was an "unfortunate misunderstanding," and added, "I came to this country to work as a chauffeur and I worked here only as a chauffeur." Federal Judge Anthony T. Augelli gave Butenko thirty years and Ivanov twenty. Both could have been sentenced to death.

Much about Butenko remained a mystery. How and when the Russians had recruited him was not clear, nor were his motives. It was not shown at the trial that he was paid to betray his country, and he seemed apolitical, certainly not ideologically identifiable. Ivanov, on the other hand, was a professional intelligence officer, and the Russians wanted him back, badly.

There are two principal reasons why the Russians try to retrieve captured officers of the KGB (or the GRU), men like Ivanov and Abel. First, there is always a chance that they will start to talk, a possibility that is eliminated if they are returned safely to the Soviet Union. Second, the morale of the entire Soviet espionage establishment is strengthened when a career agent knows that if he is caught, his government will make every effort to get him out.

Ivanov's importance in the KGB, and the Russian government's interest in protecting him, became clear three weeks after his conviction, when the Soviet embassy provided $100,000 bail for the man who had come to the United States to work "only as a chauffeur." The Circuit Court of Appeals in Philadelphia then granted Ivanov his freedom on bail pending the outcome of his appeal. Behind this unusual move was a private pledge by the Soviet government to the United States government that Ivanov would not try to flee the country. It was this assurance of the Russians that carried even more weight than the $100,000 bail bond.

Ivanov's wife had gone back to Moscow after his arrest, where she gave birth to another child while he was on trial in Newark. He now moved into the Soviet Mission to the UN, at 136 East Sixty-seventh Street, a pleasant part of Manhattan, there to wait out the disposition of his case in the courts. Ivanov's name had appeared in the headlines only briefly, and few Americans realized that the KGB's efforts to free him lay behind a series of seemingly unrelated events that followed.

In all, the Russians have attempted to trade Ivanov for at least four Americans arrested in the Soviet Union. The first of these was Peter Nelson Landerman, a twenty-two-year-old student from Riverside, California. A friendly, bright graduate of the University of California, Landerman was fluent in Russian and interested in folk music, anthropology and languages. Because his father was a U.S. foreign-aid official, he grew up in Formosa, Greece and Bolivia.

Landerman was one of a group of thirteen American students who went to the Soviet Union on a forty-day camping trip in 1963. On the night of August 15 Landerman was driving his fellow students along a road near Minsk in a Volkswagen Microbus. There was a good deal of oncoming traffic, and Landerman switched to his parking lights, as he had been told to do. One of the cars coming toward him did not, and Landerman, momentarily blinded, hit Leonid S. Popov, a sixty-two-year-old retired factory worker. Landerman was held by police; Popov died five days later, and on September 24 the young American was placed on trial in the Minsk district court. On the advice of his lawyer he pleaded guilty, but then came an unexpected verdict: three years in a corrective labor colony for negligent driving. Shunted from one prison camp to another, Landerman was set to work chopping birch logs in subzero weather, subsisting on cabbage soup and grain meal.

The Landerman case broke before the arrest of Igor Ivanov in the United States. After Landerman was shipped off to a Soviet labor colony, the Russian government hinted to U.S. diplomats that the way to gain the student's early release was to free Ivanov. Washington refused.

In December, perhaps to increase the pressure on Washington, Landerman was sent back to Moscow from the labor camp and held for a time in a KGB prison. In Moscow, an American embassy official was allowed to see him. Not until February 1965 was Landerman pardoned and returned to the United States, and by then he had served sixteen months of his harsh sentence.

An even more blatant KGB attempt to win Ivanov's release had been made two days after he was arrested in New Jersey in October 1963. Professor Frederick C. Barghoorn of Yale University was relaxing over cocktails with Walter J. Stoessel, minister of the American embassy in Moscow, at Stoessel's apartment inside the embassy compound.

It was the shy, fifty-two-year-old political scientist's last night of a month's tour of the Soviet Union. He knew the country well; he had served in the American embassy in Moscow during and after the war (attached to the press section), and he was an expert on Soviet affairs. He had collected voluminous notes on this, the latest of his six trips, which had been marred only by a brief illness in Tiflis. The single possible hint of trouble on the journey had come in the delightful form of an overly attentive, very beautiful girl who sat next to the bachelor professor on the flight to the Georgian capital. She had even given Dr. Barghoorn her telephone number. Her English was flawless, and in the light of later events it seems entirely possible that she was an agent of the KGB.

After cocktails with Stoessel, Barghoorn was delivered back to his hotel, the Metropole, in the limousine of Ambassador Foy D. Kohler. The ambassador's Soviet chauffeur, undoubtedly a KGB man, let Barghoorn off at the side of the hotel. The professor had taken about five steps when he was intercepted by a young man who shoved a roll of newspapers in his hands. Unwisely, Barghoorn thrust the papers in his trench coat, and as he turned toward the hotel entrance, KGB men jumped from an automobile parked at the curb and seized him. Wrapped inside the newspapers, they told him later, were photographs of rockets.

A British friend waiting in the hotel to have dinner with Barghoorn was not terribly disturbed when he failed to turn up, since Barghoorn had a reputation for being the proverbial absent-minded professor. Although the ambassador's driver had witnessed the whole performance, he reported nothing to the embassy, and since Barghoorn had been scheduled to leave for Warsaw the next morning, it was days before anyone in Moscow realized he had vanished. All the while, he was being held in solitary confinement in Lubianka. A light bulb was kept burning in his cell around the clock; his captors gave him a copy of Theodore Dreiser's *An American Tragedy,* which he read.

During the interrogations the KGB accused Barghoorn of spying on his trips in the Soviet Union. From 1949 to 1951, when Barghoorn briefly worked for the State Department interviewing Soviet defectors in West Germany, he had listed himself as in "intelligence" work, and perhaps this gave the KGB men a peg on which to hang their charges. Ten days went by before the U.S. embassy was told of Barghoorn's arrest; then it was privately made clear that the Yale professor could be returned in a trade for Igor Ivanov. The ploy did not work.

President Kennedy declared in a news conference on November 14, only eight days before his death, that Barghoorn was "not on an intelligence mission of any kind" and demanded his immediate release. The Russians must have been impressed by the fact that Kennedy had staked his personal prestige on Barghoorn's innocence.

At noon two days later Stoessel was summoned before Foreign Minister Andrei A. Gromyko, who read him a long, involved statement which boiled down to this: despite all that Barghoorn had done, the Soviet Union was going to release him and it hoped that the United States would follow that example. To Stoessel, it was clearly a suggestion that in return for the professor's release, the United States free Ivanov. Four hours later the Russians hustled Barghoorn on a BEA Comet jet for London. After sixteen harrowing days in the hands of the KGB he was a free man.

The next Soviet attempt to win back the KGB "chauffeur" in Manhattan had a much more tragic ending. On February 1, 1966, Senator Edward M. Kennedy of Massachusetts arose in the Senate, and in the accents and style so reminiscent of his brother, the late President, declared, "Yesterday afternoon, in the town of Sheffield, Massachusetts, a young man was buried. His name was Newcomb Mott, and the circumstances of his death are of most serious concern—not just to his family and his countrymen, but to the cause of justice, and to future relations between the United States and the Soviet Union."

Newcomb Mott was not a man one would forget easily. Twenty-seven when he died, he was six foot five, a husky, restless and romantic young graduate of free-spirited Antioch College. A favorite athletic activity of his at Antioch was "roving"—running alone through the one-thousand-acre wooded college glen.

He grew up in Sheffield, a Berkshire mountain town, where his father was a dealer in rare books and drawings. Newcomb taught at a boys' school there for a while after graduating from Antioch. In the fall of 1963, around the time Igor Ivanov was arrested, he went to work as a traveling salesman for D. Van Nostrand Company, the Princeton textbook firm. On July 19, 1965, with a long summer vacation ahead of him, Mott flew via SAS to Copenhagen. He visited Sweden and Finland, and on September 2 he flew to Kirkenes, Norway, a remote arctic town a few miles from the Soviet border. Mott received conflicting advice when he inquired about visiting Boris Gleb, the tiny Soviet enclave just over the border. The confusion probably arose because the Soviet town, consisting of little more than a restaurant and bar, a church and the border station, was open to Norwegian tourists—but not to Americans.

On September 4 he took an early morning bus from Kirkenes, got off at a crossroads and headed for the Soviet border. He later explained that his purpose was to find out for himself whether he could visit Boris Gleb. But he came to no checkpoint. Instead, he passed a yellow border pole, realized that he had strayed into Soviet territory, but for reasons never made entirely clear, kept going. At Boris Gleb he was detained by Soviet border guards. The next day a KGB officer questioned him and asked whether he was a CIA agent. Mott said he was not, but a day later he was shipped to Murmansk, formally arrested for illegally crossing the border and held for trial. On October 15 a KGB man handed a letter from Mott to William T. Shinn of the American embassy. "Something tangible would have to be given or promised in return for my release," Mott wrote. "If the only way I could be released soon was by U.S. exchange of a Russian prisoner of some sort, I hope the United States would do it."

To the State Department, it seemed obvious that the KGB had suggested this proposal to Mott. It seemed equally clear to Washington that the KGB was using Mott as yet another pawn in its untiring effort to get back one of its own, Igor Ivanov.* Later in October the U.S. embassy in Moscow sent back word: there would be no trade of a tourist for a spy.

Mott went on trial in Murmansk on November 22, and two days later he was sentenced to eighteen months in a prison camp. On the night of January 20, 1966, according to the Russians, while Mott was 350 miles east of Moscow aboard a train going to the labor camp, he committed suicide by slashing his throat with a razor blade.

The Soviet autopsy report provided to Washington claimed that Mott, "traveling in solitary Compartment 9 on the special railroad car . . . began to show signs of abnormal behavior; having placed on the shelf a picture post card of the Madonna, he spread out playing cards before it, began to talk to himself; wrung his hands; loudly shouted some words; and then with a sudden movement, gathered up the cards and tore them up . . .

---

* At the time, Mott may not have known Ivanov's name, though later his parents discussed Ivanov with him when they were first permitted to see him after the Murmansk trial. The State Department, in any event, had no doubt that the Russians were trying to exchange Mott for Ivanov.

"Having noticed blood on N. Mott's body, the guards tried to enter . . . but N. Mott . . . threw three glass jars of canned goods at the guards . . . in spite of this the convoy personnel entered the compartment and gave N. Mott first-aid treatment, which he resisted. Then N. Mott became weak from the great loss of blood and, although steps were taken to save his life, he died soon thereafter."

A U.S. embassy physician was present at the autopsy in the Moscow morgue, and an embassy statement said that "a deep laceration of the throat, five inches long, that cut across the windpipe and the esophagus . . . was the apparent cause of death."

Many questions remained unanswered. With a five-inch laceration of the windpipe, how had he "resisted" the guards? Was it not unusual that a prisoner was allowed to have a picture of the Madonna?

The Johnson Administration assailed Moscow for its handling of the entire case, and in a note to the Soviet Union declared that for lack of evidence, "The United States government has found it impossible to arrive at meaningful conclusions about the events leading up to Mr. Mott's death and the means by which his death came about." *

On October 1, 1966, the Russians arrested two more young Americans, Buel Ray Wortham, a twenty-five-year-old ex-U.S. Army lieutenant from North Little Rock, Arkansas, and Craddock M. Gilmour, Jr., twenty-four, of Salt Lake City. They were seized after checking out of the Europeiskaya Hotel in Leningrad with the hotel's bear, a twenty-inch cast-iron statue of one shot by Czar Alexander II

---

* At Mott's trial a Soviet witness testified that Mott had walked right up to the border guards in Boris Gleb and identified himself. But according to another version, told to the authors, the first person to encounter Mott in the Soviet Union was the bartender at the restaurant in the Soviet enclave, who was on his way to work when he ran into Mott in a field. He took Mott along with him to the bar, and shortly afterward Mott was arrested there. The bartender was transferred to Leningrad, given a new job and an apartment, and rewarded as if he were responsible for apprehending Mott, according to this version. In April 1967 the Scandinavian press reported that two Norwegians arrested as Soviet spies by authorities in Norway may have been meeting their Russian contacts in Boris Gleb, which might be an alternative explanation of why the Russians overreacted to Mott's presence there. The same published report said that Norwegian security police placed a close watch on Boris Gleb after a known Soviet intelligence agent turned up in the town—as bartender.

in 1865. They were questioned by the KGB for sixty days. On December 21 both were convicted of buying rubles on the black market, and Wortham of stealing the bear. Gilmour was fined $1,111 and sent home, but Wortham was sentenced to three years. The Russians hinted they would like to trade Wortham for Ivanov, but nothing came of it. On March 11, 1967, Wortham, who had appealed his sentence, was fined $5,555 and released.

In early 1967 Ivanov was living comfortably in the Soviet UN mission on the East Side of Manhattan with his wife, who had returned to this country with her children on December 2, 1966. He remained free on $100,000 bail, his case still awaiting action in the circuit court in Philadelphia. In four years, three young Americans, including one who died tragically, a Yale professor and President Kennedy, all had become enmeshed in the struggle over the fate of a single KGB agent.

In England the Russians were engaged in a parallel effort to free Morris and Lona Cohen, the KGB couple convicted as Peter and Helen Kroger in the Portland naval secrets case. Gerald Brooke, twenty-six, a lecturer in Russian at London's Holborn College, was arrested in Moscow on April 25, 1965, on charges of having distributed subversive pamphlets for the NTS (National Alliance of Russian Solidarists), the anti-Soviet émigré group. Tried in July, he was sentenced to five years. The Russians said that a stout NTS agent named "Georgi" had first approached Brooke in England and plied him with "coffee and pastries with cream, Gerald Brooke's favorite delicacy," at a London restaurant called Schmidt's. Who could resist the cream puffs at Schmidt's? After that, Brooke had little choice but to become an agent of the NTS, according to the Russians.

At any rate, Brooke was in Lubianka, where his wife, Barbara, later visited him. From the start the KGB tried to swap him for the Krogers. Early in 1966 Brooke wrote to Robin Stafford, Moscow correspondent for the *Daily Express*. Brooke said he had lost weight on the prison fare and was "very depressed," adding, "From what I read in the press, I draw the conclusion that my fate is inextricably bound up with that of Peter and Helen Kroger . . . According to the newspapers, as I am not a spy, the question of an exchange of prisoners is in my case ruled out . . . Does this mean that if I were a spy such an exchange would be practicable? . . . Why should I have to suffer more because I am not a spy? . . . voices clamor that the exchange is unfair, that two old, sick guilty spies are worth more than one young, sick innocent teacher. Perhaps this is so. I wouldn't know. Whatever the answer, perhaps one should bear in mind that human lives are being bartered."

Prime Minister Wilson appealed to the Soviet leaders to release Brooke, but two years after his arrest he was still imprisoned, as were the Cohens.

There is no reason to think, however, that the spy trades begun in 1961 will not continue to take place in the future. In fact, spies, whose activities were not even admitted by governments a few years ago, are today being glorified, commercialized, interviewed, decorated, encouraged to engage in literary pursuits and, in general, treated in a manner that would have been unthinkable a decade ago.

The trend toward exaltation of spies by both East and West was a logical outgrowth of the espionage revolution. First, captured spies were acknowledged. Then spies were traded. With that, governments realized that having gone thus far, they might as well go all the way and reap a measure of propaganda advantage from the exploits of their secret agents.

In the Soviet Union the beginning of this trend was visible even before the downfall of Khrushchev, although glorification of Soviet spies was greatly intensified afterward. Before Soviet agents could be lionized, however, they had at least to be humanized, and that process was begun several years ago.

During a conversation with Averell Harriman in 1959, Khrushchev related that Stalin had become so suspicious in his last years that when his aides or advisers called on him they were never sure they would emerge to see their families again; accordingly, after Stalin's death, his political heirs decided they could not allow that kind of atmosphere to continue—the powers of the secret police would have to be reduced. In that connection, Khrushchev told Harriman, the Kremlin leaders had a little difficulty with Beria, whom he described with a smile as "a little overly ambitious."

Striking a similar note in a speech to the 1961 Communist Party Congress, Shelepin, then chairman of the KGB, declared, "The state security agencies are no longer the bugbear that enemies—Beria and his aides—sought to make them not very long ago, but are truly the people's—in the literal sense of the word—political agencies of our party."

The campaign to honor Soviet spies began in earnest three weeks after Khrushchev's overthrow, when on November 5, 1964, the award of Hero of the Soviet Union was posthumously conferred upon Richard Sorge, the fabled GRU agent in Japan. About the same time *Komsomolskaya Pravda,* the Soviet youth newspaper, ran an eleven-part series on counterespionage, featuring a seductive female KGB agent who smoked Camels and trapped Western spies. A popular movie, *State Criminal,* had as its hero a handsome young KGB agent, and another successful film paid tribute to Sorge.

The message of *The President's Secret,* a motion picture script published in Moscow early in 1965, was that the Soviet military suffered setbacks in World War II because Stalin ignored intelligence that had been gathered at great risk by Soviet secret agents.

Spy novels flooded the Soviet Union, to the point where a Soviet literary weekly ran a cartoon that showed a line of writers waiting outside an editorial office, clutching manuscripts with titles like *Operation Rose, Operation X, Operation White Elephant* and *Operation No. 24.**

In May 1965 Moscow took an extraordinary step and admitted publicly for the first time that Rudolf Abel was a Soviet spy and had been decorated for valor after his exchange for Powers in 1962.† A

---

* *Literaturnaya Rossiya* (February 26, 1965).

† Not to be outdone, the CIA conferred a medal on Francis Gary Powers in April 1965, just before the fifth anniversary of his U-2 flight. Like the ceremony at CIA headquarters, attended by top officials of the intelligence agency, the gold medal itself was secret. One CIA man described it as "one of

Soviet television show sketched in Abel's alleged wartime background as an intelligence agent against the Nazis, and said that after his arrest in 1957 he had spurned the efforts of "foreign intelligence" to turn him into an agent against the Soviet Union ("He would not crumple. He stayed firm").

A few days after the television program, *Pravda* published a long article by Vladimir Semichastny hailing Soviet spies. During World War II, the KGB chief said, "along with open, armed combat was waged a bitter secret war . . . an unprecedented test for Soviet intelligence and counterintelligence." It was true that the Stalin era had resulted in "serious distortions and errors in the work of the state security agencies," but these "did not alter the socialist nature of Soviet intelligence and counterintelligence work, did not cut it off from the people and the party.

"One cannot fail to express special appreciation and profound gratitude to the valiant Soviet intelligence agents who, like Hero of the Soviet Union Richard Sorge or the agent known by the name of Rudolf Abel, performed difficult but honorable tasks in the struggle against the enemy . . . in resolving these tasks, the state security agencies direct the cutting edge of their activity outward, against the imperialist espionage agencies. The Chekists stand tireless guard over the interests of the Soviet people."

From the viewpoint of the Soviet Union, the international espionage revolution and the new world-wide awareness of spying neatly coincided with its own desire to come to terms with the past. The terror of the Stalin era, carried out by the state security agencies, left a deep and lasting scar that could not be removed by Semichastny's soothing words. The government's efforts to rehabilitate and sanctify Soviet spies, to remake the image of the KGB, was not a

---

those under-the-lapel medals." In November 1962, nine months after Powers' return to the United States, the CIA announced that he had taken "a routine test pilot job" at the Lockheed Aircraft Corporation in Burbank, California, "checking out U-2's." Lockheed built the spy plane and acted as the civilian front behind which the CIA's U-2 flights over Russia were carried out from 1956 to 1960. After divorcing his first wife, Barbara, Powers on October 26, 1963, married Claudia Edwards Downey, twenty-eight, a CIA psychologist and divorcee with a seven-year-old girl of her own. They lived in a modern home overlooking the San Fernando Valley near Burbank. In June 1965 they had a son—Francis Gary Powers, Jr.

casual development but a carefully planned public-relations campaign. As one Washington analyst put it, the program seemed to have as its goal an atmosphere in which Russian citizens would come to accept the image of "your neighborhood KGB man." Other Western experts saw the effort to ennoble spies as a sign that the KGB was flexing its muscles within Soviet society and was itself behind the spy-promotion program.*

Certainly the KGB was deeply involved in the round of spy memoirs which, beginning in 1964, were surfaced by the intelligence agencies of both East and West.

The first of these reminiscences was "Greville Wynne's Story," a five-part series that ran in the *Sunday Telegraph* of London in September 1964. After his arrest in Budapest on November 2, 1962, Wynne, then forty-three, was described as a British businessman, the managing director of Mobile Exhibitions, Ltd., a traveling trade show that he was taking through eastern Europe. Greville Maynard Wynne, a short man with a mustache which the *New York Times* once said made him look "a little like the actor Terry-Thomas in repose," wrote in his memoirs that he was born in Shropshire on March 19, 1919, educated as an engineer at Nottingham University and commissioned during the war as an Army officer. After the war he said he joined an electrical company as a sales engineer and in 1950 set up his own business as an exporter of heavy industrial equipment, which involved frequent trips abroad, including many to the Soviet Union. He lived in Chelsea with his wife, Sheila, and their son, Andrew. He had steel pins in one leg, the result of an accident on one such trip to Odessa in 1957.

It was in Moscow on December 1960 that he first met Oleg Penkovsky, a Soviet GRU colonel whose cover job was that of civilian employee of the State Committee for the Co-ordination of

---

* The campaign was still booming three years later and had spread to other Communist nations. A chubby Bulgarian novelist, Andrei Gulyashki, invented a Communist James Bond called Avakum Zakhov who wolfs noodles and cabbage, which would have horrified Fleming's hero. The two fictional ace spies of East and West clash in *Avakum Zakhov versus 07,* which *Komsomolskaya Pravda* serialized for its youthful readers in September 1966. (The Bulgarians were unable to get copyright permission to use Bond's name or "007," so they settled for one zero less.)

Scientific Research Work. When he realized that the Soviet official wanted to contact Western intelligence, he helped him: "Most British businessmen with my experience would have done the same."

In early April 1961, Wynne was back in Moscow. When he returned to England, he took a letter from Penkovsky to British intelligence, and for the next sixteen months he acted as an espionage courier for Penkovsky. Twice during this period Penkovsky visited London with an official delegation, from April 21 to May 6, 1961, and again from July 18 to August 8. During his total stay of thirty-seven days in London and on a later trip to Paris in September, he was extensively interrogated by British intelligence and the CIA.

Penkovsky was apprehended in Moscow shortly before Wynne's arrest in Budapest, and both pleaded guilty at their Moscow trial, held from May 7 to 11, 1963. At the trial Wynne described himself as "an electrical engineer and salesman" who had been led astray by British intelligence. In particular he blamed two British agents named "Roger King" and "Ackroyd" whom he had at first regarded as "trustworthy gentlemen" from the "Foreign Office." Wynne said he agreed to work with Penkovsky when Ackroyd's chief assured him "this was nothing to do with espionage." Asked on the witness stand what he thought of spying, Wynne replied, "If you are talking about state secrets, I would not touch it. It's a dirty business." When he worried about his role, Wynne testified, "Roger King . . . threatened me."

"You agreed then to carry out assignments for British intelligence?" the Soviet prosecutor asked.

"I agreed reluctantly," said Wynne. "A thousand miles away there are my own people—responsible people who have landed me in this dock." The picture of unsuspecting "businessman" Wynne succumbing to the blandishments of M.I.6 was not a terribly convincing one, but Wynne was on trial for his life and perhaps entitled to say what he wished. He was sentenced to eight years, but Penkovsky was sentenced to death. On May 16 Tass announced tersely: "The spy Oleg Penkovsky has been executed." *

---

* Six British diplomats in Moscow and the wife of one, plus five American embassy officials, were named in the trial. Later the Russians claimed

Wynne was shipped to Vladimir Prison, ninety miles northeast of Moscow, where, according to his memoirs, he shared a cell with Marvin Makinen during the summer of 1963—the same cell which Francis Gary Powers had occupied. Wynne and Lonsdale were exchanged the following April. After the Briton's memoirs were serialized in the fall, the Wynne-Penkovsky story dropped out of the news for a time.

Next, it was the Russians' turn to put out a spy memoir. In England, Gordon Lonsdale's story was first serialized in March 1965 by *The People,* a Sunday newspaper, and then published in book form in October.

There were reports around this time that Abel, too, was writing his memoirs. He was, in fact, permitted to write two articles and deliver a radio lecture on espionage the following year. In these, Abel claimed that he had tricked the FBI by disposing of certain evidence at the time of his arrest. "No professional spy wants to admit he goofed," the FBI replied, adding that Abel had "obviously bungled his mission," since he was caught.

In the United States, the question of whether to publish a Penkovsky memoir had been debated for months within the U.S. intelligence community. Penkovsky had dispatched many documents to the West—he confessed at his trial to having sent out five thousand frames of film; in addition, the CIA and M.I.6 had accumulated miles of tape and transcripts from questioning Penkovsky during the thirty-seven days he was in London. In November 1965, a book was published based on this material.*

From the outset, particularly in England, the book was attacked for having CIA origins. Victor Zorza, distinguished Soviet expert of the Manchester *Guardian,* wrote: "The book can have been compiled only by the Central Intelligence Agency. The CIA has been repeat-

---

that two other U.S. embassy employees were involved with Penkovsky. In all, the Russians ousted five American and five British diplomats as a result of the Penkovsky case.

* Oleg Penkovskiy, *The Penkovskiy Papers,* Introduction and Commentary by Frank Gibney, translated by Peter Deriabin (New York, Doubleday, 1965). "Penkovskiy" is a form of transliteration from the Russian favored by the United States government, including the CIA.

edly stung and provoked by the attempts of the Disinformation Department of the Soviet intelligence organization to discredit its activities throughout the world. The Penkovsky Papers are the CIA's answer."

Paul Blackstock, an intelligence specialist in the Department of International Studies of the University of South Carolina also concluded, in *Agents of Deceit,* published by Quadrangle Books in 1966, that *The Penkovskiy Papers* "is not what it is represented to be." Blackstock found much of it "an insult to the intelligence of the lay reader." John Le Carré, author of *The Spy Who Came in From the Cold,* had drawn similar conclusions in his lead review in *Book Week* of December 26, 1965.

The basic mistake made in releasing *The Penkovskiy Papers* was that the CIA had chosen the same team—Gibney, Deriabin and Doubleday—that had produced *The Secret World* in 1959. Deriabin, after all, had defected to the CIA and was identified with it, and this earlier book had publicly been praised by the CIA—only two months before the publication of the Penkovsky book—as "probably the most authoritative public account of KGB organization and activity." *

Against this background, it was natural enough that critics immediately linked *The Penkovskiy Papers* with the CIA. Supposedly, Penkovsky had typed out the Papers in his Moscow apartment under the nose of the KGB ("When I write at home I disturb my family's sleep . . . typing is very noisy"). But the publishers seemed to have some difficulty in producing the original Russian manuscript for skeptical newsmen. According to Gibney's Editor's Note, "it was Deriabin who received the Penkovskiy Papers, after they had been smuggled out of the Soviet Union, and instantly recognized their importance." † Deriabin, in a letter to the newspapers, said: "I will not, however, reveal how the Papers came to me."

The debate was silly, in a way, since who else *but* the CIA and M.I.6 would be expected to have the "manuscript" of a Soviet spy for the CIA and M.I.6?

---

* *The Soviet and Communist Bloc Defamation Campaign.* See Chapter II.
† "It [the manuscript] got to him [Deriabin] Lord knows how—I don't want to talk about that," said Gibney in a television interview. "I trusted him. I was satisfied that the Papers were authentic."

Deriabin's CIA affiliation, and Gibney's involvement, came forcefully to the attention of Robert L. Gale, a former Peace Corps official, in an interesting cloak-and-dagger escapade that took place a few years ago. At the time Gale was a fund-raising official at Carleton College in Northfield, Minnesota. He received a telephone call from Gibney, an old friend, who had a favor to ask: a Peter Deriabin, much debriefed by CIA, was being held in something close to protective custody by the agency, and was getting restless. Could Gale arrange to have Deriabin invited to Carleton College for a few days or weeks for a change of air from the CIA? Anything would be welcome, in order to give Deriabin a breathing spell in a pleasant campus atmosphere.

Gale agreed to accommodate his friend. He was instructed to go to a bar of a prominent New York hotel where he would be met. How would he know his contact? Gale asked. Never mind, he was assured, he would be spotted. At the appointed time Gale was at the bar in Manhattan when two men in trench coats approached him. They did not introduce themselves but simply exchanged a few words and gave him a telephone number to call. Then they vanished.

Gale, intrigued by this nonacademic adventure into the world of the CIA, called the number and was told to buy two airline tickets—one from New York to St. Paul via Chicago, for Deriabin, but made out in a cover name. The other, Chicago to St. Paul, would be for Gale, who was to get to Chicago on his own and pick up the flight that Deriabin was on. He would escort him to St. Paul and from there to the college.

Dazzled by this intricate travel scheme, Gale complied. He boarded the flight in Chicago, as instructed, but Deriabin was not aboard. When Gale got off at St. Paul, there was Deriabin at the airport to meet him, with a huge CIA man for a bodyguard. The KGB defector apologized to Gale and said he and his "friend" had made other travel arrangements.

As Gale had planned for Deriabin to stay at his own home, it was obvious that he would now have to put up the "friend" as well. The two men moved in with Gale and his family. Deriabin stayed for several days, enjoying the ivy atmosphere, but his hulking bodyguard never let him out of his sight for a minute. At parties, in classrooms, everywhere Gale had arranged to take Deriabin, the bodyguard went too.

The attempt to disassociate the CIA from *The Penkovskiy Papers* was foredoomed to failure, and the game was given away in the midst of the furor, by a little-noticed exchange of letters in the Washington *Post*. In December a reader named Richard H. Brightson questioned the value of both the CIA and *The Penkovskiy Papers*. This brought an angry reply, published on January 11, 1966, and signed "Phillip G. Strong, Hartland, Vermont."

"Having commenced a career as a professional intelligence officer some 30 years ago," Mr. Strong wrote, "and served subsequently in ONI, OSS, Battle Force Pacific and finally more than a decade as an official of the CIA, I feel strongly that Mr. Brightson's attack on the competency of CIA's intelligence analysis and estimative staff must be answered by someone not bemused by the tongue-in-cheek whimsies of James Bond and U.N.C.L.E. and who has not only read more than a short serialization of *The Penkovskiy Papers, but actually worked with the original material* [our italics]."

Some critics of this most famous of the recent "spy memoirs" argued that it was a "Cold War" political operation that served no useful purpose. Many high officials of the State Department, who were not consulted in advance as to the wisdom of publishing the book, felt that the real damage lay in the fact that the CIA's hand had shown through. These officials contended that much of the material in the book was accurate and valuable. But they argued that because the genuineness of the material was placed in doubt by the way the book was created, one of the greatest intelligence coups in years was placed in doubt along with it.

Such objections were directed to the manner of publication and not to the substantive issue. In seeking to deceive their adversaries overseas, the intelligence services were also confusing their audiences at home. It is doubtful whether in the long run the exploitation of spies, and the production of alleged "memoirs" and "disinformation" by each side, will serve the cause of mankind, which is already skirting close to the edge of oblivion in the nuclear age.

But espionage establishments do not think or act in humanitarian terms—their aim is to serve their own countries and they fight one another on their own level. Soviet intelligence reacted to the Penkovsky account by lighting a backfire. A British newsman was invited to visit Mrs. Vera Penkovsky and her daughters, Mariana, three, and Galina, nineteen, in their Moscow apartment at No. 36 Maxim Gorki Embankment—the point of the exercise being that if Penkovsky had typed his memoirs in their tiny apartment, his wife would have heard it; she indicated that she had not. The CIA, on the other hand, was satisfied that the "Papers" had publicized Penkovsky's—and, by implication, its own—accomplishments.

In the turbulent days after the U-2 was shot down in 1960, President Eisenhower had sought the right words to justify the espionage he had ordered. "No one wants another Pearl Harbor," he declared. "Intelligence-gathering activities . . . have a special and secret character. They are, so to speak, 'below the surface' activities. They are secret . . . They are divorced from the regular visible agencies of government . . . These activities have their own rules and methods of concealment which seek to mislead and obscure . . .

"It is," he concluded, "a distasteful but vital necessity."

Seven years after Eisenhower spoke those words, the nonvisible, "below the surface" establishments of East and West were competing in ways that would not have been thought possible before May Day 1960. An espionage revolution had been wrought. But as in the case of most revolutions, no one could say where it would end.

ix on espionage

Espionage has been a preoccupation of man throughout all of recorded history. The Bible recounts that the Lord ordered Moses to send men "to spy out the land of Canaan" to judge the resistance that might be met in making it the new home of the Israelites. Later the Bible tells of Joshua, who sent "two men to spy secretly, saying, Go view the land, even Jericho." They were sheltered by Rahab the harlot, who was, as a result, the only inhabitant spared when the walls came tumbling down.

In the fifth century B.C. the Chinese sage Sun Tzu included a detailed chapter on the "Employment of Secret Agents" in his book, *Art of War*. (He even used the term double agent in describing the varieties of spies.)

During the intervening centuries, all major nations and peoples have practiced espionage to advance or defend their interests. But until modern times, spying was largely restricted to periods of war. With few exceptions, governments did not maintain large, powerful spy establishments.

Through the centuries, the techniques of the profession scarcely changed, and the spy himself remained the "base fellow" of society. It was Montesquieu who said, "Spying might perhaps be tolerable if it were done by men of honor; but the infamy which inevitably attaches to the agent is a criterion of the infamy of the practice."

The traditional view of spies reflected the realization that espionage is the dark shadow cast by some of man's basic (although not necessarily best) instincts: self-preservation and mistrust of his fellow man.

If spying is ancient, the powerful, well-financed, highly organized espionage establishment is a unique phenomenon of our times. So, too, is the respectable, bureaucratic spy with the house in Georgetown, the *dacha* near Moscow and the country home in Sussex.

We live most of the time in a state suspended between war and peace. The more we spend on security, the more insecure we seem to feel. We demand arms for our protection and more and more secret intelligence to reassure ourselves that this protection is adequate.

Thus the large intelligence services that were developed in World War II have been retained, refined and enlarged for the prosecution of the Cold War. They claim to be the first line of defense in the nuclear age; and within their respective interpretations of the national interest, they can make a case for being preservers of the peace, in that they arm their governments with foreknowledge of the enemy's intentions, or at least his capabilities.

At the same time the espionage establishments have created grave problems, particularly in their ability to provoke events by clandestine activity. For example, during the Eisenhower years, it may be disclosed, U.S. policy was based on the assumption that the Soviet Union had set a specific date for an all-out, surprise attack on the United States. That assumption grew out of the fearful interpretations put on intelligence information at the height of the Cold War. In turn, preoccupation with "the date" led to an insatiable demand for more and more intelligence about the Soviet Union; this motivated Eisenhower to approve the superbly efficient but risky U-2 program, which led the world close to the nuclear brink. The U-2 incident underscored the fact that spying, always a potential threat to peace among nations, has become infinitely more dangerous in the thermonuclear age.

Aside from this, the espionage establishments have demonstrably created dangers within their own societies. Secret power is not easily controlled—the levers of such power too often become hidden with the rest of the machinery.

"An intelligence service," Allen Dulles once wrote, "is the ideal vehicle for a conspiracy. Its members can travel about at home and abroad under secret orders, and no questions are asked. Every scrap of paper in the files, its membership, its expenditure of funds, its contacts, even enemy contacts, are state secrets." Dulles was talking specifically about the German Abwehr; the possibility of an intelligence agency turning on its own government remains remote enough in the West.

Yet the democracies are not exempt from the subtler dangers flowing from the creation of huge centers of secret power in their midst. An intelligence establishment may err or take some action, deliberately or otherwise, that embarrasses the national leadership or even threatens the stability of the government. Moreover, it would be naïve to think that a powerful secret organization implanted at the center of a society will confine itself to operations abroad. It would be difficult to single out a major intelligence agency that does not wield enormous influence within its borders. The roots run deep.

An espionage establishment poses particularly difficult problems for the United States. The American people have traditionally dismantled their armed forces during times of peace and until World War II the United States had no formal espionage service. The prevailing prewar attitude was expressed succinctly by Secretary of State Henry L. Stimson, who in 1929 closed the "black chamber," the State Department's primitive code-breaking section, with the explanation: "Gentlemen do not read each other's mail."

After the war such scruples were declared officially obsolete. A

Cold War began and clandestine institutions were created to fight it. These institutions engaged in actions which ran counter to conventional morality and the nation's Puritan ethic. The government felt it necessary to hide these actions, to deny their existence; this in turn led it into untenable public positions and to the mistaken conclusion that it was necessary to supplement the right to life, liberty and the pursuit of happiness with the right to lie.

It is not a right; it is a wrong.

Much of the government's current "credibility" problem is a result of official misstatements designed to protect intelligence activities. The credibility crisis did not originate with Lyndon Johnson. Official untruths, misleading statements, wafflings and evasions to becloud intelligence-connected activity flourished under President Eisenhower and continued under the succeeding Democratic Administrations.

As far back as 1954, the Eisenhower Administration denied any part in the CIA's overthrow of the government of Guatemala; it issued statements disavowing any role in the CIA-supported revolt against Indonesia's President Sukarno in 1958; and it flatly denied, at first, that the U-2 had been sent over the Soviet Union. The Kennedy Administration pretended initially that someone else was invading the Bay of Pigs, and there were more misleading statements at the time of the Cuban missile crisis.

Today there is a widening sense of alienation between the government and the people. So much confusion has been sown in recent years that large segments of the population are willing to believe almost anything, no matter how wild; and to disbelieve anything, no matter how sensible, that their national leaders tell them. This is not a healthy climate for America. In such soil, extremism flourishes.

For example, one wonders to what extent the findings of the Warren Commission failed to gain public acceptance because of the intelligence undercurrent running through its report.*

---

* Marina Prusakova was living with her uncle, Ilya Prusakov, a colonel in the MVD, at the time she met Lee Harvey Oswald in Minsk. The KGB undoubtedly investigated Oswald and was certainly the source of the "Red Cross" funds with which the Russians subsidized Oswald during his stay. Oswald was interviewed twice by Soviet intelligence while in Russia; the CIA

None of the theorists of conspiracy have shown that any intelligence agency, East or West, had a connection with either Oswald or the President's death. But the fact that Oswald drifted between two ideologies and two countries inevitably made him a figure of intelligence *interest*. Because people sensed this fact, however vaguely, they were perhaps more willing to believe some of the wilder theories circulated about the assassination than if Oswald had been, say, an apolitical corn farmer from Iowa who had never traveled to Minsk or Mexico and whose name had never appeared in the locked files of Langley and Lubianka.

The point is that the Cold War and official misinformation, designed to conceal espionage activities, have created an atmosphere in which the veracity of the government is doubted even when it is telling the truth. We are on the way to becoming a nation of disbelievers.

Too often, as a society, we have fallen back on the "higher morality" of the Cold War: that the end justifies the means, that we must adopt the methods of the enemy to preserve our own system, that we must "fight fire with fire."

In a thoughtful essay on the modern spy, Jacques Barzun, Columbia University historian, concluded that "what is reprehensible is for the modern world to have made official the dreams and actions of little boys." The spy, he said, enjoys "permissive depravity," for "in exchange for a few dirty tricks there is also power and luxury, cash and free sex . . . the advantage of being a spy as of being a soldier is that there is always a larger reason—the reason of state—for making any little scruple or nastiness shrink into insignificance." *

The most extreme action, the bloodiest deed, can be justified on the ground of "higher morality." The Communist rationale in this

---

and the FBI had opened files on Oswald when he defected in 1959. Oswald went to Mexico City eight weeks before the assassination and tried to get travel visas at the Cuban and Soviet embassies. Then he wrote to the Russian embassy in Washington that while in Mexico, he had seen a Soviet official whom the CIA identified as a KGB officer, one Valeriy Vladimirovich Kostikov. The CIA advised the FBI about Oswald's visit to the Soviet embassy in Mexico.

* "Meditations on the Literature of Spying," *The American Scholar* (Spring 1965).

regard is explicit. "Morality," Lenin decreed, "is that which serves to destroy the old exploiting society . . . A Communist must be prepared to make every sacrifice and, if necessary, even resort to all sorts of schemes and stratagems, employ illegitimate methods, conceal the truth . . ."

Such a philosophy runs completely counter to America's image of itself. The Puritan heritage is deeply rooted in the United States, and officials who must deal in the most devious practices feel compelled to speak as if their stewardship is an exercise in high moral purpose.

In a speech at Catholic University in Washington in June 1965, President Johnson declared that he did "not believe it is pleasing in the sight of God for men to separate morality from their might . . . The strength of our society does not rest in the silos of our missiles nor lie in the vaults of our wealth, for neither arms nor silver are gods before which we kneel. The might of America lies in the morality of our purposes and their support by the will of our people in the United States . . . this is an America morally aware, morally aroused . . ."

On his seventy-fifth birthday, in October 1965, President Eisenhower warned of America's "moral decay" and added: "We are going too far away from the old virtues and rules of life . . . there are certain values we should keep, values like decency in our conduct and dealings with others, pride in ourselves, self-reliance, dedication to our country, respect for law and order."

However, Eisenhower's Director of Central Intelligence, Allen Dulles, saw no contradiction in his activities and the dictates of morality. "All that I can say is that I am a parson's son, and I was brought up as a Presbyterian, maybe as a Calvinist, maybe that may be a fatalist. I don't know. But I hope I have a reasonable moral standard." *

Richard Bissell, Dulles' deputy director for plans, explained that CIA men "feel a higher loyalty and that they are acting in obedience to that higher loyalty." He conceded that agents sometimes undertook actions "that were contrary to their moral precepts" but contended

---

* NBC-TV interview, "The Science of Spying," May 4, 1965.

that "the morality of, shall we call it for short, cold war is so infinitely easier than the morality of almost any kind of hot war that I never encountered this as a serious problem." *

If it is not a serious problem for the individual agent, however, it remains a serious problem for the American people. The espionage establishment has become a permanent institution. There can be no turning back to a simpler time when reality could more easily be made to conform to morality.

"Revolutions," Disraeli once said, "are not to be evaded." Neither can the fact of spying in today's world be evaded. The Soviet Union and Communist China have an active espionage apparatus. Under the circumstances, the United States needs its intelligence machinery. But it can stop treating it as something sacrosanct, separate and apart from the normal constitutional processes of congressional and executive control.

If the American vision is to be sustained, the American people must guard against the easy rationalization that anything can be excused in defense of the American Way of Life. Otherwise we may one day wake up to discover that the face in the mirror is no longer our own. And then the judgment of Jacques Barzun will have come true. "The soul of the spy," he has warned, "is somehow the model of us all."

---

* *Ibid.*

Bundesamt für Verfassungsschutz, see
Office for Protection of the Constitution
Bundesnachrichtendienst, see FIA
Burdiukov, Lev, 27, 27n
Bureau of Intelligence and Research
(INR), 136n, 173
Bureau of Public Roads, 149, 149n
Burgess, Guy Francis de Moncy,
100–5, 105n, 117, 130
Burrows, Sir Bernard, 92, 93n
Bush, Dr. Vannevar, 164
Butenko, John W., 266–8, 270
Byelorussian Mission to the United
Nations, 19, 209
Byrnes, Sec. of State James F., 162
Bytchkov, Anatoli E., 27, 29

"C," 83, 97, 125
Captive in Korea, 115n
Caramar, 167
Cardin, Min. of Justice Lucien, 29
Carnegie Foundation, 143
Carswell, Daniel L., 264
Carver, George, Jr., 154
Castro, Fidel, 143, 147, 148, 167, 194,
264
Catherwood Foundation, 156n
Center (in Moscow), 21, 21n, 23, 32,
34, 36, 204
Center for International Studies
(M.I.T.), 153
Center of Studies and Documentation
(Mexico), 155n
Central Committee of the Communist
Party (USSR), 13, 44, 46, 72, 75
Central Intelligence Act of 1949, 166n
Central Intelligence Agency (CIA),
3–6, 11n, 15, 15n, 16, 19n, 26, 39n,
45n, 49, 53, 57n, 60, 65, 71, 72,
110n, 111n, 115, 116, 127, 127n,
129, 130, 132–75, 182, 198, 229,
238, 239n, 254, 256, 261n, 263,
264, 265, 275, 282, 291, 291n, 292,
292n, 293; budget, 17, 17n; confers
medal on Francis Gary Powers,
279n; directors of, 132–9, 141,
167; domestic operations of, 144,
145, 147, 151, 160–5, 168; Domestic Operations Division, 144,
145, 147, 161; duties of, 164, 165;

headquarters, 145, 145n, 149n;
offices in U.S., 142, 142n;
organization of, 39n, 129, 135,
136n, 144, 145; for Plans,
Intelligence, Research and Support
divisions, *see* separate entries; other
buildings, 146, 147, 261n; rivalry
inside, 135, 136; size of, 10, 15, 17,
17n, 146n; and James Bond, 6,
128n, 132, 133, 269n; and Fidel
Castro, 147, 148; in the Congo, 167;
and congressional control of,
171–5; and Cuba, raids on, 147;
and Cuban invasion, *see* Bay of
Pigs; and émigré groups, 148; and
Estonian case, 148ff.; and
foundations, 143, 144, 153n, 155n,
156n; Vice-President Humphrey on,
156, 157, 158; in Guatemala, 167,
291; in Indonesia, 167n, 291; in
Iran, 167; and Interarmco, 167,
168; and President Johnson, 132,
137, 139, 157; and Katzenbach
panel, 158, 159; and President
Kennedy, 4, 170, 291; and KGB,
61–3; and labor, 159n; and legal
authority to operate in U.S., 151,
160–5; and M.I.6, co-operation with,
115-16, 127, 128–30; and Oswald,
Lee Harvey, 291n, 292, 292n; and
The Penkovskiy Papers, 283–7; and
Special Group, 169; and special
operations abroad, 165, 166, 167;
and students, 154, 155, 157, 158,
159; and Tofte case, 164n, 165n;
and President Truman, 161, 162ff.,
168, 169; and the U-2, *see* U-2 *and*
Powers, Francis Gary; and
universities, 152, 153, 153n, 154
Central Intelligence Group, 162
Central People's Government Council
(China), 178
Century House, 80
Charles I (Stuart), King, 97
Cheka, 14, 41, 42, 50, 64, 280
Chesapeake Foundation, 156n
Chiang Ch'ing, 176
Chiang Kai-shek, 177, 181, 182, 185
Chief Intelligence Directorate of the
General Staff, *see* GRU
Ch'ien Hsueh-shen, 180
China Islamic Association (CIA), 188

ABOUT THE AUTHORS

Thomas B. Ross is a native of New York, a graduate of Yale College and a former Nieman Fellow at Harvard University. He served as a junior officer in the Navy during the Korean War. He subsequently worked for the International News Service and the United Press International. In 1958 he became a member of the Washington Bureau of the *Chicago Sun-Times*. He is married and has two children.

David Wise is a native New Yorker and graduate of Columbia College. He joined the *New York Herald Tribune* in 1951, served as the newspaper's White House correspondent during the Kennedy Administration and as chief of the Washington Bureau from 1963 to 1966. He is married and has one child. With Mr. Ross, he is co-author of *The U-2 Affair* (Random House, 1962) and *The Invisible Government* (Random House, 1964).